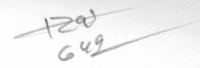

AMBER, FURS AND COCKLESHELLS

Eisenstadt was a pleasant little town, with fine displays of amber in the jewellers' windows. I took advantage of a very professional cycle shop to have Condor's wheels checked, as they seemed to be rolling reluctantly. The front wheel was pronounced too dry; it needed cream on the axle. The rear wheel had two spokes out of true, which was making it wobble at speed. While these faults were being rectified, I was treated to a good ticking-off.

'Don't you know this bicycle is illegal in Austria? You've no business to be riding around with no reflectors on your spokes and pedals, and no fixed lights. If the police catch you, you could be prosecuted and banned from cycling. I'll have to change these pedals for you and fix on reflectors. Which of these lights do you want now?'

'I don't want any of those lights,' I said. 'I don't need them – or new pedals either. I've already cycled across Austria. I'm going in to Hungary tomorrow.'

'Well, I suppose that's all right then,' he said grudgingly. 'But you'd better use the cycle paths to get there – and don't let the police see you.'

I fled to Hungary to escape prosecution and prison.

To Heather Brigstocke

About the author

Since she gave up full-time employment as headmistress of a girls' school in Sussex in 1987, Anne Mustoe has spent every winter abroad. She is a classical scholar and has run her own travel business, organising specialist tours to classical sites in Greece, Italy, Turkey and Tunisia. She is internationally renowned for her best-selling cycling adventures: *A Bike Ride*, *Lone Traveller*, *Two Wheels in the Dust* and *Cleopatra's Needle*. Anne gives talks and slide shows about her cycling adventures, and enjoys a substantial and loyal readership.

Read more about Anne's cycling adventures on her website: www.annemustoe.co.uk

AMBER, FURS AND COCKLESHELLS

Travels With Pilgrims and Merchants

Anne Mustoe

First published in 2005 by
Virgin Books
Thames Wharf Studios
Rainville Road
London W6 9HA

ISBN 0 7535 0983 0

Typeset by TW Typesetting, Plymouth, Devon
Printed and bound in Great Britain by Clays Ltd, St Ives plc

CONTENTS

INTRODUCTION

No changing of place at 100 mph will make us one whit stronger, happier or wiser. There was always more in the world than men could see, walked they ever so slowly; they see it no better for going fast.

John Ruskin

Books can happen accidentally. This is one I never intended to write. It just somehow willed itself on to the pages.

I like a challenge, and usually my cycle rides are challenging in the extreme. They are struggles across continents, which take a great deal of organisation, research and time. But occasionally, between these major undertakings, the sun comes out and I feel the urge to jump on my bicycle and take a short cycling holiday, to amuse myself on an interesting and basically comfortable ride.

The three journeys which feature in this book are all recent pleasure jaunts. I researched the routes and kept a log out of habit, but I cycled them purely out of curiosity, with no intention of writing them up – until I saw that what began as three quite separate rides were so inter-related that they formed one very satisfying whole.

All three of them are routes with a fascinating history: the Amber Route, the Santa Fe Trail and the Pilgrim Way to Santiago de Compostela. They all cross spectacular landscapes and take in magical cities, from Prague, Vienna and Burgos with their splendid palaces and cathedrals to the mean streets of Dodge City and Las Vegas.

The Amber Route is the oldest and, like all ancient trade routes, it is not one road, but a network of routes extending from the Baltic to the Mediterranean. Which route was chosen at any given time depended on the season, the political situation and the temper of the fierce local tribesmen. Amber beads from the Baltic Sea have been found in the graves at Mycenae, which means that the Greeks were importing this beautiful fossilised resin as early as the Bronze Age, from around *c*16 BC. They prized it both as a jewel and as a substance with magical and medicinal properties. The Romans were equally passionate about it, as were the Vikings, the mediaeval craftsmen, the Danish court, Peter the Great and more recently the jewellers of the art nouveau movement. Understandably so, for amber is a fascinating jewel, sometimes clear, sometimes opaque, varying in colour from the palest cream to the tawny brown of whisky. Some chunks of it contain insects and seeds, which were trapped inside the resin in prehistoric times. It was from the blood in the stomach of a trapped mosquito that Steven Spielberg's scientists in *Jurassic Park* took the DNA to recreate dinosaurs – a film fantasy which is totally in keeping with amber's magical tradition.

The Amber Route I chose to follow was one of several developed by the Romans. It ran for 2,000 miles from Scagen at the very northern tip of Jutland, then followed the river Elbe from Hamburg through Wittenberg, Meissen and Dresden, before branching off along one of the Elbe's tributaries, the Vltava, to Prague and beyond. After climbing through the mountains of the Czech Republic, the route dropped down to Linz, then followed the Danube cycle path to Vienna. Just beyond Vienna lies Petronell, a small village today, but once Carnuntum, the greatest Roman city along the Danube, and the place where the Emperor Marcus Aurelius wrote his *Meditations*. From there, the route ran south across the Hungarian Plains to the river Drava and the gap between the Julian Alps and the Carpathians, before hurtling down the mountains to the Adriatic. It finished halfway between Trieste and Venice, in the port of Aquileia, where the Romans had their great amber-working factories. It was a magnificent river and mountain ride through the heartland of Central Europe with its fine cities, music and rich cultural heritage.

By contrast, the Santa Fe Trail is the most recent, and the shortest-lived, of the three routes. By 1821, the North European settlers, known by the general name of 'Anglos', had pushed westwards from the Atlantic to the Missouri river. Then a few rugged mountain men, who trapped beaver for the top hats of the New York gentry, found their way from the Rockies down to Santa Fe in New Mexico and opened up an additional market for their furs. They were soon followed by a handful of 'Anglo' traders, who struggled across unmapped territory from the Missouri river to Santa Fe. The Spanish settlers, who had moved northeastwards from Mexico and founded the city, were far from their home base and short of life's small necessities. They were so eager to buy that fortunes could be made through trading pots and pans, needles and knives. What began as a trickle of men on horseback from the eastern states soon grew to a tide of juggernauts crossing the plains, until by 1862 the value of the trade had reached a staggering $40 million a year.

Then disaster struck. Another Western legend, the Atchison, Topeka and Santa Fe Railroad, was completed in 1880 and the first train steamed into Santa Fe on 9 February. The Santa Fe Trail withered away, along with the Oregon Trail and the Pony Express Route, all victims of the steam engine and its accompanying telegraph wires. A colourful chapter in the history of the West was at an end.

The trail began in Independence, Missouri, and crossed the cornfields and grasslands of the entire state of Kansas. There was only one variation to the route, the Cimarron Cutoff, but now as then, the cutoff road is pretty empty, so I chose to continue along the original Mountain Trail through Colorado. I crossed the Rockies (in a blizzard!) at the Raton Pass, then dropped down into New Mexico and climbed the Sangre de Cristo mountains to reach Santa Fe just before Christmas.

The Amber Route and the Santa Fe Trail were both primarily trade routes. The third route, the Way of St James, brought trade and development in its wake, but it was fundamentally different in origin. It was, and still is today, a path of Christian pilgrimage, a route trodden with devotion, for spiritual rather than commercial gain.

Santiago, or St James the Greater, the apostle son of Zebedee and brother of St John, is the patron saint of Spain. Although he was martyred under King Herod in Judaea, his body miraculously arrived off the coast of Galicia, where it was hidden to protect it from the pagans and lost for centuries. But when the Moors overran Spain, St James rose to free his chosen people. In 813, a field of stars (one interpretation of Compostela) guided a hermit to his tomb. King Alfonso of Asturias constructed a shrine there and pilgrims began to flock to Spain, Charlemagne among the first. In 846, the saint himself appeared on a white charger at Clavijo, leading the heavenly hosts into battle against the Moors. He inspired the Christian armies throughout the Reconquest of Spain and was held in such reverence that the Spanish New World is littered with Santiagos great and small, the most notable being the capital of Chile.

Unlike the other two routes, the Pilgrim Way to Santiago de Compostela in Galicia has maintained a continuum from the Dark Ages through to the present time, and is currently enjoying a boom in popularity. The shrine is remote enough and the road sufficiently difficult to provide the elements of endurance and adventure necessary to a true pilgrimage. Today, it still provides a challenge, both physical and mental, so that non-believers share the hardship of the footsore, saddle-sore Christians. As the cockleshell is the symbol of St James, going on the pilgrimage was known in mediaeval times as 'taking the cockle', and the cockleshell is still carried today by those who journey along the way.

Of the four main pilgrim routes to Santiago de Compostela – from Paris, Vézelay, Le Puy and Arles – I chose the earliest one, pioneered in 951 by Bishop Gottschalk of Le Puy. It began in the Haute Loire, in the Monts du Velay, and travelled westwards across the grain of the country, dropping down chasms to the waters of the Loire, the Allier, the Lot, the Dourdou, the Auze and the Tarn, then climbing leg-breakingly up the opposite cliffs. Leaving the Massif Central just after Cahors, it ran across the Gers and Les Landes to St Jean Pied de Port and crossed the Pyrenees at the legendary Pass of Roncesvalles. Just beyond Pamplona, the four routes converged at Punta la Reina and the bands of pilgrims joined forces to plod together across the scorched landscape of La Rioja, Castile and León. The splendid cathedral cities of Burgos and León were followed by the desolate Cebreiro Pass and the first sight of journey's end, the towers of Santiago Cathedral in the valley below. The route from Le Puy is the longest and most arduous of the four rides, but by far the most spectacular.

The Amber Route crossed Europe from north to south and the Way of St James from the north and east to the very western edge of the continent, Spanish Galicia. But there was a geographical link – the port of Aquileia. This was the Romans' great amber-working centre, so they developed excellent road and sea connections to speed the import of raw amber and the export of their highly prized amber artefacts. The port still flourished in mediaeval times, when it was also an important Christian bishopric, and it became an assembly point for overland pilgrims to Santiago and Rome, as well as sea-faring pilgrims to Jerusalem.

The Santa Fe Trail crossed another continent, but the settlers who founded the city of Santa Fe in New Mexico came from Spain, many from the poorer western regions of Galicia and Extremadura. They traded with the northern Europeans, who were pushing westwards from the eastern seaboard. So the Santa Fe Trail was in essence another European route, connecting the peoples of the English Channel, the North Sea and the Baltic with those of the Mediterranean and Atlantic coasts.

Where the routes differ is in the experience they offer to the traveller. Along the Amber Route, I cycled through Danish, German, Czech, Hungarian, Slovene, Serbo-Croat and Italian speakers. I can cope in German and Italian, and the Danes usually speak good English. But between Germany and Italy, I had my first experience of total linguistic isolation. In some places, I found it impossible to communicate, except by signs, mimes and animal noises. How else do you ask for chicken in a restaurant? It was a bit like looking at a silent film. I watched the landscape roll by and I watched the people, trying to guess what they were thinking and how they led their lives. But all I could do was smile, like a dog wagging its tail, to show that I was harmless and well-intentioned. A smile and a bicycle are badges of innocence.

On the Pilgrim Way, I had plenty of company. It was a great experience to be swept along on a strong tide, like one small fish in a shoal, all of us striving to reach the same destination, Santiago de Compostela. Here was the camaraderie of the road, thousands of us carrying the cockleshell of St James, exchanging experiences, worries, hopes and dreams, urging one another forwards in a mixture of French, English and Spanish.

But for company, nothing could compare with the American Midwest. Along the Santa Fe Trail I was entertained by a host of amazingly candid characters, who regaled me with their life histories the minute I walked through the door. The ride was a warm, happy experience from beginning to end. And it was all so easy. Everyone spoke English, the roads were good, the food familiar and the motels clean. I shall save a more thorough exploration of the United States for my old age, when I shall really value my comfort.

* * *

When I came to write up the three routes, the three narratives evolved in three different styles. The Amber Route was the most headstrong, with a mind of its own. It was born in the British Library and seemed determined to become an academic treatise on the history and uses of amber through the ages. I had to fight hard to lighten its mood and introduce a little frivolity. The Amber Route is the densest, most earnest section.

The Santa Fe Trail wheeled across Kansas and the Rockies without a care in the world, almost writing itself. I kept bumping into weird and wonderful characters, so the emphasis is on the people I met, rather than the historical background. Lewis and Clark, the American thrust westwards, the Native American peoples, their culture and destinies, scarcely figure in the narrative. It was simply a ride for the fun of it.

As for the Way of St James, it is so popular now that for a long time I resisted the idea of writing it up. The route was already too well documented. There were so many books already on the shelves, from learned treatises on the ecclesiastical architecture and the history of the monastic orders along the way, to spiritual guides, to the novels by Paulo Coelho and David Lodge, to practical handbooks for walkers and cyclists. But I eventually decided that such a powerful experience could take another third of a book, especially if I made it a personal account and looked for aspects neglected by other writers.

I chose the three routes because they had all been trodden throughout the centuries by venturers in search of riches, a better life for themselves and their children, or the salvation of their souls. Menaced by fierce Germanic tribes and Indian braves, or just by the local cut-throats and highwaymen, the merchants, settlers and pilgrims struggled on foot and horseback through unexplored mountains, plains, deserts and forests.

The lands are peaceful now and well supplied with tarmac. Travellers rush across them, unthinking, unobservant, in cars and trains; or they fly over the top of them in a matter of hours, picking at the food on their trays and watching the aircraft video. It is only the walker or the cyclist, toiling along slowly, often wearily, who can truly appreciate the achievement of those brave souls who shaped our world. It takes courage to leap into the unknown; and to continue in the face of storm, danger, disease, hunger and thirst drains the deepest reserves of perseverance and faith.

John Ruskin was certainly not a cyclist, but he appreciated the value of the cyclists' pace. All through his life, he followed the pattern established by his family when he was a child, of travelling no more than fifty miles a day, with frequent stops to admire the scenery or visit significant buildings. He found time to marvel at the small details which speedier travellers overlooked as they rushed by. Often, he would stop to draw them or describe them as accurately as possible in his notebooks, as the best way of fixing their beauty in his memory – 'to *see*, to take note rather than to look'.

When I cycle, my average distance, like Ruskin's, is fifty miles a day. I stop frequently to take a better look at my surroundings and I often jot down on-the-spot notes of scenes, buildings or incidents which I find particularly arresting. So in many ways, I am a humble cycling follower of Ruskin in his carriage.

Where we differ is that Ruskin rarely showed any signs of interest in the people he met on his travels. For him, a set of paintings of the west front of Rouen Cathedral in every light was the main product of his visit to the city. Its inhabitants were no more than ants, scurrying in front of the Gothic façade. He missed the warmth and the funny side of the human condition. Cyclists know better. They know that it is the people along the way who make the ride; and they know that there is no transport so useful as the modest, classless bicycle for making the introductions.

THE AMBER ROUTE

A Roman
Amber Route

St Petersburg
Pushkin

Skagen

Esberg

Kaliningrad
(Königsberg)

Hamburg

R. Elbe

Leipzig   Dresdenh

GERMANY   R. Vltava

Prague

Vienna

Linz   Bratislava

Budapest

Aquileia   Ljubljana

Venice   Trieste

R. Danube

ITALY

⚊⚊⚊⚊   Roman Amber Route

SKAGEN

Be like the headland amidst the crashing waves. It stands firm until the
tumultuous waters around it sink once more to rest.

Marcus Aurelius, *Meditations*

Skagen–Løkken–Løgstør–Viborg–Videbaek–Esjberg

Skagerrak and Kattegat. Even the names sound wild as shipwreck.
This low promontory, where the North Sea (Skagerrak) meets the
Baltic (Kattegat) is so storm-racked that its shifting sands cringe
eastwards, curling into a bill hook, or a back hunched against the
gale. There are rushing tides and treacherous cross-currents,
haunted on stormy nights by the ghosts of ships and the cries of
drowning men. Perhaps it was the Romans' Ultima Thule, the
fearsome coast which they glimpsed, but never dared approach.

Yet early that morning, the perfect weather of my crossing from
Newcastle held, and the treacherous seas were smooth as glass and
twice as luminous. I chained my bike to a stand in the Grenen car
park and walked along the curving sweep of sand to the very tip
of Jutland, the Skaw. It lay pale cream under a radiant blue sky,
unruffled by the slightest breath of wind. Only the sign forbidding
bathing at all times stood as a reminder of the sea's malevolence. I
joined three squealing tots in the shallows, left foot in the North
Sea, right in the Baltic. It was early June, so only a handful of
pensioners and this group of pre-school children disturbed the
shimmering calm.

I started to comb the beach, searching in the tangle of twigs and
seaweed at the tide's edge, along the line where I knew that amber,
the jewel of the Baltic, came to rest. I was looking for a talisman to
bring me luck on my ride along the Roman Amber Route to the
Adriatic. But which pebbles were what? Baltic amber can be clear
or opaque, and any colour from the palest gold to whisky brown.
I picked up stones and peered at them with my inexpert eye, then
decided to play safe in the Grenen souvenir shop. I came out with
an authenticated golden amber nugget, attached to a key-ring.

Baltic amber is the loveliest and most plentiful in the world.
Thirty million years ago, in the Upper Eocene/Lower Oligocene

eras, the lands around the Baltic, and what is now the Baltic Sea itself, were covered in vast subtropical pine forests. Amber is the resin which oozed from the bark of these conifers, often trapping insects, seeds and fragments of vegetation in its sticky path, before becoming embedded in the earth and fossilised, along with its hexapodal captives. It is nature's time capsule.

This natural curiosity caught the imagination of Steven Spielberg. In his film *Jurassic Park,* scientists extracted the DNA of a dinosaur from the stomach of a fossilised mosquito, caught in a chunk of amber. The mosquito had bitten a dinosaur and sucked in a quantity of its blood. From this mosquito meal, Spielberg's scientists were able to obtain enough dinosaur DNA to produce a clutch of eggs, which hatched into rampaging prehistoric monsters. It's a good yarn, but highly improbable. The Natural History Museum has been trying for years to extract DNA from similar fossilised insects, but their scientists have recovered only small fragments of the DNA strings, and those have all come directly from the creatures themselves, not from the remains of their dinners. In any case, no insect-bearing ambers from the Jurassic age have as yet come to light; and mosquitos in amber are extremely rare, with only a few examples in the whole world, most of those from Dominica.

Over the millennia, Earth's restlessness has submerged lands in the sea and thrown them up again. The amber of the ancient forests now lies buried deep in a deposit of blue earth, some of it underground, in Russia and Poland, where it is mined. But the most prized amber lies under the Baltic Sea. Wrenched from its submarine bed in stormy weather, it is tossed up on to the shore, already polished by the action of tides and sand.

Amber was the first precious substance used by man, preceding gold, silver and gems. In Homer, Menelaus's palace was decorated with amber, and Baltic amber beads have been found in the Bronze Age tombs in Mycenae, which means that there was an established trade route to Greece, probably by sea, from as early as 1600 BC. Amber was prized by the Greeks, not only for its beauty, but because its power to attract hairs, dried leaves and other light-weight fragments to itself, when rubbed, was thought to be magical (the Greek word for amber was 'elektron', from which we derive 'electricity').

The Greeks were so taken with amber that they wove a myth around it. Helios, the god of the sun, used to drive his chariot with its team of white horses across the heavens every day, bringing light and warmth to the world. He had an ambitious son, Phaethon, and like many other characters in myths and fairy tales, Helios made a grave mistake. He promised Phaethon that he would grant him any request that he chose to make. Phaethon immediately asked to drive his father's chariot for a day. Helios knew it would be a disaster, but he could not go back on his word. When he failed to dissuade Phaethon, he had no choice but to yoke his horses and watch the reckless boy career off into the heavens. The horses were too powerful for him and charged out of control, flying so near to the Earth that the forests started to blaze and the sea began to boil. Fearing that the world would be consumed in one great conflagration, Zeus, the king of the gods, hurled his thunderbolt at Phaethon. The boy's body fell to Earth beside the river Eridanus. His sisters, the Heliades, wept so bitterly at his death that the gods turned them into poplars on the banks of the river and their tears became amber. The early Greeks knew that amber came from somewhere in the far northwest, so they placed the river Eridanus in that vague direction, making it flow into the Northern Ocean and placing a group of amber-bearing islands, the Electrides, at its mouth. Later writers, such as Strabo, identified the Eridanus with the river Po, where some inferior amber has been found, and where there are poplar trees in abundance.

The Romans were just as enthusiastic about the versatile resin. Workshops in Aquileia produced finely carved jewellery and amulets; Roman ladies carried balls of it in their hands to keep them cool; it was powdered and used as medicine; it was burned as incense; and the profligate Emperor Heliogabalus had it crushed and spread underfoot, to perfume the porticos of his palace. Amber was so fashionable that, according to Martial, Roman ladies bleached their hair with alkali to make it amber-coloured, or wore wigs made of the golden tresses of conquered Teutons. For the Romans, it was *the* luxury material, and it had to come from the Baltic. When the Emperor Nero, ever extravagant, decided that amber beads would look pretty threaded into the mesh of the gladiators' nets in the amphitheatre, he sent to the Baltic Sea, 3,000 km away, rather than use the local varieties from Sicily or the Po.

13

Unlike the Greeks and Phoenicians, the Romans were no sailors. They preferred an overland march, however long and arduous. In Imperial times, when the trade in amber was at its height, the Romans themselves controlled the territory, and therefore the Amber Route, as far north as the river Danube. Beyond lived the wild Germanic tribes, who collected the amber on the Baltic shores and carried it south down the rivers of Central Europe to Carnuntum, the principal Roman amber market. Like the more famous Silk Road, the Amber Route was in fact a whole network of paths. Which path was chosen at any given time depended partly on the season, but mostly on the mood of the bellicose locals. Were they peaceable, or were they ravaging the land in one of their frequent wars?

Out of the many paths from the Baltic Sea to the Adriatic, I chose to follow the one which would take me through a whole series of unexplored countries. Starting at the Skaw, I would cycle down through Jutland, then follow the Elbe across Germany, continuing up its tributary, the Vltava, to Prague and the Austrian frontier. Dropping down to the Danube at Linz, I would follow the Danube cycle path to Vienna and Carnuntum (modern Petronell), where one of the few virtuous Roman Emperors, Marcus Aurelius, spent most of his troubled reign warding off the fierce Quadi and Marcomanni and writing his *Meditations*. Then I would turn south across the Hungarian Plains and the mountains of Slovenia, to reach the Adriatic near Trieste. Finally, the Via Gemina would lead me to my destination, Aquileia, once a major riverine port and amber-working centre, mighty enough in its heyday to be dubbed 'Roma Secunda', but now a tranquil backwater behind the seaside town of Grado. It would be a ride through the heartland of Central Europe, crossing the old Cold War divide to embrace the majestic cities of Leipzig, Dresden and Prague, and the forests of Bohemia.

By nature, I am a Mediterranean creature, bewitched by the ruins of classical lands, with their sunshine, cypresses, lemons and olive groves. Whenever I think of travel, which is often, I think of the south. Central Europe had never cast the same spell, and I was curious to see if a closer acquaintance would warm my cool interest to enthusiasm. It would be an unusual ride for me, because it would take me across countries where I knew not one single word of the language. I could get by in German and Italian, but how would I manage when everyone spoke Danish, Czech, Hungarian, Serbo-Croat or Slovene?

I rested for my ride with a weekend in Skagen, where the red-roofed houses are painted yellow ochre, their frilly gables picked out in white, like lace edging. The cost of the hotels came as a great shock, but cyclists have the advantage of being able to cruise around, looking for alternatives. I found a hut in an old man's garden, complete with two beds, a cooker, sink, fridge, electric coffee-maker, and a dangling witch made of two coconut shells with coconut fibre for hair. It was all fairly ramshackle, with wiring snaking everywhere and the wrong colours on the taps, but it had its own private patio, where Condor and I could both enjoy the shade of a large café umbrella. The old man wore dungarees and a check shirt, and was full of fussy instructions in halting German. He spent his days across the garden in his carport, which was lit in the evenings by fairy lights in the shape of bananas and oranges. It was delightfully eccentric accommodation, cheap and totally problem-free, until I was surprised by my portly host walking naked out of his shower at 3 o'clock one morning.

'I'm so sorry about last night,' he said, crimson in the face, when I saw him later on. 'You see, there's this beautiful little mink. He got into the house through the cat-flap one day and bit the cleaning woman. But now he's started to come into the carport when I'm having my supper, and yesterday he climbed up on to my shoe and went to sleep. He looked so peaceful nestling there that I hadn't the heart to disturb him. So I just sat there for hours. That's why I was so late having my shower.'

Everything closed on Sunday, so I walked the length of the immaculately clean high street, peering into shop-windows, trying to find the key to the split in the Danish character. Think of Danish design, and you see austerely beautiful furniture. I spent my first night in Denmark in a hotel in Frederikshavn, which was the epitome of Danish style, all varnished pine, neutral colours and understated elegance. At breakfast, each table had a crisp white cloth, white napkins, a white candle flaming in a white candlestick and one freshly picked white rose in a slim white porcelain vase. This was the Denmark I expected. What I didn't expect were shop-windows full of dwarves in nappies, elves asleep in beds of leaves, cows on roller-skates, cows with wings, winsome gonks, pigs in hats, and plastic models of naked, wrinkled old men sitting on lavatories, while others cowered naked on their knees under the whips of jackbooted madames. The key-rings labelled 'Shitting Cow' I leave to the imagination! It seemed as if all that impeccable taste in interior furnishings was so overwhelming to the Danes that they needed to freak out at times into screaming vulgarity. Kitsch was their antidote, their escape from the stark chastity of Scandinavian design.

The Natural History Museum was closed, but I looked through the window and saw lumps of amber the size of young boulders. Then I took in the paintings of the Skagen School, the shimmering sand and seascapes of Michael and Anna Ancher and P S Krøyer. Their huge canvases, such as *Death of a Fisherman* and *Lighting the Bonfire on Midsummer's Night*, were so real that every eye glistened. The woman in a long white Edwardian dress, gazing out to sea with her labrador beside her, seemed to be a figure in a photograph. You could see that realism at the end of the nineteenth century had gone as far as it was technically possible to go. Art needed to find a new direction.

True to form, the delightful weather broke during my last night in Skagen. A fierce wind rose from the southwest, spitting rain directly in my face as I cycled out of town. But it was a wild, exhilarating ride. The windswept heathland was carpeted in pink clover and buttercups, with yellow broom and low, twisted hedges ablaze with red and pink wild roses. The belfry of a church stood out against swirling clouds, all that was left of Skagen's ancient parish church; the nave lay totally buried under drifting dunes. Then I crossed a low ridge and followed cycle paths across farmland rich in barley, rape seed, flax and wheat, through villages with neat little red-brick houses and gardens of lilac and rhododendron. It struck me that Jutland was a neater, more toytown version of East Anglia – the same pines and heathland along the coast, the same crops, the same wild wind and the same infinite skies.

I crossed the entire peninsula that first day, 80 km. to Løkken on the western Skagerrak coast. Then I turned south. Skylarks soared in the overcast morning and I noticed a strange phenomenon. There were buttercups, dandelions and wild roses in profusion, but not a daisy to be seen. Then I crossed the bridge, which links the north island of Jutland to the main body of the peninsula, and found myself cycling through snowy white fields. That stretch of water, the Aggersund, was the daisy divide.

As I journeyed south, the weather worsened, with winds so strong that the turbines were whirling round and the roads were littered with the tiny corpses of songbirds, swept helplessly into oncoming traffic by the force of the gale. But the plus side of that first week was my discovery of Danhostels. I was standing disconsolately in the rain in the middle of Viborg, when a vision in white pushed its bicycle in my direction. It was a small, busy, bespectacled old lady, dressed in a white PVC mac with a matching white PVC sou'wester, white ankle socks and white tennis shoes.

'You look lost. Can I help you?' she asked, in perfect English.

'I'm looking for a hotel.'

'You can't stay in a hotel. They're much too expensive. Nobody can afford hotels. You must go to the Danhostel. Follow me!'

With that, she jumped on to her gearless shopping bike and sped down to the lake, then along a forest path, while I puffed and panted to keep up.

'I cycle all the time,' she said. 'Sometimes I go right across Denmark and into Germany. I used to cycle with two friends, but they're both dead now, so I go on my own. I'm glad to see you do the same. Most people are so spineless. They won't go anywhere unless they've got someone to hold their hand. How do you like Denmark?'

'It's very nice, but terribly expensive. How on earth do you manage?'

'We don't!'

The Danhostel was an elegant building, with perfect lawns sweeping down to the wooded lakeside. A bearded warden stood behind the pristine pine reception desk.

'She'll take a bed in the shared female accommodation,' announced my guide, without consultation. 'Singles cost three hundred Kroner and that's far too much. Sharing is only one hundred [about £10].' And having sorted me out to her satisfaction, she whizzed off down the path, a flash of white against the dark fir trees.

I was delighted with my 'shared female accommodation'. I'd expected a dormitory full of bunk beds, but in fact it was a superbly appointed twin-bedded room with private facilities. A third bed could be let down from the wall, if required. As it was early in the season, I was the only lone female, so I had this splendid accommodation to myself, at less than a fifth of the cost of some dreary, bottom-end hotel room. I was the only cyclist too. All the other visitors arrived in cars, because Danhostels are not known as 'Youth Hostels', with all the spartan connotations of that name, but as 'Travellers' Hostels'. They are the Danish equivalent of our no-frills Travelodges, with the bonus of shared rooms for the impecunious. Having discovered them, thanks to the managerial lady in white, I stayed in them whenever possible.

As I gazed out that evening over the rainy car park, I focused on what I foresaw would be the main problem of this ride. The Danish landscape looked much like our own back in England; the people looked like us; they behaved like us, being similarly reticent; their food was like ours; and so was their weather. Central Europe, I felt sure, would be exactly the same. There would be no extraordinary incidents, nothing quaint or picturesque, no extrovert locals bursting with eccentricity and charm. One old man with his pet mink, a bossy old lady in a white mac, and the softest, most delicious freshly caught plaice I had ever eaten in my life would hardly make a book. The story of amber itself was fascinating, and I had enough material to produce a learned treatise on the topic, but cycling along the Amber Route would probably be no more exotic than cycling across the Midlands. It was a problem which taxed me until I reached Aquileia, when I was able to look back over the entire ten-week journey. I realised then that there was a pattern. While my cycling weekdays were pleasant but uneventful, they were spiked with truly memorable weekends. I would concentrate on those and overleap the sameness of the distances between.

ESJBERG

The art of living is more like wrestling than dancing. It demands a firm and watchful stance against unexpected onsets.

Marcus Aurelius, *Meditations*

Esjberg–Ribe–Haderslev–Flensburg–Schleswig–Rendsburg–Itzehoe–Hamburg

I wrestled my way into Esjberg against the unexpected onset of a thunderstorm, but then the weather cleared and my second weekend was as blue and radiant as my first. Esjberg is a prosperous fishing, oil and ferry town, the main port of entry from England. Its nineteenth-century mock-mediaeval gables make a pleasant backdrop to the restaurant tables lining the Torvet, the town's main square, where my fish tasted all the better for a glass of wine, as a change from Danish beer. But what drew me to Esjberg was its amber.

The richest sources of tidal amber are the shores of the Baltic, especially the area around Kaliningrad on Russia's Samland Peninsula. But I knew from my years in Southwold that there was North Sea amber too, as it was often washed up by storms on to East Anglian beaches. The magnificent Amber Rooms in the Esjberg Museum were a celebration of all amber, wherever it was found – its origins, properties and usage through the ages – with excellent chronological charts, well-explained displays, even a video. I spent the whole weekend there, marvelling at the wealth and variety of the exhibits.

What first caught my eye were the animal pendants from the Mesolithic Age (9000–4000 BC), cute little bears and deer, all found in Denmark and perhaps used as protection against the creatures of the forest, or as hunters' magic. In the next phase, the Neolithic Age (4000–2800 BC), amber clearly began to assume economic importance, as beads have been found in rich burial sites, marking the high social standing of the dead. Then something dramatic happened. Amber disappeared almost completely from Denmark, to pop up in Bronze Age Greece (1800–500 BC) and later in Rome. The Jutes of Jutland had discovered the export trade. Amber from their shores travelled to the Mediterranean in great quantities, along routes which are clearly marked by archaeological finds. Baltic amber moved south and east in exchange for technologically advanced items, which could only have come from Greece and Rome. Bronze spears and armour, coins, gold jewellery and Roman glass are the way-marks of the amber trade across Northern Europe. Bronze armour was so prized that it was sunk as offerings to the gods of northern lakes and streams.

But fashions change. As the long Roman love-affair with amber cooled, and the export trade died out, Baltic amber became available once again for the Baltic peoples to enjoy. The Vikings set up workshops to fashion jewellery and game pieces. In the Middle Ages, the finest nuggets of amber were dedicated to the service of the Church, carved into rosaries and crucifixes. Being a resin, amber can be heated and smaller pieces pressed together to form chunks of amberoid. These were moulded into sacred vessels.

For centuries, the Danish court was besotted with amber. To ensure their supplies, the Danish kings kept amber-gathering on their shores as a royal prerogative. Princes attached turners to their courts to work amber, ivory, ebony and alabaster, and to teach their masters and mistresses the skill. Turning became a noble pastime – so much so that Queen Dorothea, in 1743, had her lathe disguised as an elegant chest of drawers, so that she could keep it in her boudoir in Rosenborg Castle and do a quick bit of turning whenever she had a spare moment. The products of this age are truly astonishing in their artistry and refinement – bowls with swans' necks and serpents' tails, inlaid boxes, intricately carved chessmen, fanciful chandeliers, gravy boats like Viking ships and altarpieces of astonishing richness. And not content with turning and carving the resin, they mounted it on decorative panels and employed the difficult 'eglomise' technique, embossing gold and silver foil to place behind sheets of translucent amber.

When the court lost interest and amber was free to move down the social scale, the rich farmers of Jutland and North Germany showed off their wealth by bestowing great amber necklaces, often weighing several kilos, on their tottering brides. That was in the nineteenth century, when there was so much amber available near Esjberg that the islanders of Fanø used it as everyday buttons, plain or multi-faceted, in the shapes of stars and flowers. What they couldn't use themselves, they exported to the Middle East to be moulded into hookah mouthpieces, as Muslims are forbidden to hold animal bone in their mouths. In fact, amber has a long connection with smoking. In the West, we used amber, often elaborately carved, for the mouthpieces of meerschaum pipes; and amazing as it may seem in these health-conscious days, amber cigarette-holders were one of the most popular confirmation presents from godparents! Amber's final fling in popularity was in the age of art nouveau.

Sunday afternoon was sunny, so I cycled along the coast to see Esjberg's most famous landmark, the statues of four gigantic men, all seated in the same stiff, monumental pose, their hands by their sides, gazing out from a small green hillock across the North Sea. They were sculpted by Svend Wiig Hansen to celebrate the centenary of the granting of Esjberg's charter as a market town in 1899. Dazzling white, they make the same powerful impact as Antony Gormley's weathering steel giant, *The Angel of the North*.

Sunday evening brought me a taste of the linguistic problems I had been dreading on this ride. Watching the national news on my television, I gathered that Poland had just held a referendum on joining the European Union, and the vote had been affirmative. This nugget of information was not easily acquired, as the report came from Warsaw, where the politicians were announcing the result in Polish – and the subtitles were in Danish!

'You should go to Norway!' declared a Norwegian walker the next morning over breakfast. I had been complaining about the priciness of Denmark.

'You have no idea what expensive is. We all play dominoes in Scandinavia. The Norwegians go to Sweden for their holidays. The Swedes go to Denmark. And the Danes go to Germany. No one can afford to holiday at home. Prices everywhere are totally unafford-able.'

He spoke to me in English, but I was fascinated, as a linguist, to hear him chatting merrily away to the waitress in Norwegian, while she replied in Danish, and they both laughed at each other's jokes. It seems that written Norwegian evolved under the Danes, as a result of some Danish conquest in the Middle Ages, so that their written languages are akin, and Old Norwegian, which my breakfast companion had learned in school, is similar to contemporary spoken Danish.

We talked about travel. He was just three months off retirement and was longing to mark it with a really long journey, perhaps in South America or Australia, both continents I had cycled across. I realised that I was the lucky one. No one would choose to be a widow, but if you are one, you might as well take advantage of it. I am free to go wherever and whenever the fancy takes me, while he was a married man, whose wife had to be considered – and she would rather stay at home. So he was faced with a very common dilemma.

'I don't know what to do for the best,' he said. 'Should I bully my wife into going with me, and have a gloomy fellow traveller who can't wait to get back home again? I know she wouldn't enjoy it if she came. It would be an ordeal for her. Or should I go on my own – in which case I would feel guilty about leaving her behind, and I know she'd resent being left. Or should I abandon the project altogether in the interests of marital harmony and spend the rest of my days regretting it?'

We chewed over the problem, along with our breakfast rolls, but he came no closer to a solution. He was a pale, wistful man and I couldn't see him taking a bold decision. I just knew he would waste his retirement, as so many other people do. He would take his dog for walks, do his DIY and potter about in his garden, dreaming of what might have been.

Denmark might be cheaper than Norway, but I did marvel at his choice of Central Jutland for a walking holiday. I spent the next few days cycling across arable land, where my only excitement was the occasional horse or cow. No one was working in the fields and the dedicated cycle paths were safe and solitary. When they ran along disused railway lines, the hedges were so high that I had no view at all and the wind was often funnelled against me through a seemingly endless green tunnel. There were no comfortable wooden gates, where I could perch for a snack under a tree to escape the intermittent rain. Everything was tremendously neat, trim, well ordered, well signposted in red on white, and somehow empty. Even in the graveyards of village churches, neat box hedges squared off the turf to isolate the tombs from one another. Every ghost had his own lonely little room.

I had never been to Denmark before, yet it all looked so familiar. I couldn't place it at first, then it suddenly hit me. It was just like suburban America. There was the same obsessive neatness, the same national flags flying from every home and public building, the same groaning restaurant tables – the Scandinavian smörgåsbord translated into the American 'Eat-as-much-as-you-like Buffet. Only $5.99!' The chunky modern Danes might be less warlike than their Viking ancestors who swept across England and Northern Europe, but they had still made their mark as migrants in the New World.

When the wind veered round to the west, it blew me, in one exhilarating day, across the whole width of Jutland. I entered Germany near Flensburg, along with traffic jams of Danes, who were piling into the border supermarkets to load their cars with cheap German food and drink. As I cycled into the city centre, I was a little surprised at myself. Sometimes in London these days I get the impression that I am living in a city of foreigners and a brief shadow of resentment clouds the moment. In German Flensburg, I was back in the middle of the same ethnic and cultural mix as we have in the major cities of Britain, and I found my spirits lifting. I realised then how much I had missed the vigour and variety of a multi-cultural society among the monotonously pink and white Danes.

Schleswig-Holstein. My history teacher at school, Mr Robinson, used to pronounce the name with tremendous relish, when he described how this territory in the south of Jutland had swung back and forth through the centuries between Denmark and Prussia. Flensburg sits invitingly on its firth. Schleswig, a great sailing centre, tumbles down through wooded hills to the Schlei, the longest fjord in the Baltic, and claims to be the oldest town in Northern Europe (its public records go back to 804).

Rendsburg has a magnificent central parade ground and the most terrifying long escalators I have ever seen, disappearing down into the gloom of the cycleway under the Ostsee Kanal. Unfazed Germans were riding calmly up and down with their bicycles, chatting as they went, but one glance down the precipitous flight and my vertigo struck. I could imagine myself whirling head-over-heels to the depths, all in a heap with my Condor, panniers and all. I froze at the top, quite incapable of stepping on to the moving stairs. Fortunately, a kindly station official spotted my distress and manoeuvred my bike on to the escalator, controlling it as we swept down. I sheltered behind his broad back, with my eyes tightly closed. The trick, it seemed, was to turn the handlebars parallel to the flight. When I reached the far end of the tunnel, I worried about the upward sweep, but my fears were unfounded. A smiling second official, alerted by the first, was waiting at the bottom of the escalator to escort me up to safety.

Those escalators were my only bad experience in Schleswig-Holstein. Between agreeable cities, the beech woods and forests of pine provided welcome shade. Unlike wet and windy Denmark, Germany had been calm, hot and rainless for months.

HAMBURG

The appearance of the country varies, but in general it is covered either by bristling forests or foul swamps . . . The Germans themselves are probably indigenous, with little foreign blood either as a result of invasions or friendly contact with their neighbours . . . For who would want to leave Asia Minor, North Africa or Italy, to go and live in Germany with its gloomy landscape and unpleasant climate?

Tacitus, *Germania*

Hamburg–Geesthacht–Wittenberge–Stendal–Magdeburg–Dessau–Wittenberg–Leipzig

I cruised into Hamburg, finding my way into the great city with no difficulty at all, thanks to the set of detailed maps which James had provided. He had even coloured the Elbe blue, in case his poor bewildered grandmother had difficulty identifying the river! James and Isabelle treated me to a delightful weekend at their home in Rissen, a leafy inner suburb. We caught up on family news, went sightseeing in Hamburg and dined outside in the mild evening air on smoked salmon, Parma ham and asparagus. In between times, I devoured their stack of English papers, *Economists* and *Private Eyes*. I had not found a single newspaper I could understand in Denmark and I felt very cut off from the world. But I had to move on quickly. A few more days of this warm, sociable idleness and I would never have stirred from Rissen again.

On Sunday morning, Isabelle produced my favourite breakfast of pancakes with maple syrup. Then James pedalled down with me to the Elbe, his tie flying in the wind (James always dresses very correctly), and saw me safely on to the cycle path which would carry me all the way across Germany to the Czech Republic.

Rows of elegant riverside villas led me along to the crowded fish market and the monumental art nouveau buildings of the St Pauli ferry terminal, all familiar territory from my weekend of sightseeing. But then my problems began. The docks of 'The Free and Hanseatic City of Hamburg' are probably the most extensive in Europe, occupying no fewer than 75 sq km. Three rivers flow through the city – the Elbe, the Alster and the Bille – as well as innumerable canals, many of them dead-end lading berths. I tried to stick to the Elbe, but got utterly lost. I was always within sight of water and often pedalled for half an hour or more, before realising that I had travelled up a broad canal, which led to nothing but a concrete wall. So I decided to try my compass. I followed it southeastwards, in an amazing sea of motorbikes, only to end up at the entrance to the Berlin motorway! But somehow, somewhere, late in the afternoon, after endless backtracking and frustrations, I found the Elbe again. I should have asked James for more of his meticulously marked maps!

Following the cycle path along the top of the Elbe embankment, I reached Geesthacht in the early evening. I had covered far less than my target distance out of Hamburg, but at least I knew I was on the right road now and clear of all those revving motorbikes. It turned out that Geesthacht was in the middle of a *Schützenfest*, a shooting festival. Hundreds of men in green coats, spattered liberally with badges, and green Bavarian hats with little feathers in them, were milling around in my hotel, accompanied by brisk, plump wives in short scarlet jackets, trimmed with black to match their dirndl skirts, and white stockings. All were consuming vast quantities of beer and *bockwurst*, and singing raucous songs. I escaped to a quiet pub in the next street.

'Ach! That *Schützenverein!*' said the landlord dismissively, as he served me with a gigantic helping of fish and chips. 'Shooting with their silly antique guns. Now they've taken to prancing about like a gang of Robin Hoods. Bows and arrows in the forest! But you must have had a terrible time getting here today. They said on the news that twenty-five thousand motorcyclists were converging on Hamburg for a rally.' So that explained the leather-clad hordes.

The shooting club was obviously a very important feature of social life in Saxony. Every small town seemed to be holding its shooting festival, and I passed a number of plaques on houses announcing proudly to the world that the occupier had been *König*, or king of his shooting club, in a particular year.

If the towns were not holding *Schützenfeste*, they were invariably holding *Spargelfeste* (asparagus festivals). There were '*spargel* happy hours' in the bars and *spargel* was on the menu in every restaurant, served up with scrambled eggs or Parma ham. The sandy soil was ideal for it.

Sometimes I followed the Elbe along the dykes separating the river and its flood plain from the arable land beyond. Sometimes I took to the road, which was less exposed to the sun. But the scenery was always the same – fields of wheat, barley, maize, asparagus and cabbages, with distant views of wooded hills. Being a townie, I find it hard to lyricise about the countryside, even at its most ravishing. And ravishing Saxony-Anhalt certainly was not! After its brief spell of liveliness in Hamburg, my mind returned to its rural Danish torpor. I generally do my most constructive thinking on my bicycle, particularly when the going is flat and easy. I plan everything from exciting new journeys to the redecoration of my kitchen. But in Saxony, I reached such a state of dullness that I was virtually brain-dead. Even my singing snagged. I had only to smell a wild rose on a hedgerow, and Schubert's *Heidenröslein* started up automatically, like a needle stuck in a groove. I couldn't get it out of my head.

I crossed into the former East Germany and stayed in shabby little towns with peeling paint and a few poor shops. There were derelict factories and depressing Communist housing estates. Old buildings were shuttered, sprouting weeds. But my own accommodation was usually excellent. Everyone who had a spare room had done it up to the highest standard, with a sparkling new bathroom, and was offering bed and breakfast. One enterprising woman, who ran the village post office, had combined it with a floristry business, while her daughter served coffee and cakes. Not content with that, she had converted the storeroom behind the shop to a perfect little bedroom and bathroom, where I stayed for a modest sum. After the more sophisticated West, life seemed somehow innocent. Teenaged boys played badminton in the traffic-free streets and passers-by wished me a pleasant '*Guten Abend.*' Shop assistants were labelled 'Frau Schmidt' with old-fashioned formality, unlike our matey 'Caroline' and 'Tracy' badges.

These East German towns have suffered a double disaster – Allied bombing in World War II, followed by decades of Communist mismanagement. Since unification, the trunk roads have been improved, but the minor roads through towns and villages have still to be tackled. My lightweight tourer rattled and juddered over lumpy cobbles on crinkle-crankle roads, and the cycle paths were no better. Their surface of higgledy-piggledy, cracked concrete slabs dipped down to broken cobblestones at the entrance to every house. Cycling was a tiring business.

But it was not all gloom and doom. The storks had arrived and taken up residence on chimney stacks, their great ramshackle nests housing clutches of storklets. One evening, I was dining outside in a restaurant garden, when a fearsome clatter erupted. We all looked anxiously up to the roof and saw two storks rattling their prodigious beaks at each other. They had built their nest on the restaurant chimney. Everyone in the garden smiled. And there were storks by the roadside too, but these were not the real thing. It seemed to be the practice in that part of the world to set up a tableau outside the front door – a pram with a life-sized wooden bride and groom, balloons, and a wooden stork dangling a pink or blue bundle from its beak. It was the signal to neighbours to come inside and see the new baby. These wooden storks were the apogee of German kitsch, rampant enough to cause death by jealousy to their rivals in kitsch, the Danes!

Beyond Magdeburg, I cycled through some remnants of the vast Teutoburgian Forest, which once covered the whole of North Germany. It was the scene of one of the greatest disasters in Roman military history, the disaster which shattered their northern aspirations and shaped the Germans' vision of themselves. In 9 AD, the Roman general Publius Quintilius Varus was marching his army of 25,000 men from the river Weser to their winter quarters on the Rhine. As they were passing through a narrow defile between dense forest and swampland, the army was ambushed by a horde of Cheruscan spearmen. If they retreated, the Romans would be sucked down into the bog, so they had no choice but to march into the dark forest, the realm of the green men, where conventional battle plans were useless against the lightning strikes of guerrillas who knew every tree and every hiding-place. The Roman army was virtually annihilated and Varus fell in shame on his sword.

The leader of the Cherusci was a chief named Arminius (Hermann). He had served in the Roman army before reverting to life in the forest, so he understood Roman military tactics and the Roman mind. The Romans had walked into his trap because they had been dismissive of the German tribes. In their view, the Germans could fight when the mood took them, but they were no more than rude savages, children of the trees, too disorganised to present any real danger. Varus's defeat at the hands of Arminius was a blow to their pride. It was a disgrace which had to be avenged.

Six years later, the Emperor Tiberius selected his nephew, a brilliant young general named Germanicus, to carry out this mission. Taking Arminius by surprise, Germanicus fought his way into the Teutoburgian forest, where he collected the scattered bones of Varus's fallen legions and gave them a decent burial. Then for three years he harassed the German tribes with superior forces, until he had wiped out enough of their warriors to establish a reasonable title to victory; after which the Romans retreated with dignity to the Rhine. They had salvaged their pride, but they had also learned their lesson. In future, they would leave the German tribes well alone. They fixed the boundaries of their empire along the Rhine and the Danube, and never again attempted to subjugate the peoples to the east or north of those rivers.

Meanwhile, the Germans had acquired their folk hero. Hermann was their strong, innocent man of the north, the unspoilt child of nature, defender of his native forests and heaths against the decadent, materialistic city-dwellers of the Mediterranean. Hermann became the inspiration for the German ideal of sylvan simplicity, which has permeated their culture ever since. The honest woodcutters of fairy tale; the Gothic horrors of the dark, bristling forest; Gothic architecture with its echo of pine trees thrusting towards the heavens; the woodland raptures of German Romantic poets; the *Wandervogel* ramblers' clubs in their lederhosen; the re-enactments of Varus's defeat by fur-clad, helmeted nationalists in the early days of Hitler's Reich – all have their roots in the Hermann legend. Even the members of today's *Schützenverein*, in their antique huntsmen's gear, are harking back to Hermann's exploits in the Teutoburgian forest. And we all know the sinister practices which resulted from Tacitus's casual remark about German racial purity. He intended it as a bit of a slight: Rome was a sophisticated cosmopolitan city, where people of all the races under Roman rule mingled and married. But his slur on the backward, rustic Germans became the murderous pride of the National Socialist Party.

As for the Amber Route, the struggle between Hermann and Varus was critical to its development. If the Romans had conquered the Germanic tribes, their own merchants would have controlled the trade in amber from its source. But when their dreams of an empire stretching to the Baltic faded, they had to rely on the free Germans for their supplies. No northern tribesmen, so far as we know, travelled the entire distance. Amber was collected on the seashores and sold on down the rivers, from one German trader to the next, until it reached the Roman city of Carnuntum on the Danube. This chain of suppliers, each with his own mark-up, made for a very expensive commodity. In an attempt to bring down the price, a Roman knight in the reign of the Emperor Nero was despatched on a mission to the Baltic by an entrepreneur named Julianus. He was to bring back a large quantity of amber himself and produce what would nowadays be called 'a feasibility study'. Would it be possible for the Romans themselves to take over the trade, or at least cut down the number of middlemen? His report must have been discouraging. The thought of all those warlike Hermanns lurking in their dark forests was enough to strike dread into the hearts of would-be Roman traders. They decided to stay safe in their cities, and leave the gathering and transportation of amber to the Germans, even if it meant higher prices.

There were excellent cycle paths through what remained of the Teutoburg forest, but I was glad to emerge into the sunlight of Dessau, a lovely open city of parks and tree-lined avenues. It was easy to see why the Bauhaus movement had chosen it as their home when they moved from Berlin. I stopped two women on Gropius Allee to check the route to Wittenberg. 'Don't go through the forest!' they said. 'Not on your own.' Even the Germans are nervous of their woodlands. They advised a quiet back road through Oranienburg instead.

'Welcome to the baroque town of Oranienburg!' said the notice. Streets of erratic cobbles, baroque in the extreme, jolted me to the perfect baroque church, where I sat in a neat baroque square and ate my lunch-time sandwich of sunflower bread and delicious black cherry jam. Then I hurtled along the flat, swept by a raging west wind, like a leaf in a gale or a yacht with its spinnaker flying. When I turned north to cross the bridge over the Elbe, a tremendous gust blew me straight off my bicycle, fortunately on a fenced-off cycle path. I tried to remount, but the wind kept tossing me down again. So I gave up the battle and walked slowly across the bridge, relishing the distant view of the towers of Martin Luther's city. The townie was back in her element after weeks of field and forest.

LUTHERSTADT-WITTENBERG AND LEIPZIG

Time is a river, the resistless flow of all created things. No sooner does one object come into view than it is swept away and another appears, only to be swept past in its turn.

Marcus Aurelius, *Meditations*

Wittenberg–Leipzig–Meissen–Dresden–Pirna–Bad Schandau

Wittenberg, now known as Lutherstadt-Wittenberg, in honour of its most famous son, is a picture-perfect German Renaissance town. Sadly neglected under the GDR, the public buildings round its cobbled market square are now freshly painted in delicate shades of pink, cream and blue, and there are flower baskets everywhere. But what really catches the eye is the magnificent, gleaming white town hall, its gables, doors and window-frames picked out in black, a Renaissance triumph, built at the height of Wittenberg's glory, when it was the seat of the Elector of Saxony and the intellectual fulcrum of Central Europe.

The old town was small enough to be enjoyed on foot – which was just as well, for there were more of those baroque cobbles, which made for very uncomfortable cycling. I braved the evening gale to stroll through the meadows beside the trickling Elbe. It was a river starved of rain, its sandbanks poking through like the bones of a famished creature. The largest of the river-boats had already been tied up and there were fears for the summer tourist traffic.

Before me rose the bulky might of the Schlosskirche, the castle church. Its tower was a round structure, which would have looked exactly like a lighthouse, had it not been charcoal grey; and it had a small, rather comical Gothic spire sticking out of its pinnacle-fenced dome, like the spikes on the kaiser's helmets in the First World War. It was not a thing of beauty, but it finally drove *Heidenröslein* out of my head and replaced it with a new obsession. For under its bulging dome and fancy ironwork was a plain band of stone with golden words – the first line of Martin Luther's majestic hymn, *Ein feste Burg ist unser Gott* ('A safe stronghold our God is still').

Humming my new tune, I walked round the church to look at the famous door, where Luther nailed up his 97 theses on 31 October 1517. These criticisms of papal indulgences were the first significant act in the Reformation which was to sweep across Europe. Luther wrote his theses in Latin, the language of the Church and the Universities; but later, with the aid of his friend and fellow professor, Melanchthon, he translated the Bible into German, to make it more accessible to the people. And Melanchthon went even further, campaigning for German to replace Latin as the language of instruction in Germany's schools and universities.

The chancel of the Marienkirche, the other church where Martin Luther preached, has wonderful wooden panels, painted by the Cranachs, father and son, who lived and worked in Wittenberg in those exciting times. My favourite is a spirited picture of Luther, Melanchthon, Lucas Cranach the elder and a bevy of clergymen, modestly dressed in black, all hard at work tending one end of the Lord's vineyard. The other end is crowded with princes of the Catholic Church, overweight cardinals and bishops in their decadent gold vestments. Unlike the devout reformers, they are maliciously tearing down the vines of the Lord and trampling them underfoot.

What the painting does not show is the nugget of amber which Martin Luther always wore around his waist, to protect him from kidney-stones. Amber was worn as a prophylactic against all manner of afflictions – toothache, delirium, weak sight, digestive problems and every kind of malfunction of the internal organs. Archaeologists have unearthed amber necklaces discoloured by the pyrophosphoric crystal secreted by rheumatic sufferers, evidence of the use of amber from the earliest times to relieve rheumatism. It was poured down ears in a mixture of honey and rosewater to cure earache; and it was administered internally too, crushed and taken in honey as a remedy for sore throats, and mixed with water for stomach upsets. It was even fed to babies to soothe them when they were teething. Amber was not just a beautiful ornament, 'the gold of the north'. It was a wonder-working substance, both magical and medicinal. Little wonder the Romans were prepared to pay such a high price for it.

I woke on Saturday to an overcast morning, hot and stuffy under a blanket of grey, which still produced no rain. There were a few stalls in the market, selling the inevitable *Spargel*, locally grown, but most of the shops were shut for the weekend. Used as we are in England to supermarkets and corner shops opening seven days a week, I just couldn't adapt to the limited German hours and was always running out of fruit.

'I thought the Germans were supposed to work so hard,' I said to James, when I found that shops, even in central Hamburg, were closed on a Saturday afternoon.

'They do work hard,' he said. 'But their weekends and holidays are sacrosanct. They take their leisure as seriously as their work.'

So Wittenberg was a weekend ghost town, deserted until a file of American teenagers trooped out of the Best Western Hotel, all masticating slowly and dragging reluctant feet towards Luther's house. They were soon joined by a coach-load of their fellow countrymen. I heard the languid drawl of the Deep South. They were Lutherans from America's Bible belt, on pilgrimage to the fountain of their faith.

These Americans were the first foreign tourists I had come across since entering the former East Germany. Most visitors there were retired Germans on day trips. Again, I missed the international flavour. Even the tourist destinations seemed somehow lacking in vitality. Their buildings had been painted up, but on warm sunny evenings, when the rest of Europe was sitting outside, enjoying ice-cream and cold beers at the pavement cafés, the old East Germans stayed firmly indoors. Were they still so short of cash that they couldn't afford a meal out? Or had years of bleak socialism ground them down? Whatever the reason, there seemed to be no fun in their lives, no *joie de vivre*. In Wittenberg, I expected something livelier when I saw the tourists, but they did a businesslike round of the Luther and Cranach sights, then disappeared in their coaches. When I went out for dinner, I walked down empty streets. There was not even a lighted shop-window to pierce the darkness and give me something to look at. The statues of Luther and Melanchthon presided over a desolate market square, where my footsteps echoed. I was glad of the cruising police cars, and relieved to turn into Collegienstrasse, the one bustling thoroughfare, where I dived into the safety of a well-lit Italian trattoria.

The gloomy detachment of the East Germans was partly, I think, a linguistic problem. The landlady at my pension congratulated me on my German.

'It's not very brilliant,' I said. 'I learned it at school and I've never really practised it. It's just about good enough to get me by.'

'I wish we'd learned English at school!'

'What did you learn? Russian?'

'Yes, Russian. And I've forgotten all of it now, though my husband still speaks it a little. But, you know, we feel so cut off. So foolish. We'd love to travel to the West, now that we're free to do it, to see Paris, London, Venice, all those wonderful cities. But how can we, when we don't speak anything but German and a few words of Russian – neither of them languages that are commonly spoken these days. So we stick to the places we're used to. We still take our holidays at the seaside in Romania and Bulgaria, countries which share our past, where we feel comfortable.'

Then she brightened up. 'But things are changing. My son speaks quite good English. As for my grandchildren,' she added proudly, 'they're absolutely fluent already, both of them, and they're only eight and ten.'

She kindly volunteered to take care of my bike and most of my gear, while I took the train to spend the rest of the weekend in Leipzig. It was not on my direct route along the Elbe, but it was only 70 km away, and it was the German city I most needed to visit. Leipzig, not Luther's Wittenberg, was the site of my own personal pilgrimage.

When I was nine or ten years old, I was rummaging one idle afternoon through my mother's piano music, looking for pieces that I might conceivably be able to play. I found a neglected green book, her copy of Bach's *Two-Part Inventions*. The pieces were a revelation. I rushed into my next piano lesson, clutching the book. 'These are what I really, really want to learn! Do you think I could manage them?' Since that day, for me, there has been music, and then there has been Bach. Bach is transcendent. He is the sun, whose light blots out the feeble rays of other composers. There are many whose music I enjoy, but I would throw their entire opus on the bonfire to save one fugue of the divine Bach.

I had almost given up on enjoyment in the old East Germany, when Leipzig knocked me off my feet. Could this beautiful, exuberant, swinging city really belong there? I marched out of the gleaming railway station (the largest in Europe) and across the Willy-Brand-Platz, free and unencumbered. It felt good to be 'on holiday' from cycling. An antique Paris bus was just about to leave the tourist office, so I jumped aboard and did an effortless sightseeing round of the lavish villas and parks of the ring road. Here was the house where Schiller lived, and Goethe, and Mendelssohn, Wagner and Richard Strauss. We were treated to lists of dates, costs, heights, weights, numbers of workmen employed, all those mind-bending facts beloved of tour guides the world over. I was glad of the convenient tour, but it was peripheral to my purpose, and when it was over I dumped my rucksack in my hotel room and sped off down Nikolaistrasse.

What followed was the highlight of my summer journey, even one of the highlights of my life. I entered the Thomaskirche, where the great Johann Sebastian Bach served as organist and choirmaster for 27 years, until his death in 1750. Sunlight streamed through his memorial window. His tomb was a simple slab of black marble on the chancel floor, engraved with his name and dates. A vase of pink and white lilies stood beside it, and there was a scattering of red roses. Best of all, by a great stroke of good fortune, I chanced on a Bach recital. It was being given by his present-day successor on the new organ, specially built to show off the glory of Bach's music. The church resounded with the thunder of one of his majestic fugues, that contrapuntal marriage of intellect and heart-rending beauty. It was almost more than I could bear. I left the church in a daze.

Still in pursuit of Bach, I retraced my steps along Nikolaistrasse to his other church. With twenty children to support, he needed extra work, so he took on the job of organist and choirmaster at the Nikolaikirche, and raced back and forth between his two churches. The Thomaskirche was a plain Gothic building, with nothing exceptional about it. But the stunning classical interior of the Nikolaikirche had the most extraordinary pink fluted columns, topped with long waving spiky green leaves, which looked more like giant pineapples than capitals. It was in this church that the people of Leipzig began their silent vigils and services of peaceful protest in May 1989 – one of the first steps in the quiet defeat of Honecker's brand of socialism.

Everything after that was bound to be an anti-climax. I wandered past the cafés which, amazingly for the former GDR, were buzzing with life and laughter. Then I treated myself to dinner in

Auerbach's Keller, the famous Leipzig watering-hole where Goethe's Faust made his pact with Mephistopheles. I did no more sightseeing, for what could compare with Bach and his churches?

There followed another week of miles under the wheels, with more fields, trees and derelict industrial estates. In Grossenhain, I slept under a giant poster of a jungle lady, voluptuously clad in leopard-skin, lolling seductively beside an unimpressed leopard. I wondered what sort of clientele usually patronised that hotel. Certainly not lone lady cyclists. That was the day I passed my first vineyard and heard my first tentative cricket. Meissen had a stunning cathedral and castle, towering on their crag above the Elbe. But Dresden was a nightmare of excavated roads, traffic diversions, building sites, cables, cobbles and pipe-laying gangs. They were tearing up the city from its foundations, to repair the damage of those disastrous and unnecessary Allied bombing raids, followed by decades of Communist neglect. I pressed on to the monumental centre, the Theaterplatz and the Brühische Terrasse, high above the Elbe. These vast, cold open spaces were the setting for a display of overblown eighteenth- and nineteenth-century baroque, crude statements of Saxon power, buildings as arrogant as they were lavish. I took one look at them and lost all heart for their picture collections. There was a paddle-steamer down on the river, just preparing to cruise upstream. I pedalled furiously down to the quay and was just in time to jump on board. It was only a 10 km cruise to Schloss Pillnitz, the summer castle of the kings and queens of Saxony, but it got me clear of haughty Dresden and its terrible bone-shaking roads.

After four weeks of flat fields, I had reached 'The Saxon Switzerland', and my road was gently rising. The Elbe flowed through a craggy landscape, where castles perched on sandstone pinnacles, carved into fantastic shapes by the action of wind and water. It struck me as more gloomy than the real Switzerland, possibly because I saw it through the eyes of that painter of Gothic eeriness, Caspar David Friedrich. As I cruised along excellent cycle paths in perfect weather, the landscape seemed unthreatening. But paint in a ghostly mist or a Friedrich storm, and it could easily turn into another of those bristling prospects which had so terrified the Romans. It was another leg of the Amber Route best left to the local

Hermanns, especially as the river itself could be temperamental. In the tourist towns, such as Pirna and Bad Schandau, the houses had been repaired and given a cheerful lick of paint, but there were marks high up on the first floors to show the astonishing level the Elbe had reached in the floods of 2002. In 2003, months without rain were bringing the opposite problem: the Elbe would soon be too low for the paddle-steamers. Like everywhere else in the old GDR, Bad Schandau was dead by nightfall, so I spent my last evening in Germany watching Wimbledon on my television (23 channels, all of them in German) over a solitary picnic of ham, cheese, cherries and wine.

LITOMERICE AND PRAGUE

The performance is always the same. It is only the actors who change.
Marcus Aurelius, Meditations

Litomerice–Prague–Votice–Tyn nad Vltavou–
Ceske Budejovice–Ceske Krumlov–Rozmberk nad Vltavou–
Freistadt–Linz

All change! At the Czech border, the Elbe changed its name to the Labe, place names became unpronouceable, and the smooth German cycle path changed to a rugged road, perpendicular as a cliff-face. Roman surveyors would never have countenanced such a gradient. The mountains and forests of Bohemia were clearly another Roman no-go area on the Amber Route.

I had no idea what to expect of the Czech Republic. It was unknown territory, where the language was gibberish to my Latin ear, and the place names were littered with so many weird diacritical marks that I gave up attempting to pronounce them. Even life's basics were a mystery. I had to lurk behind a tree, spying like a pervert on the people using the public loos, to find out if I was a *muzi* or a *zeny* (I'm a *zeny*!). There was no frontier post and no currency exchange, so I hadn't a Czech koruna to my name and couldn't see a bank. But I did see something which cheered me enormously – a notice pointing to Tesco's! The comfort of the familiar brought a smile to my face and I set off for Prague in good heart.

Decin and Usti nad Laben were grimy industrial towns, but the countryside between them was a delight. The river was tightly sandwiched between two roads. The one on the left bank took all the heavy traffic, while my minor road along the right was green and peaceful, with views through the trees to the water's edge. After just one modest climb, I cycled into Litomerice and was bowled over by its beauty.

I found an ATM in its magnificent market-place and a newly refurbished pink and white pension, awash with geraniums, down a quiet cobbled street nearby. Opposite stood the tiny church of St Wenceslas, a white baroque jewel with fanciful trimmings in salmon pink and a charming little green onion dome, topped with a filigree cross. This was baroque with a light touch, elegant and gay, a world away from the ponderous grey monuments of Dresden. Every building in the town was equally delightful. The Gothic churches had little baby spires sprouting from the sides of the important ones, so that they looked like castles out of a fairy tale. And all the baroque was deliciously pastel, with extravagant icing-sugar swags and flounces. It was architecture for the fun of it.

For dinner, I thought I had better go to the best restaurant in town, where the waiters might, with luck, speak English or at least a bit of German. They did, serving me with great charm, but considerable slowness. It was all delightfully old-fashioned. The lights were dim and there were real lace tablecloths and lace-trimmed linen napkins. All the tables were round six-seaters, each one of which was filled up before the next one was broached. I dreaded the embarrassment of having five Czechs foisted on me, when I didn't speak a word of their language. But my waitress left me in peace, lapped into nostalgia by the restaurant pianist. 'Smoke Gets in Your Eyes', 'September Song', 'The Man I Love'. If I were of a melancholy disposition, I would have been in tears by the end of my solitary dinner.

The next morning, I overslept. I had cycled diagonally across the whole of Germany in less than a fortnight, with some intensive sightseeing on the way. It was time I took a day off, and where better to enjoy my leisure than this beautiful town of Litomerice?

I was offered an omelette for breakfast, which made a pleasant change from the fat pork, salami and processed cheese of recent weeks. Over my third cup of proper coffee, I got into conversation with two motorbikers, on their way home to Sweden.

'Did you come through Dresden?' they asked. 'It's a wonder we've got any teeth left in our heads after those cobbles and potholes! And the wind was so strong, we could hardly control the bike. We hated it. There were so many diversions, we got hopelessly lost and utterly fed up. We'd intended to stay there for a few days, but we couldn't face it.'

'Exactly my experience,' I said. 'It was murder trying to cycle there, and I hated all that leaden baroque. The Theaterplatz was milling with tourists and there was nowhere to leave my bike. I couldn't get out fast enough.'

'We moved straight on to the Czech Republic and we're so glad we did. We've had a wonderful time here. You'll love it!'

They went on to talk about last year's floods along the Elbe and Vltava, and how amazingly well the Czechs had got themselves together again. The husband was an economist, who confidently asserted that the cost of the damage was greater than the country's Gross National Product, so in most cases, the Government could afford to pay only ten per cent compensation to people whose houses and businesses had been ruined. Yet somehow they had managed to repair and repaint them, and everything looked spick and span.

Litomerice city was high on a hill over the Elbe, now named the Labe, so its gorgeous buildings had not been badly affected. I wandered round the streets in a daze of delight, snapping away like a Japanese tourist. When I got home, I realised that I had more photos of Litomerice than of any other place. I just couldn't resist the pretty pastel façades and the black on white murals. Two walls of the Salva Guarda Hotel were completely covered with childlike paintings of the Creation, Adam and Eve, Noah's ark, the Annunciation and the Ascension, all muddled up with Bacchus and his grapes, saints and their lions and mediaeval Bohemian warriors in helmets. It was a feast for the eyes.

When I reached the cathedral, I found that Saturday morning Mass was being celebrated by a visiting cardinal. The cathedral was packed. Every pew was crammed, with standing-room only at the rear of the nave. One family with four young boys, aged from about sixteen down to six, were occupying the porch, and all were on their knees, praying devoutly.

But marriages were civil ceremonies, and Saturday was the day for them. Four doddery old men were standing at the bottom of the town hall's stone stairs, playing baroque music on their trombones, while the bridal couples passed. The grooms wore shiny new suits and the brides were in flouncy white confections. As for the guests, there seemed to be no dress code at all for them, as some were dressed to kill, while others came in their shorts. But all were there to enjoy themselves. One high-spirited young man had parked his beribboned car, with a bride doll on the bonnet, across the entrance to the town hall, and had clamped the wheels with purloined police clamps. A crowd had gathered in the square and everyone was laughing. Eventually, the police arrived, but instead of administering a stern reproof, they joined in the amusement. One officer was so tickled that he rushed off to get his video camera and started to film the scene, but he had to give up, because he was laughing so much that his camera was shaking.

It was my first taste of the legendary Czech humour. The Czechs have lost their independence several times in their history but have survived through satire and mockery. Under the Habsburgs, *The Good Soldier Svejk*, a Prague dog-catcher, was drafted unwillingly into the Austro-Hungarian army, where he caused military chaos by carrying out his orders to the letter. The creator of this innocent wrecker, Jaroslav Hasek, is one of a tradition of Czech writers who have gnawed away at authority, undermining its rules and red tape with ridicule. Most recently, the underground writers of the 1970s and 1980s in Prague were the power behind the 1989 'Velvet Revolution'. Of those known abroad, the knife-sharp satirical novelist Milan Kundera was stripped of his Czech citizenship in 1979 for his collection of wry tales, *The Book of Laughter and Forgetting*; while the most famous of all, the playwright Vaclav Havel, had several spells behind Communist bars before the Berlin Wall fell and he emerged from the darkness to become president of his newly democratic country.

'Don't even think of cycling into Prague!' After Saturday's Swedes, I had Sunday Germans over my breakfast coffee. They were a retired couple who had flown with their bicycles from Dresden to Vienna and cycled back as far as Litomerice along the route I was planning to take. As I had cycled along their route to Litomerice in the opposite direction, we were able to swap information of the kind that cyclists really need.

'The road along the Vltava, from Austria into Prague, was fine. But coming out of Prague in this direction, it was absolutely terrifying. There were no cycle paths, and the space on the hard shoulder, behind the white line, was no wider than our tyres. The surface was cracked. It was full of stones and broken glass, and the trucks were roaring past. We're lucky to have got out of it alive. And there was nothing to see between Prague and Kralupy anyway – just motorway and factories. Take the train into the city.'

I promised to think about it, and set off for Prague via Litomerice's Penny Market. Everywhere I looked in Germany and the Czech Republic, the trees were dripping with cherries, my favourite fruit, the pavements beneath them stained purple. But there was rarely a cherry to be seen in the shops. Litomerice's supermarket was no exception. There were fine displays of mangoes, bananas, citrus fruits, kiwis and pineapples, all expensively imported, but nothing from local growers. For better or worse, the Czechs had joined the global economy. I made do with a couple of New Zealand Braeburns.

Germany had been comfortably overcast, but now the sun was beating down on the orchards and hop fields, the soil was cracking for want of rain, and roadside trees were shedding their leaves, like autumn in June. As I cycled towards Melnik, I felt a mixture of sadness and anticipation. I was sad because it was my last morning on the Elbe, the river which had been my constant companion since Hamburg. But I had to admit that the Elbe had often been a boring, bucolic friend – all those days of mechanical pedalling through cabbages and maize – so I was quite excited at the prospect of leaving the flat agricultural landscape behind me and switching to my next river, the Vltava. The mountains and forests of old Bohemia lay ahead, not to mention one of the most elegant cities on earth, Prague.

For the Hindus, the confluence of two or more rivers is a sacred spot, where a single bathe will wash away a lifetime of sin. I am no Hindu, but I share their awe at the silent meeting of great waters – the merging of the sky-blue Indus from the mountains of Kashmir with the turbulent brown Kabul river; the spruce-green Rhone from the Alps with the darker, slower Saone; or the sinister Rio Negro, which flows for miles in a parallel stream, till it finally mingles its clear black waters with the nutrient-rich brew of the Amazon, dense and brown as oxtail soup. These are majestic spectacles. But I was disappointed in Melnik. I missed the confluence of the Labe and the Vltava. A new main road, which was not on my map, led me hopelessly astray, a canal adding to the confusion. When I next sighted the river, I was halfway up the road to Kralupy, where the factories on the outskirts of Prague began. The traffic thickened, even on a Sunday afternoon, and the sun beat down without mercy. I took the advice of the cycling Germans and sped through Prague's industrial suburbs on a local train. It was the only time I cheated on the ride.

* * *

When Marcus Aurelius made his theatrical analogy, he was obviously thinking of Rome and Athens. But if ever a city was a magnificent stage set, that city is Prague; and the pomp of its performance is always the same. Only the actors change.

Luxuriant tree-clad mountains, crowned with castles, provide its backdrop, while the centre stage is occupied by the city's stunning architectural vistas. Prague has been fortunate in its builders. The Holy Roman Emperor Charles IV provided Gothic at its purest; the Habsburgs were responsible for its sumptuous baroque; and art nouveau was favoured by its wealthy industrialists. The city's mediaeval ground-plan was not destroyed to clear the way for nineteenth-century boulevards; few of its buildings suffered in World War II; and the Communists were not strong on modernisation. So Prague has remained an unspoilt relic of its more gracious past, remarkably coherent in style. The least attractive bits of the stage set are the actors out at the front, the mobs of touts and tourists.

For Prague is now the proverbial victim of its own success. Maybe I'm an old curmudgeon these days, but it did strike me that the city was over-full of beer-bellies, tattoos and filthy dreadlocks – the indigent and uncultured of the West there for the cheap booze. My hotel turned out to be the venue for an English stag weekend. Thirty young men partied the afternoon away over tankards of strong Czech beer, went out clubbing at night, and came back, uproariously drunk at 4.45 a.m., waking the whole hotel. Their shouts ricocheted off the trellis-clad walls of the inner courtyard, and when the poor night porter tried to hush them, they turned nasty and threatened to rough him up. I heard it all from my bed and was ashamed to be British. When I dropped my key with the receptionist the next morning, I thought I ought to make some apology for the terrible behaviour of my compatriots.

'And they're booked in for another night!' she moaned. 'We were so pleased to get such a big booking so early in the season. But the agency didn't tell us it was this sort of a group. We were expecting English ladies and gentlemen. We have always considered the English to be such courteous people. This behaviour has been a great shock.'

Fortunately, the stags were incapable of appearing at breakfast. Instead we were treated to a party of honking, neighing Italian jackasses, all in reverse baseball caps.

One of the joys of Prague is its compactness. My four-hour walking tour of the city, guided by a handsome young student of English, took in virtually everything from Wenceslas Square on the low left bank of the Vltava up to Hradcany, the spectacular hilltop castle, and the Gothic cathedral of St Vitus. On the way, we passed all the fairy-tale spires, pastel baroque and gilded, curvaceous art nouveau that anyone could wish for. And just as fascinating to me, we passed numerous shops selling amber. Entire window displays were devoted to amber, and nothing but amber, in all shades of its tawny yellow splendour. Other jewellers were specialists in both Baltic amber and local garnet, set in Bohemian silver. The designs were traditional, evidence that amber had passed through Prague and been fashioned into jewellery for centuries. I was certainly on an authentic Roman Amber Route.

In the Jewish quarter, we passed the house of Franz Kafka, where the Czechs have put up a plaque to please the tourists. They were surprised at first that foreigners should be so interested in a writer who was virtually unknown and certainly little regarded at home. For the Czechs, he has always been on the wrong side of the fence. Born in 1883, when the country was part of the Austro-Hungarian Empire, he wrote his books in German, just at the time when the Czech independence movement was stirring. This meant that he was shunned by the intelligentsia, who were making a point of writing in Czech. When the Nazis overran the country in 1939, his works were banned because he was Jewish. Then after the war, his works were still suppressed, because the anguish of the little, bewildered man, struggling against a mechanistic authoritarian regime in *The Trial* and *The Castle*, was far too near the bone for the ruling Communists. It is only now that the Czechs are beginning to appreciate one of their own most famous writers.

A walk through the mediaeval Jewish quarter is an excursion into the darker recesses of the human mind. To begin with, the buildings are lower than those in the rest of Prague. The level of the city has been raised a few metres to protect it from the Vltava's floods, so what used to be the ground floor of many old buildings is now the basement (my hotel had a beautiful underground restaurant). But the Jews had to leave their homes and synagogues at the original lower level, because their religion was 'lower' than

Christianity. The Jewish quarter has been plagued with flooding ever since – which is a pity, as it has one of the oldest synagogues in Europe (1270 Gothic) and a delightful pastel blue and white town hall, with a normal clock and, beneath it, a clock from the sixteenth century, which has Hebrew numbers and works widdershins. The whole district is now the Prague Jewish Museum, founded by the Nazis in 1942. It is where they assembled artefacts of interest and value from all the Jewish communities throughout the former Czechoslovakia, intending to create 'The Museum of an Extinct People'. The Pinkas Synagogue, with the names of over 77,000 Czech Jewish dead, shows how close the Nazis came to achieving their objective.

The weekend heatwave erupted into a violent midnight storm, but it had calmed down to a few gentle spits and spots of rain when I started my ride south along the Vltava. There was a cycle path of sorts as far as Zbraslav. Then came a long, thickly wooded hill, which I was pleased to find I could manage without having to get off and push. The climb was so steep that I was expecting a long run down from the summit, but Czech hills turned out to be quite unusual. This one opened out at the top on to a wide, high plateau, which felt like the roof of the world. Far below me, to the north, the whole city of Prague lay outspread, while fields and woods stretched to the horizon in every other direction. With a strong northwest wind on my tail, I bowled effortlessly through charming villages and pleasantly undulating country. It was a Czech holiday area, watered by the Vltava and its tributaries.

As evening fell, so did the rain, and I left the quiet riverside for the main road, where I hoped it would be easier to find accommodation. Votice looked a big place on the map, the sort of town where they were bound to have hotels, but its wet streets were deserted and there was no sign of anywhere to stay. Motorists have an easy life; they can always move on to the next town. But Tabor was another 26 km along a hilly road, much too far for a weary cyclist at the end of the day. I had to find something in Votice.

There was a butcher's shop in the main street, where a buxom, pink-cheeked girl was giving a final scrub to the counters. Although she spoke nothing but Czech and was a bit slow on the uptake, I closed my eyes, folded my hands under my cheek and snored violently, until the fog of her incomprehension finally cleared. She shook her head. Then a customer came in, a much brighter old lady, who smiled and beckoned to me. In the very next street stood the Wenceslas Pension. It was bolted and dark, but the old lady was undeterred. She signalled to me to stay where I was, while she went home to phone the owner. Ten minutes later, she was back with a hefty man, whose face was half hidden behind a luxuriant black moustache. He spoke no English either, but he handed me his mobile, so that I could talk to someone who did. I agreed the terms with this disembodied female voice and the man gave me a set of keys to the empty house and a card from his restaurant. Then he disappeared into the rainy night.

The experience became even more bizarre at dinner-time. I found the restaurant with the aid of two Czech-speaking Korean girls (what on earth were they doing in Votice?) and confronted the menu. It was all in Czech and no one spoke English or German. I pointed to a section, flapped imaginary wings and crowed.

'*Ano,*' said the waitress. Of course, I took that to mean 'no', when in fact it is the Czech word for 'yes'. Once that misunderstanding was cleared up, I went on to the next section, where I honked like a pig.

'*Ano,*' she said again. Everyone laughed. In fact, the snug, crowded restaurant was full of laughter, as families, couples of all ages and large groups of friends enjoyed an evening out. I was amazed to find such a vibrant social life in such a poor little dump of a town. They raised their glasses to me as I tucked into my delicious pork casserole with red peppers, onions and leeks, served with mixed vegetables, roast potatoes, chips and a side salad, washed down with a litre of beer and polished off with a double Glenmorangie – all for less than £4! I decided that rural Bohemia was a fine place.

It was an idyllic week. The country had everything that Switzerland or Austria can boast, except snowcaps. There were mountains, rivers, forests, smiling meadows, steepled churches tucked in the folds of green hills, and villages with ducks on the ponds and flowers in the gardens, even geraniums decking the bus shelters. The people were good-humoured, the roads virtually traffic-free and prices were still far lower than those in the West. The only snag was the impenetrable language. The young people, who now learn English in school, must all have migrated to Prague to find jobs in tourism, because outside the capital even a little rusty German was hard to find. I cycled through a picture-book landscape, delightful even to an inveterate city-lover, but it was frustrating not to be able to communicate.

The Vltava was rising, but I scarcely noticed it, as each climb took me up to a broad plateau where I cycled easily, without losing altitude. I passed through Ceske Budejovice, which as Budweis, to give it its Austro-Hungarian name, is the town where they still brew the original Budweiser beer; then on to Ceske Krumlov, a dramatic mountain eyrie embraced by an almost circular sweep of the river. The town was a tourist honeypot, where groups of Americans, as well as the ubiquitous Germans and Japanese, swarmed up its steep cobbled streets. Every house seemed to be offering rooms. The evening sun was fleeting and it was bitterly cold up there. I have no idea of the altitude, but I know that I shivered my way home from the restaurant under a sliver of new moon, admiring the fine displays of amber in the shop windows.

My last day in Bohemia was remarkably beautiful. When I flew down to the Vltava from Ceske Krumlov's crag, I found myself on a winding road which ran along the water's edge, through beech woods and conifers, almost to the Austrian frontier. The river was shallow now and swift-flowing, with the most extensive campsites I have ever seen on the opposite bank. It was Independence Day, so crowds of Czech holidaymakers were riding the Vltava in canoes, or gliding along on crowded rafts. The current was perfect for family water-sports – so fast that there was no need to paddle downstream, but not fast enough to be dangerous.

There were no cars on my quiet road, but in the middle of the morning I was overtaken at speed by a Chinese boy on a mountain bike. At the top of the next rise, he was waiting for me, puzzling over his map. I got out my map too and together we worked out his route to the source of the Vltava, which struck me as rather an ambitious ride for someone who had hired his bicycle for a mere six hours. He asked me where I was going, and I told him I was aiming for Venice.

'Venice! I could never do that. I'm afraid of so many things, so nervous. I'm such a coward! I really admire someone with the courage to go on such a long ride alone.'

I tried to be encouraging and modest at the same time. 'I think you will find that you get braver as you grow older. You have less to lose. Anyway, I think you're the brave one, cycling on your own in this remote part of the Czech Republic, such a long way from home.'

We sat on the grass beside the road and talked for a while. The boy was from Singapore and was very happy to hear that I had been there – on my bicycle too. He asked if he could take my photo. Then he whizzed off like a rocket in the direction of the Vltava's source. English was his first language, and it was such a pleasure for both of us to have a real conversation, our first for many days.

Shortly after the picturesque village of Rozmberk nad Vltavou, I left the riverside to cycle into Austria at Dolne Dvoriste, running the gauntlet of the roadside prostitutes, who always gather where the truckies converge. One of the girls shouted to me, asking the time. In my innocence, I rode over and showed her my watch. Then the penny dropped. For the first time in my life, I was being offered a quick trick by a bisexual miniskirted bottle-blonde with predatory carmine lips!

FREISTADT AND LINZ

Do not indulge in dreams of having what you lack, but reckon up the blessings you do possess. Then reflect with gratitude how you would crave them if they were not yours.

Marcus Aurelius, Meditations

Freistadt–Linz–Grein–Ybbs–Melk–Krems–Tulln–
Klosterneuburg–Vienna

Frau Pirklbauer was short and dumpy, in a knee-length dress with puff sleeves, a frilly white pinafore and white ankle socks. This was the uniform of the women of Freistadt, even when they went out for a beer in the evening. As she showed me to my room, Frau Pirklbauer said, 'Well, I suppose there's hope for me yet, if you didn't take up cycling until you retired!' I smiled at my mental picture of Frau Pirklbauer's fat little legs in their dirndl skirt chugging up the mountains of Austria. She took it for a smile of encouragement and seemed pleased. My German was creaking back into motion and it was good to be able to share a joke again.

In Freistadt, I was back among the *Schützengemeinschaft*. Here the members of the local shooting club were dressed up in the full rig of dark-green hussars, all boots and frogging, their helmets draped in spectacular plumes of glossy black feathers. They marched about town with their rifles over their shoulders, looking very important, while their women pranced along beside them in dark-green suits and white stockings. They were rather stumpy little people, very different in physical type from the tall Czechs. It was chilly up there, only 12° C according to the chemist's thermometer. As I drank a warming mug of tea, the hills disappeared in a pall of drizzle. First Ceske Krumlov, now Freistadt. I do dislike these cold mountain resorts. I couldn't wait for the morning, to swoop down to Linz on the milder banks of the Danube.

But I was disappointed. It was not as much of a descent as I'd expected. My road out of Freistadt began with a 15 km climb, followed by a sharp descent. After that, there seemed to be just as much uphill as down, and it was maddening to watch the parallel Linz motorway striding across deep valleys on stilts, perfectly flat, while I was struggling on all the neighbouring slopes. Just off the road ran the tourist *Pferdeisenbahnwanderweg*. Such a mouthful could only be German – or perhaps a Welsh place name. It translates as 'the ramblers' path along the horse-drawn iron way'.

It poured with rain all morning and the clouds hung too low for me to see the Danube from the hills above. I consoled myself by thinking of Mozart, and all the times he must have travelled this very road between his favourite city of Prague and the court in Vienna. His horses and carriage probably took about the same length of time, five days, to make the journey from Prague to Linz as I was taking on my bicycle. It would have been a long haul for a man with his delicate constitution – bumpy, miry eighteenth-century roads and insalubrious coaching inns – but at least he had the luxury of travelling in a dry coach!

With Mozart on my mind, I hurried along to the Mozarthaus, despite the torrential rain. The flowery central courtyard was filled with music, the sublime *Linz Symphony*, which Mozart composed there. The mansion belonged at the time to Count von Thun, and Mozart was his guest. The count asked him to give a performance one evening, but Mozart was just passing through Linz and had no music with him. So, not wishing to disappoint his host, he sat down and tossed off the symphony. It took him just three days!

Still in musical mood, I spent the early evening in the Alter Dom, the old Linz cathedral, listening to a recital on the organ which Brückner played during his twelve years as organist and choirmaster there. Then I went to a real Italian restaurant, run by Italians, for a pizza with anchovies and olives. After three weeks of hearty helpings of pork and beef, it tasted ambrosial. I enjoyed my carafe of Montepulciano too.

In some ways, Linz was a disappointment. The shops were shut at the weekend, and so was the art gallery with the Klimt collection. In the vast baroque main square, a stage had been erected and there were jazz bands, refreshment stalls and balloons. But it was all rather a damp non-event. The rain persisted. I felt weary and my left knee, which often causes me problems, was twinging ominously after yesterday's mountains. I whiled away an hour or so in a chat with the hotel receptionist, a pleasant young man whose girlfriend came from Coventry, and I spent a lot of time sleeping.

I was now in Roman territory, the garrison town of Lentia, so it seemed appropriate to get out my Marcus Aurelius. He soon put things into perspective, as he always does. There was I, mooching about, full of trivial complaints, when I should have been counting my blessings. I was in a situation which most people in the world would envy – at ease in an elegant city on the Danube, with an interesting project to occupy my days and a comfortable hotel to sleep in. If I were stuck in my rut at home, I would be longing for the excitement of just such a trip. Suitably chastened by the wise Marcus, I shrugged off the rain and went out in search of a good dinner, pausing on the way to enjoy the amber in the jewellers' windows. Life was not so bad after all.

I spent the next four days wheeling effortlessly along the famous *Donauradweg*, the perfectly engineered cycle path which runs beside the Danube from Passau to Bratislava. At first there were few cyclists, but the nearer I got to Vienna, the more crowded the path became, until it was almost gridlocked. If I deviated, I had to wait for a gap in the cycle traffic in order to rejoin the flow. It was a popular holiday run for cyclists of all ages and levels of fitness, riding every conceivable kind of machine. There was no disgrace in pedalling along, in the middle of the Lycra-clad racers, on a gearless shopping bike, or a specially designed invalid tricycle, or a bike with a baby-carriage in tow. All were equal companions in cycling.

In England, we cyclists are rather looked down upon. We are seen as weird anoraks, or pathetic losers, too unsuccessful in life to rise to the magnificence of a car. The disdainful 'Can I help you, madam?' of English hotel receptionists, when I arrive on my bicycle, always amuses me, the implication being that no cycling nerd could possibly afford to stay in such splendid accommodation. Along the Danube valley, I noticed the difference immediately. Groups of seriously affluent Austrians and Germans were cycling the path, their luggage carried for them in vans and their rooms booked in the most expensive hotels. Most of them were elderly couples, cycling in style. I got into difficulties with one such group in Tulln. We were now well into the July holiday season and the only room I could find was in the town's multi-star. I arrived early, chained Condor to a rack in the empty cycle shed and spent the afternoon in the Roman Museum. When I got back, I found that a party of 'silver cyclists', a hundred strong, had arrived in the hotel and piled their hundred bicycles on top of mine. After a five-course dinner, plenty of wine and a hearty Austrian breakfast, they were in no mood at all to set out early the next morning. I had to kick my heels in irritation for two whole hours, mocked by the hotel's parrots, before I could finally extricate my bicycle and get on my way.

Judy Garland and 'Follow the Yellow Brick Road' kept flashing through my mind. The Danube path was so very easy – in truth, rather *too* easy. There was no need for a map or a compass. I just followed the little green bicycle signs and read all the instruction notices. I was told where to take care (on windy bridges and intersections) and where to dismount (to cross shallow fords, or negotiate a rare uneven patch in the tarmac). I had nothing to work out for myself. It seemed as if I was cycling in lead-reins, with a fussy, old-fashioned nanny to look after me. The scenery was delightful, the surface was good, and there was no danger. And in the unlikely event of a problem, I was never far from a cyclists' centre, where I could get information, first aid, drinking water, coffee, ice-cream, buy rainwear or summon a special minivan to take me and my bike to my next hotel. It was safe cycling for families and the timid of all ages. I like a bit more of a challenge myself. I like to cycle in the real world, dicing with destiny and cars, not wrapped in cotton wool.

Cruising along in my cyclist's safety bubble, I found it difficult to shake off my low spirits. My pedals turned reluctantly and I tried to persuade myself that the heavy weather was to blame. Clouds snagged on the mountain tops, and if it was not actually raining in the river valley, it was overcast and oppressive. But I finally had to face up to the fact that I was terribly lonely, in the area where I had least expected it. I had expected language to be a barrier in countries like Denmark and the Czech Republic, but in fact I had found all sorts of people there who had been happy to chat to me in English or German. The problem with the Danube path was that everyone there was on holiday, either in jolly touring groups or family parties. They were enjoying their time together and had no need of anyone outside their close-knit little travelling communities. So although I could have talked to them quite easily in German, I never got the chance. And I never bumped into a fellow 'outsider'. The cyclists on my route were all Austrian or German. I couldn't even gossip with a friendly waiter, because it was high season and staff were rushed off their feet. I'm usually quite content on my solitary journeys, because I find people to talk to. What is hard is being alone and unregarded in the middle of happy, self-contained groups; sitting alone at dinner, when everyone else is laughing and joking. I shall never again go on my own to a holiday destination. It's far too depressing.

Fortunately, on this ride, I had the fascinating story of amber to keep me going. Provincial museums are often the last resort of the rain-soaked holidaymaker, but the ones in the Danube valley were particularly fine. I spent most afternoons there, picking up amber clues. In Tulln, for instance, I learned that many Roman soldiers, who had fought in Germany and picked up the languages of the tribes there, stayed on in the garrison towns after retirement as amber dealers. They could bargain with the German middlemen in their own language, when they brought the amber down to sell it on the Danube; and they could act as general interpreters and emissaries between the Romans and Germans.

Tulln was just one of a string of Roman forts and garrison towns along the Danube. The river valley was the natural corridor between the East and Western Europe, as well as the boundary between the Roman Empire and the fierce German tribes to the north. It had to be secured by the stoutest fighters. The Roman name for Tulln was Commagena, after the cavalry troop stationed there, the Ala I Commagenorum. These were crack horsemen drafted all the way from eastern Turkey, near Nemrut Daği, to defend this key position, just across the river from a number of mountain streams, all natural paths for marauders going down to the Danube.

The Romans built their walled garrisons on the low-lying land beside the river. Later rulers went for the high ground, crowning every hilltop with a castle or fortified monastery. The most spectacular of these is the Benedictine monastery at Melk, familiar now to cinema-goers as the setting for the film of the mediaeval whodunnit, *The Name of the Rose*. Built on a granite crag, towering 60 m above the river, its original fortifications became the foundations for a delirium of extravagant, eye-popping nineteenth-century baroque. The architect was a local farmer's son, Jakob Prandtauer, who had built a few houses before, but nothing of any size. Then he was given his head on the monastery, and nothing was too grand or theatrical. In fact, the chapel, with its six boxes for the imperial family, is so theatrical that there is even a painted curtain behind the gilt statues at the high altar. There is a vast marble hall, and the main library is covered in gilded panelling. The fluted pilasters between the bookshelves sprout golden-haired caryatids with ebony bodies in golden draperies. When the money grew a bit tight, Prandtauer resorted to tricks of perspective. The flat ceiling of the marble hall was painted to look domed and the imperial corridor was narrowed in one direction from the centre, to make it look longer. But for me, all the grandeur was as nothing compared with the magnificent collection of books. There are over 100,000 volumes, housed in twelve libraries, among them illuminated manuscripts – an early Virgil, an early printed German Bible and a ninth-century Venerable Bede. It was all so overwhelming that I needed a breath of air. I staggered out on to the terrace and calmed my dizzy senses with the long view of the Danube, flowing peacefully below.

After Melk, I crossed to the left bank and rode under towering crags, through terraced vineyards and apricot orchards. At Krems, the cycle path took the right bank and changed its name to the Mozartweg, as it cruised along through woods and farmland. Every town of any size had its amber displays in the jewellers' windows.

I reached the outskirts of Klosterneuburg, in the heart of Austria's wine-growing region, just as the heavens opened. I ran for shelter to the tourist office and found that fleets of buses and trains covered the 15 km distance to downtown Vienna. So rather than fight my way into the capital on my bike, I checked into a Klosterneuburg hotel and travelled in to explore the city by bus and U-Bahn, Vienna's efficient tube.

VIENNA AND PETRONELL

You may break your heart, but men will still carry on as before.
Marcus Aurelius, *Meditations*

Vienna–Petronell–Eisenstadt–Sopron

The Viennese have the Romans to thank for their wine. The dangerous Danube frontier was not a popular posting, so the Emperor Probus had vineyards planted on the slopes of the Vienna woods to cheer his disgruntled legionaries. Those vineyards are virtually all that remains of Roman Vindobona. Vienna belongs to the Habsburgs and the Counter-Reformation.

The movement which Martin Luther began in Wittenberg in 1517 swept across Europe, and by the middle of the century most of Austria and Bohemia had turned Protestant. Then came the Habsburg crackdown. Catholicism was made a condition of citizenship throughout their empire and attendance at Mass became compulsory. Vienna, which was roughly four-fifths Protestant, was understandably short of Catholic priests, so monks and nuns from nine orders were invited to the city to plug the gap. Most were recruited from Italy, and they built their monasteries and churches in the fashionable new style of Italian baroque.

Baroque was the Catholic Church triumphant, with trumpeting angels, haloed saints in ecstasies of religious fervour, overblown frescoes, gilded altars, swags and scrolls, barley-sugar columns and magnificent domes. It was theatre at its most extravagant – *spectaculum mundi*, the world and the Church as spectacle. When Bohemia's Protestants were thrown out of the windows of Hradcany Castle in the notorious Defenestrations of Prague, and routed in the Battle of the White Mountain in 1620, baroque arrived in Bohemia with the re-imposed Catholic Church. But the Czechs brought their customary light touch to the style. Czech baroque is almost playful. Its pastel colours and whimsical flourishes have a charm which the grandiose heaps of Viennese masonry lack. I thought how lucky we were in England to have had Inigo Jones and Sir Christopher Wren, whose admiration for Palladio set the fashion for London's more seemly classical Renaissance architecture. Theirs was a vision of order and harmony, as different as it could possibly be from the extravagant distortion of continental baroque.

One glance inside a few of those overwrought Viennese churches was quite enough for me. I turned to my list of priorities, top of which was the Belvedere, where I spent my first afternoon gazing at the golden Klimts. Then I visited the café. No visit to Vienna would be complete without a slice of one of the famous *tortes*. I hesitated for a while over an authentic dark chocolate *Sachertorte*, but succumbed in the end to the museum's own *Belvederetorte*. It was a pale, melting, moist chocolate and almond sponge, with a thin layer of almost bitter marzipan on top and crushed almonds down the side. It was the most delicious piece of cake I have ever eaten in my entire life.

As far as amber was concerned, Vienna was simply one garrison town among many along my Roman route. I stumbled upon one amber display in a back-street jeweller's window, but Vienna is too rich and amber too cheap for the glittering emporia along Kärtnerstrasse. So Vienna was outside my brief and I could just enjoy my two days there, picking what glittered, like a jackdaw.

To fit in as much as possible, I went on a coach tour of the city. We were sorted into language groups and I went on the 'English' coach, where I was the only English person in a crowd of Japanese, Americans, Hungarians and Romanians. We toured the famous Vienna Ring and admired Otto Wagner's art nouveau urban railway stations. But what struck me most was the way the Empress Maria Theresia had turned the extensive, barracks-like Schönbrunn Palace into a cosy family home. Giant pot-bellied stoves in white porcelain, with gold decoration and gold crowns on top, provided the warmth in her charming rococo and Chinese rooms. Between putting the imperial finances in order, overhauling secondary education, the law courts and the army, and staving off the Prussians in the Seven Years War, the empress found time to produce sixteen children, twelve of whom survived, and to run her home in a comfortable, unaffected style. She was such a cosy monarch that the six-year-old Mozart is said to have jumped up and sat on her knee after his first piano recital in the palace. By the time she died in 1780, she weighed almost 110 kilos (over 240 lb) and had to be carried around in a chair, but she had kept up the

Habsburg tradition. She had arranged some shrewd alliances for her great brood of children, giving strength to the Austrian saying that other rulers made war, but the Habsburgs married. As for Schönbrunn Palace, she might be pleased to know that her modest lifestyle is still in evidence there. When the Habsburgs left in 1918, the Social Democrat administration of Vienna converted the top two floors into flats for the people. They are still occupied by the lucky descendants of the first tenants, at the original rent!

Vienna was such a daunting city. It would take a whole lifetime to explore it thoroughly, so I just gave up and did what the Viennese love to do. I sat in the cafés, watching the world go by over coffee and slices of heavenly cake. Most of the tourists seemed to be grey-haired American couples, walking hand in hand, like aged Jacks and Jills going steadily downhill in matching trainers. In the evenings, I went multi-cultural on Hungarian goulash and Turkish kebabs. Vienna has always been one of Central Europe's great melting-pots, drawing peoples along the Danube from east and west. In the great days of the Austro-Hungarian Empire, the Orders of the Day had to be issued in fifteen languages. None of them was Turkish.

The Turks had craved the city they called 'The Golden Apple' with the fierce longing of a nomadic people from the Asian steppes, whose life was a folding of tents and a ceaseless wandering. For them, Vienna was the city of dreams, the rich and glittering prize. They laid siege to it twice – in 1529 under Suleiman the Magnificent, and again in 1683. In the second siege, they came within an inch of success. They were on the very point of breaking through the city wall, when the combined forces of Christendom rode to the Austrians' rescue, under the command of the King of Poland, and drove the Turks back to the Balkans, opening up the southeast to Habsburg expansion. Typically, the cake-loving Viennese celebrated their relief in a frenzy of baking! The croissant is so much a part of breakfast across the Channel that it seems like a French invention. But in fact it is Viennese. Its shape celebrates the Christian victory over the Turkish crescent. With a nod to its origin, the French call all such pastries (*pain au chocolat*, *pain aux raisins* and *brioches*, as well as croissants) by the name of *Viennoiseries*.

Although the Habsburg eagle no longer flies there, Vienna is still strikingly international; and among her migrants, Turks are one of the most significant groups. Running kebab shops, station buffets, market stalls and taxis, these working people have succeeded where Suleiman the Magnificent failed. They have breached the barriers of their dream city and are making a modest living inside it. And what of the future? The Turkish birth-rate stays high, while the Austrian birth-rate shrinks. In a century or three, will the muezzin finally sound across Vienna and the crescent of Islam fly from the spire of St Stephen's Cathedral, converted into the Grand Mosque?

I always try to cycle in and out of capital cities at the weekend, when the traffic is lighter. The way from Klosterneuburg into the centre of Vienna was very straightforward, as it followed the Danube Canal. Towards the east of the city, I crossed over to Vienna's playground, the vast Prater Park, and cycled through its funfair under the shadow of Harry Lime's famous Ferris Wheel from *The Third Man.* Then I got hopelessly lost, just as I did in Hamburg. It's always easier to get into great cities than to find the way out of them. My main problem in Vienna was that the Danube has been divided into four channels – the Danube Canal, the Danube, the Old Danube and the New Danube. I spotted a few cycle signs, but they were all pointing away from the water towards Hainburg, a place I had never heard of. So I ignored them and stuck to what I hoped was the Danube proper, looking for directions to Petronell or Bratislava. I crossed and recrossed the waterways, braving nudist beaches and fishing competitions. It was mid-afternoon before I finally got round to doing what I should have done in the first place. I put on my specs and took a really close look at my map. Hainburg, which I had taken for some insignificant suburb of Vienna, turned out to be the border post (in small print) between Austria and Slovakia. I should have been on the Hainburg cycle path all along. I turned back and took an unpromising lane away from the water, but it curved around and I was soon bowling along the top of a well-signposted embankment to Orth. I was back on the Yellow Brick Road, but there was one crucial difference. I was the only cyclist. The groups had all finished their ride in Vienna.

That evening in Orth, the waiter was delighted to welcome me to his sea of empty tables, and he and the proprietor settled down for a chat about my journey. Next morning, Maria in her cheerful bed and breakfast poured herself a mug of coffee and joined me, elbows on the table, for a nice gossip. It was a paradox that I had felt utterly alone along the crowded stretch of the Danube cycle path, but now that I was cycling on a deserted stretch, I had plenty of friendly company. I set out again with a light heart. My lonely days were over.

I was planning to take the ferry from Orth across to the right bank and follow the main road directly into Petronell. But there had been so little rain that year that the Danube, like the Elbe, was a mass of sandbanks, no wider than a stream. The jetties stood high and dry over pebbled beaches, far away from the flow, so that even the modest little ferry-boat was grounded. I had to continue along the cycle path, across flowery meadows, almost to the frontier, to reach the bridge at Engelhartsstetten. Then I crossed over and backtracked through Bad Deutsch Altenburg (what mouthfuls these names are!) to Petronell.

This was the heart of my journey, Roman Carnuntum, the centre of the spider's web. Amber poured into its markets from every corner of the Baltic, to be traded on to all the cities of the empire. Carnuntum was to amber what Kashgar in the foothills of the Pamir was to silk. It was the glowing emporium of this precious, versatile tawny-gold resin.

Almost as intriguingly to me, it was Marcus Aurelius's city, for the amber market was not Carnuntum's primary purpose. It stood on the Danube as Rome's chief bulwark against the fiercest of the Germanic tribes, the Marcomanni and Quadi, who raided across the river whenever they were given the slightest opportunity. They presented such a danger to Rome that the emperor himself, Marcus Aurelius, took command of the Carnuntum garrison in AD 167. A tragic figure, he ruled for nineteen years, and spent thirteen of them in this bleak and dangerous outpost, far from the comforts of Rome. Unusually for a Roman emperor, he was a virtuous man, devoted to his family, and it was his greatest sorrow that he lost his wife, Faustina, and four of his five young children on the Danube. He lived there alone, a simple, peace-loving soul, frail in health, doing his duty as commander-in-chief of the Roman army, and consoling himself with his Stoic philosophy. In this melancholy spot, he wrote his *Meditations*, jottings which he never intended to be published. He got on with the job that fate had allotted him and kept his grief to himself, pouring it out only in his private journal. 'You can break your heart, but men will still carry on as before.'

Being such a great admirer of his, I had to check in to the Hotel Marc Aurel in Petronell, a lovely pink-washed building with a façade of suitably imperial columns and pediments. Roman Carnuntum was extensive, a city divided into three distinct areas which stretched for 9 km along the Danube. Petronell was part of the civilian zone; the religious zone, with the main temples, stood in what is now the fashionable spa town of Bad Deutsch Altenburg; and the military camp, which could accommodate four entire legions (around 24,000 troops, plus their camp-followers), lay between the two. Each of the three was important enough to support its own amphitheatre. Fortunately, Petronell and Bad Deutsch Altenburg are both small places, with farmland and flood plain between, so that most of the ruins of Carnuntum are accessible to archaeologists – unlike other major Roman cities, which have remained important throughout the centuries and so have been constantly built over.

I was free at last of the rain-bearing mountains to the north. I had cycled into sunshine, and it was suddenly baking hot. I wondered how the archaeologists in Petronell could carry on with their patient trowelling and scraping in such merciless heat. A girl in a toga was leading a gaggle of excited infant school-children through a series of tents, each showing an aspect of Roman life. They sat in desks in a Roman schoolroom, tried their hand at a few Roman games, then climbed up the reconstructed Roman watch-tower. The site was wonderfully accessible to all ages. Even the military camp down the road, an area usually of interest only to specialists, had features which everyone could enjoy. Models of Roman soldiers had their kit clearly labelled, and their daily chores at war and peace were described in the sort of detail that brought them to life. Even the soldiers' rations were listed, down to the last bean and bread-crust. And the food theme was developed in an area devoted to Roman cookery. Articles on the subject were displayed around a garden and herbarium, which was stocked with every vegetable and herb known to the Romans. The two sites were both imaginatively treated. Only the museum in the religious quarter of town was a disappointment. The amber jewellery there was sparse and dull, much less attractive than the polished replicas on sale in the Petronell shop.

I was glad I had my Condor to cycle back and forth over this extensive site, but it was hot work and I was forced to follow the example of the locals and take a siesta in the cool of my bedroom. In the evening, I explored the charming little Romanesque church next to the Marc Aurel. It was a simple round stone structure, with a roof that rose to a high point, like a witch's hat. The only elaboration was in its deeply recessed porch, where the tympanum held a carving of the Baptism of Christ. There were the usual figures – Saint John the Baptist, Christ in the river and the Holy Spirit hovering in bird form above. What was unusual, and delightfully down-to-earth, was a winged angel, who was waiting on the bank with an outstretched towel, ready to dry the baptised Saviour.

I had entered Carnuntum along one of many Amber Routes, which I chose because it seemed to offer an interesting summer cycle ride across a variety of landscapes – rivers, mountains and cities, many of them beautiful and unfamiliar. But my route was probably of secondary importance in Roman times, chiefly because the Quadi and Marcomanni of the territory loosely known as Boihaemum (Bohemia) were aggressive peoples living in dense forests. Evidence is hard to find, as there are few written sources, but it seems that the western and eastern routes carried the bulk of the traffic.

Along the western routes, amber was waterborne. It was carried by sea from Jutland to ports on the Channel and the North Sea coast, travelled by river through safe Roman territory to Marseilles, and completed its journey with a sea-crossing to Italy. But most of the amber in Roman times came from the southern coast of the Baltic, from what is now Poland, Russian Kaliningrad and Latvia – still the main sources of amber today. The natural route south from the Baltic followed the river Vistula and its tributaries across the plains of Poland, passed through the Moravian Gate, the gap between the Sudeten and Carpathian mountains, and finished on the river Morava, which flows into the Danube near present-day Bratislava. There were many variations, up the Elbe, the Rhine and the Oder, as we know from the Roman artefacts which archaeologists have found throughout Central Europe, but all of these overland routes led eventually to Carnuntum. There was one exception, and that was the route which ran directly south from the Danube to Innsbruck, then took the Via Claudia over the Brenner Pass to Trento and Verona, arriving in Aquileia from the west. The Greek routes across Russia, along the rivers Dnieper and Dniester to the Black Sea and thence to Mycenae, Byzantium and points further east fortunately need not concern us. The Roman routes are complicated enough!

Unlike most of the other cities along my route, Carnuntum was easier to leave than to find. Many roads led into it, but there was only one Roman road which led out of it to my destination, Aquileia. That was the Via Gemina.

I set out on one of the hottest mornings ever, cycling through sun-baked vines, dying trees and wilting sunflowers. In Rohrau, I passed the pretty little Schloss Rohrau, where Haydn was born in the wheelwright's cottage. Then I took the cycle path which skirted the Neusiedler See. The blazing morning turned into an incandescent afternoon, and I began to think that I should collapse and die of heatstroke on the road. But I managed to struggle into Eisenstadt, and made for the Gasthof zum Haydnhaus. It was a gloomy place, but my window looked out on Haydn's modest little house with its flowery courtyard. I had done well on this journey. I had met my three very favourite composers – Bach in Leipzig, Mozart in Linz and now Haydn in Eisenstadt. He was court musician to the Esterhazy family, and I liked to imagine him walking up the hill every evening for nineteen years, regular as clockwork, to make music in their magnificent castle, in the hall which now bears his name. He was a genial man, as calm, clear and self-assured as his music. '*Ein harmonischer Gesang war mein Lebenslauf*' ('The course of my life has been one harmonious song') was the way Haydn summed up his journey through this world.

In my mind, I bracketed Haydn with Marcus Aurelius. By coincidence, they spent their working lives within 45 km of each other. Two different epochs, two very different careers, two different systems of belief (Haydn a devout Christian, Marcus Aurelius a Stoic), yet both were men who had come to terms with life's challenges and were totally resolved and at peace within themselves. Their quiet presence gave strength to others. People in Eisenstadt used to say, 'When Haydn's around, nothing can go wrong.' And the people of Rome wept when Marcus Aurelius died.

Eisenstadt was a pleasant little town, with fine displays of amber in the jewellers' windows. I took advantage of a very professional cycle shop to have Condor's wheels checked, as they seemed to be rolling reluctantly. The front wheel was pronounced too dry; it needed cream on the axle. The rear wheel had two spokes out of true, which was making it wobble at speed. While these faults were being rectified, I was treated to a good ticking-off.

'Don't you know this bicycle is illegal in Austria? You've no business to be riding around with no reflectors on your spokes and pedals, and no fixed lights. If the police catch you, you could be prosecuted and banned from cycling. I'll have to change these pedals for you and fix on reflectors. Which of these lights do you want now?'

'I don't want any of those lights,' I said. 'I don't need them – or new pedals either. I've already cycled across Austria. I'm going into Hungary tomorrow.'

'Well, I suppose that's all right then,' he said grudgingly. 'But you'd better use the cycle paths to get there – and don't let the police see you.'

I fled into Hungary to escape prosecution and prison. My illegal bicycle crossed the frontier on a path for cyclists and walkers, where there were fortunately no police or border guards to arrest me. The remains of a temple to Mithras, the soldiers' god, showed that I was on a Roman road. In front of it, a little Noddy tourist train was waiting to ferry passengers into Sopron for one euro. I puffed up the hill behind it, then overtook it at speed as I whizzed down on my newly trued wheels to the city centre. I was making for my rendezvous at the railway station and couldn't get there fast enough.

KÖSZEG AND SZOMBATHELY

When you need a tonic for your spirits, think of the good qualities of your friends. One is a capable person, another self-effacing, another is generous. There is no more certain cure for dejection.

Marcus Aurelius, *Meditations*

Sopron–Lövö–Köszeg–Szombathely–Mursko Sredisce–Ormoz–Ptuj–Celje–Ljubljana

Since I took it up myself, I have persuaded many people that cycling is the perfect way to travel. I've even started to make inroads on my own sceptical family. For the first time, two of them – my stepson John and his wife Irma – were joining me on a leg of my journey. They had never done such a ride before, and we had never cycled together, so it was all a bit of an experiment.

The logistics of meeting in Hungarian Sopron were far from simple. I had left England at the end of May, with the loose arrangement that they would join me in mid-July, wherever I happened to be. In June, I phoned from time to time, to let them know where I was and give them a rough idea whether they would be joining me in the Czech Republic, Austria or Hungary. They were wonderfully laid-back and flexible, in a situation which would have worried most holiday-planners to death. By July, it was clear that I would be somewhere within a few hundred kilometres of Vienna, so they decided to travel there by train, and go backwards or forwards to meet me along my route.

On Tuesday, 15 July, John and Irma drove from Bedford to Mulhouse with their bicycles, to visit friends there and park their car. It was an exhausting one-day drive and quite unnecessary, as we learned later, because Mulhouse was on one of the European Bike Express routes and they could have been picked up on the M1, spent a restful day on the coach and been dropped off just round the corner from their friends' house. I contacted them in Mulhouse, before they left by train for Vienna on Thursday 17. By that time, I was already in Eisenstadt. I went to the station to check out the trains, and found that Sopron, the first major town across the Hungarian border, was on a direct line from Vienna. I phoned them on their mobile and we agreed to meet at Sopron station at noon the next day. I phoned again mid-morning from my last village in Austria, and was relieved and delighted to hear that they were safely on the Sopron train and due in the station at 11.40. I wheeled in myself at 11.25.

Then I waited. Trains came and went, and there was no sign of John and Irma. For the first time in all our complex dealings, I began to worry. Was there another Sopron station? I checked. There was only one. Had they perhaps arrived early and gone for a ride round the town? Was I waiting in the wrong part of the station? I left the entrance hall and circled the entire site. No John and Irma. Finally, I spotted them on one of my station patrols, waiting in International Arrivals for their bikes to be unloaded. We all waved enthusiastically. Their train had broken down just on the outskirts of Sopron, and they had sat there for one and a quarter hours, gazing out on the railway sidings, while an Austrian physicist held forth in broken English about the inadequacies of the Hungarian train service.

That was just the last incident in an over-eventful journey. They had arrived in Vienna at midnight, in bucketing rain, hours late, because an unexploded bomb from World War II had been found near the railway track. Then, in their early-morning sprint across Vienna to catch the Sopron train at another station, John's bicycle wheel had slotted neatly into a tramline and sent him flying. He had a badly grazed arm and leg, but had fortunately not ended up under a tram. My gentle ride from Eisenstadt was simplicity itself by comparison. We decided they had earned a nice lunch.

The restaurant in Sopron had its menu in German as well as Hungarian, and there were German posters of special offers in the supermarkets, German price-lists in the hairdressers' windows and German signs on the dentists' doors. Just as the Danes flooded across the border into Germany for cheap shopping, so the Austrians arrived in droves in Sopron, not only to shop, but to have their hair done and their teeth filled by well-qualified dentists at a fraction of the Austrian price. But once we were out of Sopron, away from the border, we were in another land of unpronouceable, unspellable names. For me, it was the Czech Republic all over again. I couldn't understand a word. And Hungary was an even stranger place, because I knew next to nothing about Hungarian history or architecture. For readers bored with my effusions on the Habsburgs and baroque, this will no doubt come as some relief!

The difference in Hungary was that I was in the company of friends. There was the added advantage that John and Irma knew Eastern Europe very well and felt at home there. John had often travelled to trade fairs in the former Iron Curtain satellites when he was working in industry, and in recent years, when those countries opened up to tourism, he and Irma had spent many happy holidays there. While I always gravitate towards the sunlit olive-groves, they can think of nothing more delightful than packing a few essentials in their car and driving off to explore Poland or the former East Germany. 'We breathe more deeply out there,' said Irma. Hungary was one of their favourites, and I was looking forward to travelling with them. Perhaps I should come to see the landscape and its people through their eyes and be converted. My one visit to Budapest, three winter days on the road to Damascus by bus, had not been particularly appealing; and I had no experience of the countryside.

We set off in convoy down the only route south, on what was a baptism of fire for my two cycle companions. For the first 7 km, all the traffic to Budapest, Lake Balaton, Györ and Szombathely was crammed into one narrow road with an inadequate hard shoulder. Most of the traffic was heavy trucks, many with trailers, whose back-draught destabilised our bikes. It was scary even for me, and I'm used to such situations. When the Györ traffic peeled off at the first fork, there was some relief, but not much. We gritted our teeth, determined to cover the worst stretch that afternoon, the first 26 km to the junction at Lövö.

As Lövö was the turn-off for Köszeg and Szombathely, two important places, we were confident of finding a hotel or a bed and breakfast there. We arrived at a bleak crossroads, where a petrol station stood in isolation in the middle of fields. The village of Lövö lay down a hill, off the main road, but it was small and there was nowhere obvious to stay. John marched into the bar. On my own, I should have been forced to do the same, so it was a nice change to have a man to do it for me that evening. The bar was crowded and cigarette smoke rose in thick clouds from every table. There was not a woman in sight. I caught a glimpse through the doorway of one splendid character in shiny nylon shorts of an electrifying emerald green, purple wellingtons, a trilby hat and nothing else. Irma and I stayed outside, holding the bicycles. Fifteen minutes went by and our hopes began to rise: John must be on to something to be spending so much time in there. He emerged with a man who said he could fix everything.

The result was a dusty, dilapidated house, with broken furniture and a yard full of nervous little dogs, who yapped, then ran to the safety of a barn as soon as the front gate opened. The local doctor had inherited the property from his mother, but had no money to do it up. His wife and two gorgeous daughters arrived with armfuls of sheets and towels, to make up three beds for us and turn on the water. Our feet left trails in the dirt and rubbish on the floor, but at least we had clean beds to sleep in. The only place to eat was the petrol station. 'You can get everything there!' they told us in the village. 'Everything' turned out to be hamburgers and beer, but they went down quite nicely. We cycled back to the bar for another beer, and treated our toothless fixer, Josef, to a wine spritzer. On that night, we all felt that we had passed some kind of test. If we could cope with that degree of uncertainty and discomfort, and even find it funny, we knew we would get on easily together. Most of our friends would have fled in horror from that derelict house.

The doctor's wife arrived early with a flask of Turkish coffee and six deliciously crisp rolls, stuffed with ham, cheese, onion and peppers. We stopped at the petrol station for longer coffees, then cycled west through fields of sunflowers along the Kőszeg road. Hungary is still very rural, a country of villages. Most were too small to appear on the map, but they were all beautifully neat and flower-filled, with raspberry canes in the gardens and tiny chapels in the centre, no bigger than roadside shrines.

Kőszeg was a perfectly preserved mediaeval town, swarming with tourists, but agreeable for all that. John and Irma measured the heat in ice-creams. That day was declared a 'two ice-cream day', and we ate our first in the sunshine outside a café on the central square. We looked at a few churches and monuments, but it was the heroism of the people of Kőszeg which had drawn me to the town. With no more than 28 hussars, 18 German knights, the town home-guard and a band of peasants, Kőszeg held off the 100,000 troops of Suleiman the Magnificent in 1529. They had to surrender in the end, but they had given the forces in Vienna precious time to strengthen their own defences against the Ottoman army. Suleiman spared the people of Köszeg for their valour. At 11 o'clock, we heard the bells of the star-spangled Church of the Sacred Heart ringing out over the town, as they still do every morning, to celebrate Suleiman's withdrawal.

We sped across the Hungarian plain to Szombathely with a strong north wind on our tails, stopping for the second ice-cream. 'Savaria' was the Romans' more manageable name for the city, and it was in the art nouveau grandeur of the Hotel Savaria that we stayed. The bedrooms were fitted with curvaceous, mirrored wood furniture, almost too grand to sleep in. But the saddest relic of former glory was the vast and virtually empty restaurant, peopled with the ghosts of the dancers who once twirled under its balconies. The railways had brought wealth to the city, and its society glittered in those heady years just before the fall of the Austro-Hungarian Crown. I produced tea and biscuits in my bedroom, to which Irma added raisins and pineapple jelly cubes. It was still baking hot, so I rested on my magnificent bed, while John and Irma sneaked out for a third ice-cream. The unrelenting heat had turned it into a 'three ice-cream day'.

The flat road was quite busy as far as Körmend, where almost everyone else took the main east–west highway between Graz and Budapest. We continued south along the straight Roman road through tranquil, wooded country. It was so hot that the tarmac was melting. From time to time, we bought a ripe canteloupe melon from a roadside stall and crouched in the shade over its juicy, perfumed freshness. There were villages along the way, but no sign of a hotel, and we started to fear another Lövö night. But in Zalalövö (Roman Sala), they were converting an old building into a pension. It was not officially open yet, but we were given two of the completed rooms, both sparkling new.

John cycles more strongly than I do, especially now that he has started to cycle to work every day in London, leaving an old bike overnight at St Pancras Station. He could have gone much faster. Irma struggled more, on a heavier bike with seat problems. Being enviably slim has its disadvantages. Without natural padding, no bicycle saddle is ever entirely comfortable. She also lacks some layers of insulation against the heat and cold. 'I'm a reptile,' she says cheerfully. But in Hungary she was very game, enjoying the ride despite its discomforts, and even talking of buying a new bike specially for long-distance touring. Like me, she enjoys *going somewhere* with a purpose. Cycle runs round the village, or even around Bedfordshire, have no appeal at all for her.

Just beyond Redics, we crossed the border into Slovenia and paused in Lendava for our first ice-cream of the day. Then the nightmare began. Croatia has a long panhandle, which pierces Slovenia along the river Lendava. We entered it at Mursko Sredisce, planning to cut across country, along the hypotenuse of a triangle, rather than cycling its two sides on busy main roads. The day seemed hotter than ever and we panted along under the unforgiving sun to the border at Bukovje, to get out of the panhandle and back into Slovenia. There was a fair-sized town about 10 km beyond the frontier, where we were hoping to sink into a cool hotel.

The border post was manned by two Croatian Jacks-in-office, obvious relics of the old Communist regime. They barred our way. 'This is a crossing for the convenience of Croatians and Slovenes. It is not an international crossing. You must go back to the main road and cross at Trnovec.'

By this time, we were so hot and weary that we could have wept. We pleaded. There was no indication on any map that this was not an official crossing. We could understand them barring trucks, as there were no customs officers there to inspect the cargo. But three poor, harmless cyclists, elderly and exhausted . . . What was wrong with exercising a little discretion on a quiet country road and letting us through?

This reasoned approach got us nowhere, so John decided to get tough. He telephoned on his mobile to the men's superior officer, whose number he had spotted behind the counter. Their boss was sympathetic, but said that he could do nothing to help us, as the decision on individual cases rested entirely with the border guards. We had no alternative but to cycle wearily back to Mursko Sredisce. As a final throw, John did his Colonel Blimp impression.

'I understand that you people wish to enter the European Community,' he boomed. 'Well, you'll have to change your attitude if you're going to join us in the West.'

Anger gave wings to our wheels. There was nothing we wanted to see in Croatia, apart from our dinners and our beds. We reflected on the heavy load of responsibility every single one of us carries for our country's reputation among foreigners. As far as we were concerned, two officious border guards had entirely ruined Croatia.

Struggling from one patch of shade to another, we crossed the border successfully at Trnovec. After the pretty little villages in Hungary, we were disappointed with both Croatia and Slovenia. A building boom was marring the countryside with ribbon-development. People got jobs in Germany or Austria, worked and saved for years, then came back to their home villages and built the biggest, flashiest houses they could afford. They landscaped their gardens, bought a car, then pulled up the drawbridge. Community spirit was nowhere to be seen. Garbage was dumped by the roadside, there were no social amenities, no houses offering bed and breakfast, no enterprise. It was every man for himself in the brave new post-Communist world.

But one small town was a delight. From the castle terrace at Ptuj, where the Romans established their river port of Poetovio on the river Drava, there were spectacular views down the cobbled streets of the mediaeval town. Beyond the red roofs and onion domes lay the Roman river crossing and the vast expanse of open farmland beyond. I could see the Amber Route disappearing across a shimmering plain on its way to the river Sava and Celje (Claudia Celeia), the capital of the Roman province of Noricum.

In Ptuj, the Dominican monastery was dissolved by Maria Theresia's son, the Emperor Josef, who decreed that monks and nuns should do useful work in the community, like teaching and nursing the sick, instead of spending their days in prayer. The building now houses the archaeological museum, with a Mithras temple in the crypt. I was shown around by an eager, plump little boy of about twelve. His English was excellent. 'My auntie is an English teacher and I talk to her as much as I can.'

There was an Egyptian Room in the museum. 'You may perhaps be wondering,' he said, with great earnestness, 'why we have so many Egyptian artefacts in Ptuj. It is because an archaeologist from Ptuj went to Egypt in the nineteenth century and brought them here. I will show you what is very, very special for me.' He led me reverently over to a glass case and showed me a mummified pigeon.

I asked about amber and he had to consult his father, the curator, because he didn't know the English word. His father had not met it either, but he knew the German, *Bernstein*. The Slovene word was *jantar* and, surprisingly for such an important halt on the Amber Route, there was none at all in the museum. There was none to be seen in the shops either.

We stayed in the Grand Hotel Mitra, a warm terracotta-coloured classical building with pink geraniums pouring down from every window-sill and a leafy café outside. It was just up the street from Ptuj's famous second-century monument, sculpted in honour of Verus, who once administered the town. Orpheus with his lyre was charming an assembly of animals, including an elephant and a camel. Ptuj was less restored than towns of similar size and quaintness in the Czech Republic; and many of the shops were still signed with the Communist 'Mercator' (merchant), with no owners' names or indications of what they were selling.

A ride along the valley of the Dravinja led us to Poljcane, where John had a puncture. Then we had serious hills to climb before our descent to the outspread city of Celje on the river Sava. In Roman times, it was so wealthy that it was known as 'Troia Secunda', and it was still a great industrial and commercial centre. Sadly, it was the parting of our ways. John and Irma were taking the train from Celje to Ljubljana, then the night train to Zurich, and on to Basel and Mulhouse. I was cycling on alone to the Adriatic and Aquileia. We had all got along extremely well, and had accommodated ourselves quite comfortably in terms of speed. No one had had to puff and pant to keep up, and no one had been irritated by the others' slowness. We had chattered amiably, with never a cross moment or a bad-tempered exchange. It was a joint enterprise which was certainly worth repeating. We celebrated with a photo-shoot and a farewell dinner – but not at the restaurant next door, where they were advertising 'Hod dog' and 'Horse burger', among other unfamiliar delights!

When I cycled out of Celje, I was on the main Ljubljana road. The weight of traffic was so appalling that I dreaded the end of the dedicated cycle path. But I was in for a pleasant surprise. When the motorway began in an outer suburb, it was compulsory for vehicles above 7.5 tons; my old Roman road was empty, apart from a few local vans. I cruised, slightly downhill, along the Lower Savinja Valley to the Roman necropolis at Sempeter.

The tombs of the richest and most important citizens of Claudia Celeia used to lined the main road out of the city, as the tombs of the famous lined the Appian Way out of Rome. Most of them were destroyed in a great flood in AD 268 but, strangely, those closest to the river Savinja survived, preserved in the gravel of the river bed. The high quality of the stone-carving is evidence of the sophistication of this wealthy city on the Amber Route. On one tomb, Heracles is leading a shrouded Alcestis back from the dead; on another, Zeus is such a vigorous bull that he seems to be leaping right off the monument, with Europa on his back, robes flying. And there are beautifully sculpted family groups seated in miniature temples, many with Medusa's heads on the gables, to frighten off tomb robbers. It was a grassy site, blissfully cool under the trees after the merciless heat of the tarmac.

After Sempeter, the lovely wooded mountains on either side of the valley drew closer together until they met the road in the distance and I could see no way through. It was going to be a tough ride up a narrow pass. When I reached it, I found a long, steady ascent, gradual enough even for me to ride. The gap in the mountains was too narrow for my Roman road and the motorway to travel through together, so the motorway had to stride overhead on giant piers. When it crossed above my road, it offered welcome pools of shade on a blistering afternoon, and I rested for a while in each one before tackling the next exposed stretch. At what I hoped was the col, at 609 m the easiest pass between the Savinja and Ljubljana valleys, I collapsed into the Hotel Trojane, where I sat on my balcony, gazing back down the mountain. A white church tower was the only building to be seen in the dense forest of deciduous trees below me, while a solitary farm broke the stands of conifers on the mountains high above. I am not often affected by scenery: I generally prefer towns with people and buildings to untamed countryside. But in Trojane, I was encircled by such astonishing beauty that I was quite bowled over. The Romans who manned the trading station and military lookout of Atrans had an enviable posting.

There was a large group of Italian workmen in the hotel, and I wondered what they were doing there, when the Slovenes were net exporters of labour. It was usually Slovenes who went to find jobs in Italy, not the other way round. All was explained the next morning. The highest stretch of my road was jammed with trucks, inching their way along narrow lanes through road works. Today's Italians are carrying on the Roman road-building tradition. The men staying in the hotel were the foremen, supervising the difficult construction of the final piers and tunnels over the col. Beyond the muddle, the traffic sped off again down the motorway, and I cruised downhill through sleepy Saturday morning villages into the centre of Ljubljana.

LJUBLJANA

*I travel the roads of this world until the time comes when I shall be at rest
. . . sinking down upon the earth which for so many years has provided my
daily food and drink and, though so grievously ill-treated, still allows me to
walk upon her.*

Marcus Aurelius, *Meditations*

Ljubljana–Postojna–Sezana–Trieste–Monfalcone–
Grado–Aquileia

'I've never heard of anyone having a good time in Ljubljana,' said
John. 'It doesn't have that sort of a reputation.' I thought he was
being gloomy and was determined to prove him wrong. After all,
Ljubljana was Roman Emona, the capital of Pannonia Superior. It
must be a fascinating place.

I hurried to the National Museum, expecting hoards of amber
jewellery in such a wealthy Roman city, but the permanent
collection was closed for refurbishment. The shops were all closed
too on that Saturday afternoon. Even the newspaper kiosks had
their shutters up. I wandered disconsolately through the streets,
looking at such sights as the Dragon Bridge, the usual clutch of
churches in Counter-Reformation baroque, and the gilded replica
of a statue of an Emona citizen, wearing his toga. Today's citizens
were all out and about, sitting in the sunshine at café tables, but I
didn't join them because the air was riven with deafening music of
the most monotonous kind. Call me stuffy, but I refuse to listen to
'Do you want to buy my body? Do you want to buy my body? Do
you want to buy my body' or '*Vamos a la playa. Vamos a la playa.
Vamos a la playa*' (Let's go to the beach), repeated fortissimo,
without variation, from the beginning of a track to the end. The
restaurants were my final disappointment. I was only two days' ride
away from Italy and my grilled chop and salad in Trojane had been
delicious. I thought I had moved into the orbit of lighter Italian
cuisine. But Ljubljana could offer nothing better than the same
greasy escalopes and chips that I had endured throughout Central
and Eastern Europe. I had to concede that John was right after all.

Like all capital cities, Ljubljana was expensive, so I had to make
do with an ugly Communist barn of a place, more like a run-down

institution than a hotel. There were no telephones in the rooms and the Slovene entrepreneurs, who seemed to be the main customers, had to make their calls from the one and only telephone at reception. One poor man was trying to raise capital in Canada for a new business. The line was bad and he was making call after call, yelling down the phone, while other would-be tycoons fumed and fretted in the queue behind him.

While all this was going on, I was sitting in the lobby reading the English-language *Slovenia Times*. There was not another Briton in sight, so I was surprised to read that, in a *Guardian* survey, the British had rated Slovenia as their second-favourite holiday destination, after Iceland (first) and just before Finland (third). I wondered if they had read the chart the wrong way up! There were a number of references in the newspaper to the racial purity of the Slovenes, and their antagonism to immigrants was clear. Of the countries of the former Yugoslavia, Slovenia may create fewer waves than Serbia, Bosnia or Croatia, with their mixed populations, but the ancient prejudices are still there, bubbling beneath the surface. The Balkans are never quiet.

I had dropped down from 609 m at Trojane to 298 m in Ljubljana, but it was lost altitude. I had to climb back to 550 m to reach Postojna, my last halt in Slovenia. Postojna is famous for its vast network of caves. Tourists ride down through the tastefully lit karst on a miniature train, gazing at the stalactites and stalagmites, and the strange little salamander-like creatures without eyes. They have always lived in the dark underground and have no need of them. I went there years ago and, not being into speleology, decided that once was enough.

The town was milling with tourists, none of them British, as far as I could see. A row of coaches lined the approach to the one hotel in town, the run-down Kras. My lavatory lacked a seat and needed an application of bleach, my curtains were dropping off their hooks, the formica cladding on the furniture was chipped and peeling, the carpets were filthy and the lift groaned like a creature in pain. The problem was not so much lack of funds as indifference. There was no competition. The tourists would keep coming anyway, so why bother? It was a depressing hotel in a shabby, depressing town. And the people depressed me too. In contrast to the hospitable, inquisitive Hungarians, the waiters were surly in Postojna. The hotel staff walked through the doors in front of me, then let them slam in my face. I was glad it was my last night in their country.

Among the coach parties in the hotel, there was one from Russia – and you have not seen gluttony until you have seen a Russian coach party at a buffet breakfast. One man piled eight slices of bread on his plate and three hard-boiled eggs. I watched in awe as he slathered a whole packet of butter on the top slice and a whole individual jam, then added two slices of ham and a slice of cheese. He gobbled this from his left hand, while chomping one of the eggs from his right. Then he repeated the process, going back to the buffet counter for more butter and a few extra eggs. It seemed as if the years of shortage in Soviet Russia had left such a scar that food had to be grabbed with both hands, in case it was taken away again. The group in general poked at the food, picked it up, inspected it, put some of it back, and stacked the rest on to their overburdened trays. Many of them were smoking and sprinkling the buffet table with ash. Against all expectations, there was one enterprising Slovene waitress. She gave me an apologetic look, then came across to my table with two unmauled bread rolls and an ash-free slice of fruit-cake.

In Postojna, I was only about 40 km from the sea. The road ran downhill out of the town, then crossed a wide grassy plain, sprinkled with wild flowers, before climbing again into wooded hills. The mountainous south of Slovenia was much more appealing than the northern valleys, and by this stage of the ride I was cycling strongly, with plenty of energy left to admire the sparkling landscape. It was one of those joyful mornings, when I know exactly why I cycle. There was nothing on earth I would rather be doing than bowling along that road, through stunningly beautiful mountains, with the prospect of Italy before me in less than an hour's time. I started to hum one of my happiest tunes, pedalling fast in time to Strauss's *Radetsky March*. As I neared the coast, the region's karst, which had lurked underground in Postojna, burst through to the surface in dramatic limestone outcrops and wild scrubland. I passed through dreary towns like Sezana, which seemed to offer cheap shopping, nightclubs and casinos to the Italians. Then there was a maze of new roads, with all their notices in Slovene, but I managed eventually to find my way to the frontier.

'*Buon giorno, signora.*' After a fortnight adrift, I was back among people I could understand, who actually smiled at me!

I had hardly lost altitude at all. The great drop to sea-level came at Villa Opicina, where I had my first view of the Adriatic above the port of Trieste. There I had a choice. I could either take the main road down a gentler slope into the city centre, or fork right, down a narrow lane that looked almost vertical. I had climbed so high, and now I had to drop down a precipice. Had Nature been kinder, I would have glided gently and lengthily all the way from Trojane to Trieste.

As I hesitated on the cliff edge, an ultra-fit young cyclist came gasping up the lane and collapsed on a bench in a heap of red and yellow Lycra. I gave him a few moments to recover, then asked his advice.

'It's a fantastic ride down the lane, but you need good brakes. Cars are banned from the middle bit. It's too steep for them. The gradient's twenty-five per cent.'

'And you cycled up it?' He smiled modestly.

'Well, my brakes are pretty good,' I said, 'so I think I'll go for it.'

'Take care, then. *Coraggio!*'

Quite apart from the excitement of the ride, I was keen to swoop down the lane and bypass Trieste, because that was the Amber Route. The main Via Gemina from Aquileia took a short cut behind Roman Tergeste.

I began my headlong descent, stopping now and then to let the wheel-rims and brakes cool down. The steepest section was cobbled, with pavement steps and a handrail. It gave me an attack of vertigo just to look at it, so I manhandled the bike down the steps, clutching the rail as I went. When the road levelled out slightly, I hurtled down a right fork and found myself, appropriately enough, on a street called Via Aquileia. There was a cycle path along the coast to Barcolo, where the Triestines go to bathe and sun themselves over newspapers and games of cards. Spotting a pleasant sea-front hotel, I checked in at just the right time for a siesta on another blisteringly hot afternoon. I stretched out on my bed with an enormous sense of relief. I felt like a Roman legionary, newly returned to Italy from service at the end of the civilised world. I was home again.

Sea breezes, shade and cycle paths led me next morning to the gleaming white castle of Miramare, clinging to its rocky outcrop in the Gulf of Trieste. The doomed Archduke Maximilian, younger brother of the Austrian Emperor Franz Josef, fell in love with this wild promontory when he was forced ashore there in a storm. He bought it and built his dream castle, with a massive crenellated tower, landscaped gardens and a flight of steps leading down from balustraded terraces to his own landing-stage. He was a professional sailor, responsible for separating the Austro-Hungarian navy from the army and developing it into an important service in its own right. He was so obsessed with the sea that he even modelled his own suite of rooms in the castle on the cabins of his favourite ships; and he installed a quadrant and arrow on the dining-room ceiling, attached to a weathervane on the roof, so that he always knew the direction of the wind. But he neither completed his naval reforms nor saw the completion of his spectacular snow-white castle. A small painting in his study shows the Archduke and his Archduchess Carlotta setting out in a lighter from the castle landing-stage, at the start of their voyage to Mexico. They sailed there by invitation, to be crowned Emperor and Empress of Mexico, but their reign was short-lived, as Maximilian was soon assassinated by the Mexicans. The unhappy Carlotta returned to Miramare, where she eventually went mad.

The castle remained uninhabited until the Duke and Duchess of Aosta took out a lease in the 1930s. Maximilian and Carlotta had lived on the ground floor of the castle, while their servants lived upstairs. The Aostas, with great good sense and discrimination, decided that the archducal quarters were too perfect a period piece to tamper with and should be left undisturbed. They moved up to the former servants' floor, which they refurbished in the fashionable art deco style. The result is a fascinating exhibition of interior design – one castle with two showpiece floors, each lavishly furnished in a completely different style.

Today, the castle is beautifully maintained, with informative notices in every room, in English as well as Italian. I found the English perfect, except for one small mistake, which somehow looked so ridiculous, it made me laugh aloud. The feminine of Duke and Archduke appeared as Dukess and Archdukess. I thought it was a kindness to point out the error to the curator.

The castle of Miramare was the last bit of sightseeing before my journey's end. I sped along the Via Gemina through Duino and

Monfalcone with wings on my wheels. Aquileia at last! But there were no signposts to such a small town and a new road had been built which was not on my map. In my eagerness to get there, I rushed past my turning and found myself at lunch-time in the seaside resort of Grado. I stopped for a sandwich and a granita, then cycled across the Grado Lagoon, along a spectacular causeway, back to the mainland. So in the end, it was the scenic Via Julia Augusta, not my old Via Gemina, which led me into the Roman amber city of Aquileia.

AQUILEIA

Pass on your way then with a smiling face, under the smile of him who bids you go.

Marcus Aurelius, *Meditations*

Aquileia's tourist office was deserted when I went in to enquire about hotels, and the young man running it was busy at his computer. While he was digging around in a drawer to find me a map, I happened to glance at the monitor and saw a picture of a Persian cat. This flicked off, to be succeeded by a basket of tabby kittens. He was not working. He was drooling over a cat-lovers' website!

'You're looking at cats,' I said.

'Yes. I absolutely adore them! I could look at them all day.'

'So could I. I love them too.'

At that, he drew up another chair for me behind the counter and we sat there, two dedicated ailourophiles, in raptures over the photos on the website. It was a good start to my time in Aquileia. The young man's English was very good, the result of a summer school in Norwich.

'I went to London last month to look for a job. I love London. But I had pains in my stomach and I got frightened and lonely, so I came home. I shall try again in the autumn. If you're staying here for a few days, do come in and look at the cats again, any time you like. It's nice to have a bit of company.'

As I entered the Hotel Aquila Nera, the first fat drops of rain for three months began to fall on to the parched earth.

'I'm arriving with the rain,' I said.

'And you're most welcome, both of you!'

There was thunder and lightning for five minutes, then it settled down to an afternoon of steady, gentle rain, exactly what was needed. I was once in Rawalpindi at the onset of the monsoon, and I remember the girls next door rushing out into the garden. They danced in the rain, hugging one another and laughing like crazy, until their hair was a torrent of water and their saris clung to their whirling forms. The people of Aquileia were more restrained, but I watched them come out to the square and stand with their faces uplifted, drinking in the freshness. Even I, used as I am to English rain, could hardly tear myself away from my open window.

Aquileia stands on an apron of absolutely flat land, which scarcely rises above the shallow waters between Trieste and Venice. It is an area of lagoons, of low-lying maize fields, reed-beds and marshes, criss-crossed with streams and drainage canals. The only vertical features are the campanile of Aquileia's basilica and the lines of poplars along the straight Roman roads. On a clear day, you can look across the shimmering heat of these wide flatlands and see the snow-capped Alps in the far distance.

It seems an unpromising site for a major Roman city, but the Natissa and Torre, which today are no more than pretty little streams, were once two broad navigable rivers. Together with a network of canals, they formed a riverine port, just 5 km upstream from the Grado Lagoon and the open sea. Aquileia was in the perfect position to receive and store not only amber, but the furs, cattle and slaves which were traded through the Alpine passes from north and east. In exchange, the merchants could offer all the seaborne gems, ivory, silks and spices of Africa and Asia, as well as home-produced olive oil, wine, pottery, glass and metal artefacts. Aquileia was the great commercial hub of the Roman Empire. And with a legion stationed there, it was also Rome's bastion against Germans, Celts, Gauls and Huns, any of whom might take it into their heads at any time to pour through the mountain passes on the rampage, or simply to settle. Like today's migrants, these people were not necessarily out for conquest or destruction. They were just poor people, who wanted a share in Rome's prosperity.

Excavations have revealed two docks, the larger one for sea-going vessels being 48 metres wide. There were monumental buildings on its west bank and flights of wide harbour steps leading up to three paved roads. On the water's edge stood one enormously long construction, which was not entirely enclosed. It could not have been a warehouse for safe, dry storage; more probably, it was a huge covered space for the initial sorting and trading of newly arrived goods. The remains of Roman bridges over a wide surrounding area are evidence of important connecting waterways.

The little river Natissa was still flowing swiftly as I strolled along its banks in the shade of the cypress trees, trying to make sense of the lay-out of the port. The broiling sun had returned with even greater ferocity, as if to make up for yesterday's lapse, and I soon gave up the excavations and fled into the cool of the basilica. This fine Romanesque building, founded when the Patriarchate of Aquileia was established in AD 314, is what today's sprinkling of tourists come to see. Theodore, the first Patriarch, covered the floor of its nave and aisles with mosaics which remained hidden under later layers until their rediscovery in the twentieth century. The result is a wonderfully preserved display of Christian and pagan imagery, still as fresh and brightly coloured as the day it was laid. There are intricate patterns, garlanded angels, Bible stories and scenes from the sea, where Jonah's whale gambols improbably with shoals of the local flatfish, octopi, lobsters and prawns.

But for me, Aquileia's chief interest lay in its amazing little museum. The city once supported hundreds of amber-workers, who were probably crammed together in the multistorey blocks known to the Romans as *columbaria*, or dovecots. They used edged tools and lathes to turn out their finely carved jewellery, which was then polished with powdered gypsum. The finished items are a delight to the eye, but we learn more about the techniques employed from the half-finished pieces which were left on the work bench, or discarded because of faults in the material or because one of the craftsmen had made a mistake.

I spent two days poring over the wonderful display. Rings were particularly important as Roman status symbols. In Republican times, only the freeborn could wear them. The rule was relaxed under the Empire, but rings were still a sign of distinction. There were seal-rings, signet rings and portrait rings (dateable from the hairstyles), some of them elaborately carved on the top and sides, and far too large to wear. In his book of dreams, Artemidorus says that to dream of a huge ring brings good luck, especially if the dreamer is a woman and the ring is amber. Sleeping puppies were popular too, as rings, pendants and small ornaments, because dreaming of puppies was a promise of the best and sweetest things in life. There were also charms relating to the cults of the gods: doves for Venus, and fish and scarabs for devotees of the oriental religions. But amber was chiefly prized because of the magical protection it offered against sickness and the evil eye. As a further safeguard, strings of amber beads would carry a central pendant in the shape of a crescent moon, a phallus, a head of Medusa the Gorgon, or simply a splinter of bone, all symbols intended to ward off evil. Then there were the frivolous, purely decorative items, such as the fine gold necklace with a row of tiny amber cockleshells; and my favourite piece, a small amber oyster shell, with the most delicate little amber and ivory spatulae for mixing cosmetics.

Aquileia was obviously a centre of excellence in craftsmanship. Ivory and bone were worked into combs, toys, hairpins, mirror handles, strigils and distaffs, often in amusing designs. Then there was the wealth of semi-precious stones, prized for their magical properties as well as their beauty. Indian agate, for instance, which comes in bands of colour, could be incised in layers to produce cameos. But it was also very useful against poisons and storms, and for settling family disputes. Onyx was potent against witchcraft. Heliotrope, a leek-green mineral speckled with red, gave protection against nightmares and helped to foretell the future. Amethyst was worn against nose-bleeds, neuralgia, tachycardia and, most importantly, drunkenness. But the stone which was clearly the most prized in Aquileia, after amber, was cornelian. This stone could be carved with a high degree of precision, and its red colour was associated with fire, blood and the sun. It was a strong safeguard against misfortune in general and haemorrhages in particular, and it brought victory to the wearer.

In AD 295, the Emperor Diocletian capitalised on the engraving skills of Aquileia's master jewellers and established a mint there. Coins from Aquileia were in circulation as far afield as Britain and North Africa, and the museum holds a fine collection of clearly incised coins, many of them newly minted.

Another room in the museum is devoted to exquisite Roman glass, which was another Aquileian speciality; and it was in this room that I made the obvious connection. The city was overrun in AD 452 by Attila and his Huns, and many of its residents fled to the safety of the Venetian lagoon. It is highly probable that the Venetian glass-makers of today are the direct descendants of the glass-blowers and engravers who produced the beautiful glassware of Aquileia.

Amber was all around me. Even the small daughter of my hotel was called Ambra. There were displays of amber in the shops, and

I thought I should mark my visit to amber city with a really significant piece. After the exhibits I had seen in the museum, it obviously had to be a ring. Some years ago, I had bought an antique Turkish ring, with a great opaque golden egg set in silver. As something quite different, I thought it would be interesting to have one of the pieces of clear resin containing flora or fauna. I didn't really fancy wearing a forty-million-year-old fly or mosquito, so I settled on a transparent whisky-coloured chunk, in whose refracted heart I could see an elegant scattering of grass seeds.

For my last outing in Aquileia, I cycled along the Via Gemina to the Museo Paleocristiano to see more mosaics, but the heat was so overwhelming, even late in the evening, that I was forced back to the shelter of my hotel. On the television news, I saw forest fires raging on the Carso around Trieste, where the very road I had cycled along was enveloped in black smoke. The police had closed it to traffic, which added to the already horrendous problems of the first weekend in August. It seemed that the whole of Italy was on the move – if sitting in day-long tailbacks on the motorways could be counted as moving.

I still had a week to spare before I was booked to go home on the European Bike Express from Cavallino, so I decided to cycle out there, find a seaside hotel and spend some days bathing and relaxing in the shade, between trips across the lagoon to Venice by vaporetto. If the fine weather held, I might check in to one of the luxury campsites for a night or two and try out my new bivvy bag.

I set out from Aquileia on Monday, 4 August – a day I shall not forget in a hurry – aiming for La Salute di Livenza, where I knew there was a modest hotel, just around the halfway mark. By noon, I had reached the outskirts of Latisana and was cycling along the hard shoulder of a quiet road with scarcely any traffic, when a short-sighted old buzzard of a nonagenarian, who had no business at all to be driving, rammed his ancient Fiat Panda into my rear wheel. I tumbled off, landing flat on my back in the path of the car. Fortunately, my assailant managed to brake in time, and I was spared a running-over. But I was not spared a spinal fracture.

The accident occurred just outside a Renault garage, where two mechanics happened to be working in the forecourt. They rushed to my assistance. One of them telephoned for an ambulance and the carabinieri, while the other slid a sheet of plastic under my head, to prevent my hair from sticking to the melting tarmac. He even ran to a café down the road to borrow a large umbrella, which he held over me as protection against the ferocious sun. The paramedics and the carabinieri could not have been more efficient, and I was soon whisked off to Latisana Hospital.

When the senior physician did his evening round with the colleague who was taking over for the night, he stopped by my bed to introduce me.

'This lady,' he said, 'is a friend of Mrs Thatcher's. She's an iron lady, who has just cycled on her own all the way from the Baltic to the Adriatic. She has cycled through great cities like Hamburg, Vienna, Prague and Trieste – all without incident. Then she comes to sleepy little Latisana. She's cycling along a quiet road at midday – perfect visibility – no traffic – and a driver in his nineties, with poor eyesight, mows her down and fractures her spine.' He gave one of those delightful little Italian shrugs. 'Life,' he sighed, 'is full of ironies.'

It was a nasty accident, but I was lucky. There was no damage to the spinal cord and my back mended within a year, while Condor speeds along nicely now on a new rear wheel. It could all have been so very much worse for both of us.

THE MYSTERY OF THE AMBER ROOM

Of the hundreds of thousands of works of art which the Germans and Russians looted from each other during World War II, the most precious treasure of all was the Amber Room from Tsarskoe Selo, the summer palace of the tsars of Russia. Hitler planned to make it the centrepiece of his Museum of World Culture in Berlin, but it disappeared in 1945 when the Allies invaded Europe. Where is it now? The internet bubbles with theories and fortunes have been spent by private treasure-seekers, but so far the whereabouts of this fabulous room remains a mystery.

So what is the Amber Room? In 1701, Frederick I of Prussia, on a tour of his realm, visited Königsberg on the Baltic Sea, one of the richest sources of amber in the world. There he commissioned a set of amber panels. For ten years, a team of craftsmen pieced together thousands of amber fragments in every shade of cream, yellow, gold and tawny brown, to produce mosaic scenes of rare beauty. Frederick installed them in a small parlour in his main Berlin palace, where he enjoyed playing noughts and crosses in their golden glow.

Peter the Great of Russia saw the amber panels on a state visit to Prussia and admired them so much that Frederick's son and successor, Frederick William I of Prussia, presented them to the tsar to cement the Prussian–Russian Alliance of 1716. Peter installed them in his winter palace in St Petersburg.

In 1755, Catherine the Great decided to move the panels to the Catherine Palace, the summer palace of the tsars in Tsarskoe Selo, now called Pushkin, some 15 miles south of St Petersburg. It took 76 of her burly guardsmen 6 days to carry them there. Never one to do things by half, Catherine used the amber panels to create one of the most magnificent rooms the world had ever seen. It was known in its day as the Eighth Wonder of the World.

Frederick's amber panels were amazing creations in themselves. Weighing around 6 tonnes, they were formed of 100,000 pieces of amber mosaic, worked into flowers, fruit, armour, Prussian royal insignia and biblical scenes. To give them extra radiance, they were backed entirely with gold leaf. Catherine the Great extended the room by alternating the amber panels with mirrors and incorporating four eighteenth-century Florentine mosaics in marble and onyx. She added richly carved and gilded pilasters, gilded busts of women from around the world, gilded swags, gilded leaves, gilded scrollwork, gilded arabesques, gilded cherubim, gilded medallions and gilded sconces. Trompe l'oeil amber wallpaper and amber objects completed the glorious whole, and the room glowed like burnished gold in the setting sun. Most magical of all were the nights, when the gleam of 565 candles set the room ablaze.

The Amber Room survived the Russian Revolution and all was well until the German invasion of Russia in World War II. As the German army advanced in 1941, the Russians whisked most of the furnishings away into safe-keeping and papered over the amber panels, hoping to hide them. As we know, the Germans never took Leningrad/St Petersburg itself, but they did get as far as Pushkin – and they were not fooled. They stripped off the wallpaper and their 'Art Protection Officer', the Prussian Count Sommes Laubach, who had a degree in art history, decided that the Amber Room must be taken to Germany 'for safety'. It took 6 men 36 hours to dismantle it and pack the panels into 29 crates. These travelled southwest by train, back to their birthplace, Königsberg, where the Amber Room was reconstructed in Königsberg Castle in 1942.

In 1945, the victorious Russian army reached the outskirts of Königsberg. The Germans hastily dismantled the Amber Room and packed the panels into crates in the castle basement. This is their last reported sighting. The Russians captured Königsberg (now Kaliningrad, because they kept the city after the war) and razed the castle to the ground.

The Amber Room was one gigantic, fantastic piece of jewellery. It was a unique creation, impossible to evaluate, though a rough estimate of £150 million has been put forward. Little wonder that teams of investigators have spent the last fifty years trawling seas, reopening derelict mine shafts, digging up forests and exploring former Nazi strongholds in the greatest treasure hunt of modern times.

There are almost as many theories about its location as there are pieces of amber mosaic in the Amber Room. Here are a few:

1. A charred fragment of amber found in the ruins of Königsberg Castle suggests that the Germans might not have been able to

move the panels quickly enough. They might have been burned to ashes when the Russians demolished the castle or destroyed in Allied bombing raids.

2. The Amber Room escaped on a German liner, the *Wilhelm Gustloff*, bound for one of the German Baltic ports, but was torpedoed on the way by a Russian submarine. After the war, Russian divers found the sunken ship, but a large hole had been cut in the hull and there were no crates inside.

3. The crates travelled by train to Weimar and were buried under Weimar County Hall.

4. On a visit to Germany in 1991, Boris Yeltsin said he had proof that the Amber Room was hidden in a particular Nazi bunker, but a thorough search by the authorities revealed nothing.

5. One of the private investigators, Helmut Gaensel, was in touch with former SS officers living in Brazil, who claimed that the Amber Room was buried in a silver mine 60 miles south of Berlin. The local residents talked of great activity around the mine in 1945, but to date no crates have been found there.

6. Stasys Mikelis, the Mayor of Neringa in Lithuania, has claimed that the Amber Room was sunk in a nearby lagoon. The SS were seen in 1945 hiding a consignment of wooden crates on the shoreline, but the lagoon has since risen, so the crates, if they were in fact hidden there, must now be underwater.

7. According to a German TV documentary, the crates were hidden by a Nazi airman, Brigadier Albert Popp, in old mine workings near Elsterberg.

8. The Amber Room panels were hidden in Gottingen.

9. They were hidden in France.

10. They were hidden in Finland.

11. They were buried in the forests of Bavaria.

12. The Baltic seabed, countless caves, disused mines, lakes, rivers, Nazi strongholds, bunkers and wartime ruins all have their advocates.

So far, none of the trawling, wading and digging has produced even the slightest hint of a fragment of amber. And superstition surrounds the search. Like the tombs of the Pharaohs, the Amber Room carries a curse: several investigators, who have spent fortunes looking for it, have died in mysterious circumstances. But for

Catherine the Great, it was her 'lucky room'. When she played cards there, she always won.

Recently, there have been two exciting discoveries. In 1997, an item appeared in a Potsdam sale room. It was a Florentine mosaic panel, made of marble and semi-precious stones, which a German lawyer was trying to sell for $2.5 million on behalf of a client, who had inherited it from his father. The client claimed that his father had come across the panel when he was serving in the German army on the Russian front, and had somehow managed to acquire it and send it home. Shortly afterwards, a German art restorer reported that he had repaired a lacquered Russian chest in the 1970s, which seemed to match the description of a chest displayed in the Amber Room.

The director of the Tsarskoe Selo Palace Museum, Ivan Sautov, examined the two items with his team of experts and verified their authenticity. The marble and onyx mosaic was one of the set of four panels acquired by Catherine the Great. It was stolen separately, as is clear from photographs of the Amber Room in Königsberg Castle, which show only three of the four panels in place when the room was reconstructed. Ivan Sautov also identified the lacquered chest as one of a pair specially made for the Amber Room in the 1760s.

When these two items came to light, the Russians began to hope that the entire room might still be lurking somewhere, intact. As Sautov said, 'Maybe these discoveries are threads leading to the finding of all of the Amber Room.'

The German government bought the two items and presented them to President Putin in April 2000, as a goodwill gesture. So there are at least two original pieces in the Catherine Palace. The rest of the Amber Room is a reconstruction.

Despairing of finding their Eighth Wonder of the World, the Russians decided to reconstruct it in time for the celebration of the 300th anniversary of the foundation of St Petersburg in 2003. Work was begun under the auspices of the Soviet Ministry of Culture in 1979, using only a handful of black-and-white photographs taken shortly after the 1918 Revolution and one colour slide. Between 1979 and 1991, they invested £4.7 million on the project. Then work was halted for almost a decade after the collapse of the Soviet Union, as amber had become unaffordable.

Tatiyana Zharkova, the director in charge of the reconstruction, explained the problem: ninety per cent of the world's supply of the resin comes from the Baltic States. When they were part of the USSR, the Government could issue a directive and buy the amber for a few roubles a kilo. But once the Baltic States became independent, the Russians had to pay the full market price – about £190 a kilo for medium quality amber and up to £650 for a ball-sized piece of the best. It looked as if the project would fail, but the German firm Ruhrgas AC saved the day with a donation of £2 million, enough to purchase four tonnes of amber and pay the craftsmens' wages.

The restoration was a Herculean task. Russia no longer had amber workers, so a team of craftsmen had to be specially trained in the Leningrad Art School before work could begin. Fifty of them then spent twenty-five years on the project. It took them eleven years simply to complete the preliminary job of sorting through all the available fragments of amber and grading them into shades of colour and degrees of transparency. Each of the ten small panels round the bottom of the room took a team of four craftsmen a full year to complete. As for the 56 large panels, the work seemed endless. According to Tatiyana Zharkova, the mosaics of couples reclining in the countryside of Renaissance Florence were particularly difficult to recreate.

The craftsmen worked with tiny drills, placing each fragment of amber on a black velvet cushion and looking through a microscope to carve tiny breastplates, apples or flowers. Vladimir Domrachev, one of the workshop's directors, explained the frustrations of the work: 'Amber is a capricious material. It's light and soft, but brittle, like glass. A carving will be almost ready, then you give it one shave too many and it shatters.' He also worries about the future. 'We no longer live in a world where there is demand for amber rooms, so what will my specially trained craftsmen do next?' Produce amber knick-knacks for the tourists?

The reconstruction of the Florentine stone panels was more straightforward. When work began, the USSR was still intact, so there was an ample supply of cheap semi-precious material, notably onyx from Kazakhstan and lapis lazuli from Afghanistan. As for the design of the panels, a copy of one of them, painted by an artist, was found in Italy, and that gave the craftsmen a good idea of the original colours. Then, more importantly, one of the original four panels turned up in Potsdam.

The restored Amber Room was opened with great celebration just in time for the Tercentenary of the foundation of St Petersburg, and President Putin hosted the G8 summit there in May 2003. The glittering jewel of a room glows golden again, and visitors can once more marvel at the Eighth Wonder of the World. But where is the original?

THE SANTA FE TRAIL

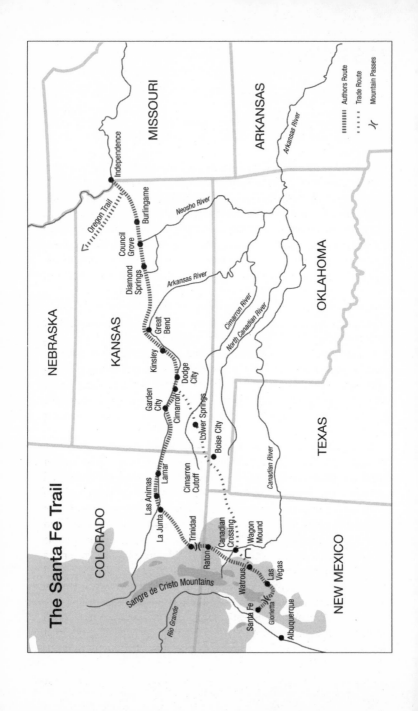

MISSOURI

listen, there's a hell
of a good universe next door; let's go.

e.e. cummings

I'm glad I didn't start travelling when I was young. Had I got the wind in my hair and my bicycle wheels at an early age, I should never have settled down with a husband or a serious job. Careerless, penniless and homeless from a lifetime of wandering, I should now be an ageing hippy, eking out my scant resources in some cheap guest house in Penang, or spreading my sleeping-bag under the stars on a Kerala beach, dreaming of England, but unable to afford to return. As it is, my life has worked out rather better. My conventional youth has earned me a reckless maturity.

People often ask me which comes first – the journey or the book. Most travel writers start young and try to make a career out of their writing. They have to think of a journey which will make an interesting book and earn them some money. But I have already had my career and earned my money, so I have the luxury of being able to travel wherever the fancy takes me. For me, the journey always comes first. I go where I really want to go. I enjoy the journey (usually), and I may or may not write a book about it afterwards.

I'm usually restless in November. The days are rainy, the evenings are dark and I long to go on a warm ride. I remember reading a Henry Miller book, in which he described his childhood in New York. He wrote of the bitter cold, and the intricate webs of frost woven inside the windows of their unheated apartment. The only warm room was the kitchen, where the whole family crouched round the stuffy paraffin stove. Years later, he realised that people didn't *have* to live in such a dreadful climate. Most of us have a choice. It's a choice which I'm now free to exercise every winter. I leave the wind and the rain behind me, to cycle in the sun by day and stroll under the palm trees in the balmy evenings.

Yet one November, my restlessness took a strange turn. I itched to go off on my bike, but not to the warmth of Asia. The ride that haunted me was the Santa Fe Trail. The more I thought about it, the more I knew that I had to ride it, and ride it that year, taking a chance with the weather. The newspapers showed that the temperatures out there were still pleasantly high, but winter comes swiftly to the American Midwest. One day it's hot, then the wind changes quarter and, overnight, the mercury drops to zero. But the ride still lured me. I had already cycled the Oregon Trail, the California Trail, the Mormon Trail and the Pony Express route. The Santa Fe Trail was the one yawning gap. I needed to ride it to complete my pioneering set.

Studying the maps, I saw that the city of Santa Fe stood at an altitude of 7,000 feet, and the trail climbed gradually, but surely, all the way up there from the Missouri river. It was also clear that the prevailing wind swept down from the Rockies and whistled eastwards across the prairies. The sensible direction to cycle would therefore be from west to east, starting in Santa Fe and cruising downhill with the wind behind me. But sensible seemed so dull. 'I'm cycling to Kansas City' somehow didn't have the same ring about it as 'I'm on my way to Santa Fe'. And in America, travelling west is to leave the cities behind and make for the freedom of the open skies and wide empty spaces, where buffalo roam and the cowboys and Indians of our youth gallop on magnificent horses across the silver screen, bullets and arrows flying. Cycling west, the air would shimmer like crystal and every day would be more exhilarating than the last. But cycling east, I would be travelling away from the magic, through increasingly built-up areas, with nothing to look forward to but thicker exhaust fumes. The romantic in me chose the impractical. I flew out to Kansas City.

DAY 1

I had booked to fly out on United Air and was pleasantly surprised to be greeted at the Heathrow check-in by a 'Two Flag'. 'Two Flags take care of bicycles,' said the polite Indian boy, as he relieved me of my Condor. No other airline had ever made it so simple. For some reason, I had to reclaim my bike and check it in again at Chicago's O'Hare Airport, which was a bore, but changing planes there was worth it for the gleaming view over the city's towers and the vast seascape of Lake Michigan.

A computer expert from Silicon Valley sat next to me in economy class, because he had chivalrously given his business-class, expense-account seat to his wife. She kept coming up the aisle to check that 'Daddy' was comfortable. 'She's still a vegetarian,' Daddy confided over our chicken lunch. 'We come from Madras and it's hard for her to change. I've got used to meat now. I eat it all, even beef, which is damnation for a good Hindu! But I'm in business, and it causes too many problems at conferences to insist on pure vegetarian food. We shall stay in the States. Our daughter was born here and she's married an American. So I think we have to adapt.'

I arrived in Kansas City in the late afternoon, and the November darkness fell while I was sorting out my baggage and pumping up my tyres. I was counting on finding an airport hotel, as I always avoid cycling in the dark – so much so that I never bother to carry lights. But there was no hotel to be seen, and I had to set out for the city centre, on the only available road. It was a fast, busy freeway, where three lanes of traffic thundered along in each direction, and I knew that cycling was illegal. But I had no choice. I said my prayers, then launched my lampless Condor on to the hard shoulder. At first, along the airport perimeter, the road was well lit, but the lights eventually petered out and I was cycling in deadly blackness. I pedalled like mad, trusting to the headlights to pick me out from behind, until I reached the safety of a service station and spotted an Econolodge just off the freeway. I staggered in, weak with relief. There was no restaurant nearby, but the Econolodge van obligingly drove me to the Hilton, a few miles down the road, where I recovered over a giant turkey-and-cranberry club sandwich and a glass or two of wine.

DAY 2

In the great days of the wagon-trains, settlers and traders bound for the west assembled at Independence, Missouri. Founded in 1827, this small town, poised on the very edge of American civilisation, as it was then, was the acknowledged starting-point for the Santa Fe, Oregon and California Trails. When rivers were still the main highways, Independence was perfectly placed on the westernmost bend of the Missouri river, just before it turns north to the Dakotas. Eastwards the Missouri links up with the Mississippi at St Louis; and the Mississippi links up eastwards with the Ohio. So travellers, manufactured goods and livestock had an almost seamless river journey from the settled east. Every spring, would-be migrants, merchants, gold-prospectors, gamblers and anyone else going west to seek a fortune gathered in Independence. There they bought their wagons, teams, livestock and equipment, formed up into trains to protect themselves against the local Indians, and took on provisions for their months on the move. The place was buzzing.

Today, Kansas City and Independence have joined up into one massive conurbation. Fortunately, I found a service road parallel to the Interstate, which kept me safely away from most of the traffic. But I still had to contend with Missouri's wretched roller-coaster hills, which I remembered well from my crossing of America in 1988. There were many of them in quick succession, all sugar-loaves, short and steep – too short to build up speed on the down-run, and too steep to cycle up without a great deal of toil. As I panted over crest after crest, I remembered renaming Missouri 'Misery'.

It was the first morning of my ride, I had not done any training, and it took me a shaming 7 hours to cover the 34 miles to Independence. 'Must do better,' I wrote in my diary. I passed factories, quarries, landfill sites and miles of road works, where the hard shoulder was broken up and stony. There was nothing along the road to lift the spirits, until I reached the Missouri river itself, which ran through a sylvan gorge, its high, wooded banks glowing gold and dusty green in the autumn sunlight. It was surprisingly hot for November. As I walked out to dinner at 7 p.m., the digital display in downtown Independence still registered 60 degrees Fahrenheit.

DAY 3

This was my day for research. Independence, 'The Queen City of the Trails', has a National Frontier Trails Center, which incorporates the Merrill J Mattes Research Library. Here, I thought, was the place to learn all about the Santa Fe Trail. But I was rather disappointed. The exhibition concentrated heavily on the Oregon and California Trails, presumably because these were the main migrant routes, the ones taken by families who travelled out of Independence to make new lives for themselves in the American west. The library's 2,200 trail diaries, which these would-be settlers wrote by candlelight between 1820 and 1870, give vivid day-to-day accounts of the dangers, hardships and camaraderie of the road, shot through with their hopes for the future. They are intensely personal documents, from which quotations are taken to infuse life into the yokes, wagon wheels, looms, pots and pans of the displays. The Santa Fe Trail had its groups of settlers too, but the primary purpose of the trail was trade, which is not so rich in human interest. As far as the National Frontier Trails Center was concerned, my chosen trail was the poor relation.

Santa Fe was not a popular destination for American settlers, because the place had already been settled, as early as 1609, by Spaniards moving up from Mexico in search of the fabled cities of gold. Their lifeline was El Camino Real, the Royal Road, or Chihuahua Trail, which connected their colony of New Mexico with Vera Cruz, the closest Mexican port, 1,800 miles away. The New Mexicans felt isolated and neglected. They paid their taxes to Mexico, but they were given little protection against the marauding Apache, Navajo, Kiowa and Comanche tribes; and because their supply line was so long and mountainous, they were desperately short of those small manufactured items, such as knives, needles, buttons and saucepans, which contribute so much to life's convenience. They may be humble and dull, but just imagine trying to cope without them! A market was ready and waiting for traders from the east.

At first, it was the fur trappers who traded with New Mexico. They had found their way up the Missouri and into the Rockies to supply their eager customers in the east with the thick, warm pelts of mountain creatures. Some of these intrepid mountain men followed the Native American paths southwest through the Sangre de Cristo mountains and sold their furs in Santa Fe.

From this small, furry beginning sprang one of the world's most romantic trade routes. The development of the Santa Fe Trail is too complex a story to take in on a cycle-ride, so I shall just tell one dramatic tale – the story of William Becknell. On 29 January 1822, four riders galloped into Franklin, a dusty little backwoods town on the banks of the Missouri. They were returning from a four-month trading expedition, but they seemed to have little to show for it. Then William Becknell, the leader of the party, slit open a small rawhide sack and out tumbled a cascade of Spanish silver coins.

Becknell and his friends had left Franklin with a stock of small trade items to barter with the Native American tribes, but then they had heard of the fur-trappers' profits and rode into unmapped territory, searching for a direct route from the Missouri to Santa Fe. The journey was so desperate that they were forced to cut off the ears of their mules and drink their blood in order to survive. But they found a way through, and the Mexicans mobbed them in their eagerness to buy the needles, mirrors and trinkets which Becknell had intended for the Indians. And they paid for them in silver, which was just what Missouri needed. The state had been admitted to the Union in 1821, but the banks had failed and the people were on the verge of a barter economy for want of coinage and reliable paper currency. On their side, the Mexicans had gained their independence from Spain in the same year and, unlike their former Spanish rulers, were keen to trade with the 'Anglos'. Missouri and Santa Fe were trading partners made in heaven, fulfilling each other's needs to perfection.

On that first journey to Santa Fe, Becknell made a reasonable profit. When he returned the next year, with wagons instead of pack animals, his profit rose to 2,000 per cent. Other wagons laden with pots, pans and calico began to roll along the trail. Mexican silver coinage became the hard currency of the state of Missouri, and the mules for which that stubborn 'show me' state is famous were imported from New Mexico in droves. What began as a trickle turned into an amazing westward tide of five hundred wagons a day. By 1862, trade along the trail was worth $40 million dollars a year. Roads were surveyed, forts built to protect the traders from Indian attack, and settlement followed. The Santa Fe Trail was the spearhead of American expansion to the southwest. It opened up a quarter of the North American continent.

Which is why I was rather peeved to find it so under-represented in the National Frontier Trails Center. I cycled off in a huff to view the city's other claim to fame – the home of the former president, Mr Harry S Truman. It's a stately Victorian house, finished in white clapboard, with flights of steps leading up to the entrances, bay windows and verandahs with fancy wrought-iron trim. I could see its detail well through the railings, as the trees and hedges were November bare. The Stars and Stripes swirled around their flagpole on the lawn, marking the house as a historical site. (That was the year before September 11. Today, defiant patriotism rules and every house in America, historical or not, seems to fly the national flag.)

The house, I was pleased to find, had a connection with the Santa Fe Trail. It was built by one George Porterfield Gates, half of the Waggoner–Gates partnership, which milled the settlers' grain and went on milling until 1967, when an explosion and fire destroyed the mill. President Truman's wife, Bess Wallace Truman, was George Gates's granddaughter.

Harry S Truman was a loyal son of Independence. He went back there when his term at the White House ended, and lived the quiet life of a retired employee. He strolled round the town, greeted his neighbours, sat on his verandah with Bess and minded his grandchildren, as if his job had been no more important than any other. He never sold his story to the press, wrote his memoirs or went on million-dollar lecture tours. Instead, he gave all his papers to his home-town, where they form the Truman Library. Perhaps he just wanted to forget those grim years in the White House – the atomic bombs on Nagasaki and Hiroshima, the start of the Korean War and the painful division of Europe, when the Iron Curtain fell.

Coachloads of reverential pensioners were touring the Truman sites, picking up pamphlets in the Truman Information Center and perusing them as they shuffled along, Darby and Joans, hand-in-hand in their matching trainers. Main Street and Independence Square were real old-town America, an oasis of quiet respectability in the middle of roaring ringroads and neon strips. Kansas City had felt like anywhere and nowhere, but downtown Independence was small enough to have some character of its own. Here, people had more time to chat, and I was 'honey' to everyone, an American form of address which I love. As a child in Nottingham, I was 'duckie' or 'duck'. That's quirky, and it always made me smile. But these days, in England, I am at the age to have become 'dear', which I hate for its patronising tone, though I'm more accepting of it than some. My friend, Heather, who could be quite imperious at times, was once boarding a British Airways flight behind two dark-suited business men. The hostesses greeted the men with a smart 'Good morning, sir.' When it came to Heather's turn, they smiled and said, 'Hello, dear,' to which she replied grandly, 'Either they are Sir and I am Madam, or I am Dear and they are Dear.' 'Honey' is by far the best appellation. It carries no connotations of age or sex. Being 'honey' in Independence just made me feel glamorous, like a Hollywood star.

KANSAS

women and men (both dong and ding)
summer autumn winter spring
reaped their sowing and went their came
sun moon stars rain

e.e. cummings

DAY 4

I awoke in Independence to the rattling of windows and doors. The girl at reception told me that winds of 60 mph were forecast, blowing from the south – just the direction I was travelling in. The winds always know when a cyclist is about to take to the roads, and do their worst. I set off southwards into Gobi-type gales. Even when I turned west along Bannister, rogue winds swirled between the buildings in sudden gusts, which made it difficult to control the bike. Fortunately there were sidewalks, which slowed me down, but at least they were safe.

I crossed the state line back from Missouri into Kansas, the state of Judy Garland and *The Wizard of Oz*. I was hoping to clear the Kansas City conurbation by evening, but the wind was exhausting and I had underestimated the distance. The city outskirts seemed never-ending, mile upon mile of suburban housing. I reached Overland Park, once an assembly point for the trails, and rode into a shopping mall to buy a reviving coffee and enquire about places to stay. I was trammelled in a mesh of roads, too small to feature on my map, and there was not a hotel in sight. Then Glenda, a recently retired geography teacher, appeared. Unlike everyone else I had consulted that day, she was a person who could read maps! She showed me exactly where I was.

'What an urban sprawl!' I said.

'Yes. Kansas City's booming. It's one of the most prosperous cities in the USA. And the pressure on housing's enormous, with all the people flooding in to take up jobs. Then, to make matters worse, the state schools in Missouri are so poor that they've been derecognised, or whatever the term is. So families with kids are desperate to move over to the Kansas side of the line. We just can't build houses and apartments fast enough. The city spreads and spreads. I'm not surprised you got lost.'

I told her I was following the Santa Fe Trail. Glenda lit up. 'How very interesting! I've done quite a bit of research on the trail myself. My grandfather was born beside it. His father came over from Wales when he was nineteen, and he and his wife were going out west to farm, at the time when the Government was giving land grants in Kansas to settlers. But my great-grandmother died on the trail, just two days after my grandfather was born, so his father brought him up on his own.'

The trail was arduous and fraught with danger for everyone who undertook it. Traders and the wealthier settlers had 800 miles of uncharted, roadless prairie to creak across in their ox wagons before they even reached the Rockies; the poorer migrants struggled across this vast wilderness, pushing their meagre possessions in handcarts over sandhills, through knee-deep riverside mud and grasses that were sometimes head-high. Travelling in convoy, the wagonmen could combine two or three teams of oxen to struggle over the worst stretches, and form stockades of wagons at night as protection from Indian attack. But there was no way they could protect themselves from freak weather, cholera, typhoid, hunger, thirst and exposure. The women had the hardest time of all. They had to look after the children, nurse the sick, prepare the food, and help with the livestock and the general chores around the camp. They struggled to keep their families together in the most primitive conditions, with none of the high-tech equipment designed for the convenience of today's campers. But the greatest miseries for them were pregnancy on the journey and childbirth by the roadside, with no medical attention. Many of them died on the way.

A few years ago, there was an outcry from the women of Salt Lake City over an exhibition on the history of Mormon migration. The notices throughout referred to 'The pioneers and their wives', as if it was the men who had opened up the West, while the women had simply tagged along for the ride. But the women were pioneers too, and they had to show more courage in the face of their own particular dangers than the men. I'm pleased to say that the offending notices were speedily altered.

There were no hotels in the centre of Overland Park, so Glenda drove me in her van to a motel on the outskirts, giving me what she called 'a Kansas hug' in parting. Like most motels in America, mine was beside an Interstate, and there were no restaurants within walking or cycling distance. Everyone drives a car. I could have rung for a pizza or a Chinese take-away, but both outlets had a minimum delivery menu big enough for about six ravenous workmen. So I made do with three packets of Doritos and Cheetos from the motel vending machine, which I helped down with a swig or two of whisky from my emergency supply. Before that meagre dinner, I had eaten a cinnamon bun at breakfast, two bananas on the ride and an Italian almond stick with my coffee. I hoped I was losing weight.

DAY 5

Between Kansas City centre and Olathe, its wealthiest suburb, there were only two fields, but after Olathe I broke free of the city streets and finally reached the countryside. The day before, I had been sweltering in a short-sleeved shirt. Then the night had brought one of those sharp drops in temperature for which the Midwest is notorious. Despite the brilliant sunshine, I needed my long johns, jersey, anorak, balaclava and woolly hat.

After a few days on the road, I was cycling strongly and enjoying the ride – until I pulled in at a gravel lay-by to read a historic marker and got a puncture in my front tyre. Fortunately, it was such a slow puncture that a good pumping-up would carry me about half a mile; and the next town, Edgerton, was less than two miles away. It all went well until I was in the middle of my third pumping, when a sudden gust of wind blew the bike over on top of me. I was unharmed, but the pump got wedged at an awkward angle. The valve snapped off the inner tube and got stuck inside the pump. I was just debating whether to walk the short distance into Edgerton or hitch a lift in a Chevvy pick-up, when a battered car pulled up and out jumped Don, flashing his ID card. 'I work in the Sheriff's Department, ma'am. Let me help you.' How lucky can you get?

Don roped Condor in the car boot and drove me to the garage in Edgerton, but they were disdainful of vehicles without engines. So he drove me all the way to Lawrence, more than 25 miles away, stopping first outside Edgerton to show me the very point where the Oregon Trail branched off to the right from the Santa Fe. The prairie grasses were short, but he told me that in the season they grew 'as high as trees'.

He found the cycle shop in Lawrence and said to the cycle mechanic, 'I want to offer this lady a cup of coffee while we wait. She comes from England, so where can I get her some real English coffee?' The mechanic looked puzzled.

'I'm quite happy with American coffee, Don. That will do fine.'

'No it won't! You've got to have some proper English coffee.'

A customer in the shop suggested the big bookstore in the next block. They in fact served Italian coffee, but I told Don that we drank that all the time in England, so he was satisfied. He treated me to an 'American muffin' to go with this 'English coffee', and we took our tray over to a table in the midst of students swotting for their mid-term exams.

'Anyone here from England?' shouted Don. 'This lady's from England. She could talk to you.' The students buried their noses in their books.

Lawrence is the seat of the University of Kansas. Don took me on a tour of the campus, where the halls of residence house 2,500 students. But he told me that many students are too poor to pay for a room there. They spend their nights in the 24-hour library, stretch out on park benches, or sleep in their cars, moving them on every couple of hours to stay within the law.

Don was a great chatterbox, a mine of information who knew the price of everything – the houses we passed, student fees, the rents they paid, the price of cars – but unlike Lord Darlington's cynic in *Lady Windermere's Fan*, he also knew their value. He talked of winning the lottery which he always played.

'What would you do with all that money if you won it?' I asked.

'Oh, give it away. There's only so much a person can use, and there are plenty of needy folk out there.'

With his gentle manner and big owl spectacles, Don didn't look much like a law-enforcer, and I was curious to know what office he held within the Sheriff's Department. It turned out that he worked in the Olathe jail from 5 p.m. to 1 a.m., in charge of maintenance and cleaning. When he did a maintenance job, he had to register every tool, nail and bit of wire, and work under escort, as he was carrying potential weapons. He finished work at 1 a.m., then collected 190 newspapers and spent the next two to three hours delivering them.

'I have to do two jobs to pay my nine hundred dollars a month maintenance to my ex and my three children. Her dad was always complaining that I was useless and didn't earn enough, and I think that eventually got to her. It turned her against me, after fifteen years of marriage. It was a real blow, I can tell you. But then, I suppose you can just get fed up with a person,' he concluded wistfully.

He told me how much he missed his children. He took them camping in the Rockies in the summer, and he was picking them up that evening to take them bowling. But it wasn't the same thing as having them at home.

'I hope this trip to Lawrence hasn't made you late for the children.'

'No. It's made my afternoon. I've just started a week's holiday and I was at a loose end. I'm going to my dad's tomorrow. He grows Christmas trees as a retirement occupation and I'm going to start chopping and bagging them for him, while he goes off for a week's hunting with his friends. Pheasant. He likes that.'

We collected the bike and Don, despite all my resistance, insisted on paying for the repair. The mechanic had fitted a new inner tube and managed to extract the piece of valve from the pump, to save me from buying a new one. I asked to be taken back to Edgerton, to the point where I'd had the puncture and stopped cycling. I never like to be helped along my way. It seems like cheating on a ride.

'If I drop you at Edgerton, where are you going to stay? It's getting late.'

'I shall cycle on to Baldwin City. They tell me there's a motel there, just as you go into town.'

'You can't stay there! That motel's wild. It's full of crack-heads on welfare, paying one hundred dollars a week and snorting their brains out. Half the inmates at Olathe come from there. I'll take you on to Burlingame, to a respectable place.'

We drove through Overbrook, where he lived. 'The last little business here folded up this week. It was a lumber yard, but the owner's died and no one in the family wants to carry on. The motel closed down some time ago. It's just another small Kansas town going belly-up. People want to live in small towns, because they like the life, but they all drive into Kansas City, Topeka or Wichita to work and shop. The only small place that keeps going is Osage City, because they've got a really popular line in pre-constructed homes.' I was to be overtaken on the road by many of these terrifying structures – towering two-storey houses, fully finished down to the last window-pane and door-knocker, wobbling precariously in the wind as they thundered past on articulated trucks.

It seemed that Burlingame was another casualty of the economic shift to the cities, because the motel had just closed down, as had the village store. So we drove on to Council Grove, to the Old Trail Motel. Don told me to sit outside in the car, while he went in to make enquiries. He was gone for some time, but eventually came out with a look of triumph on his face.

'I've fixed it all up for you. There's a fund for the needy in Council Grove. They pay a night's accommodation for people passing through with no money. She's just rung the secretary and the fund is going to look after you. I wanted to make sure about it, because if the fund wouldn't pay, I was going to pay the bill myself. I couldn't let a lady from England pay.'

I was deeply embarrassed, but Don had taken so much trouble and been so well intentioned that I pretended to go along with his plan. As he drove away, he warned me not to stay in any motel if it looked at all dodgy.

'If you're stuck for somewhere to stay, go to one of the local churches and ask for help. You know what a church is, do you? You have them in England? Good. Failing the church, you can always go to the deputy sheriff. He'll see you right.'

I waved goodbye to one of the kindest, most generous, most guileless men I have met in my long life. Then I went inside the motel and unmade all the thoughtful arrangements he had made on my behalf. I insisted on paying my own bill, so that the fund could be reserved for the really needy. The proprietors kept asking me if I was absolutely sure that I could afford the $25. When I convinced them, they thanked me effusively for my kindness – when it was I who was reduced almost to tears by the kindness of the people I had met so far in Kansas.

DAY 6

I awoke to a hard white frost, so I took my time over my Nescafé and buns, observing 'the American dream' from my window. The Old Trail Motel stood on a dirt road, where people lived in mobile homes and prefabricated wooden houses in various stages of decrepitude. It was Saturday morning and the man next door was out in the field behind his trailer with his small son. The trailer, four windows and a door long, looked pretty beaten-up, and the car parked beside it was an old model, crumbling away into a heap of rust. But there was a satellite dish outside and the small boy was roaring round the field on a gleaming new miniature motorbike, which must have cost a year's wages, or been bought with one of the loans advertised on every hoarding. 'Pay-day' loans. Keep your Car. No Questions Asked. Lowest Rates in Town. I have seen families in India and rural Thailand glued to their televisions, watching *Dallas* and dreaming of American luxury. They have no idea that the reality for so many Americans is not a wide-acred ranch, a string of thoroughbreds and cocktails by the swimming pool, but a dilapidated trailer up a dirt road.

As I was wheeling my bike down the motel path, the husband of the man-and-wife team who ran the motel came puffing along behind me. He was a big, hefty man in the uniform of the Kansas retired – blue overalls, a checked flannel shirt and a baseball cap. His face screwed up with worry, he asked if I was really sure that I could afford to pay for my room. If I was at all short of money, he would return my $25.

'I could write a book about this motel – two books! People who try to take advantage of the free-room scheme, when they've got plenty of money. And hunters who sneak in their horrible 120-pound dogs after nightfall and let them tear up the new screens with their claws. One great slob got aggressive. He said, "If my dog busts that screen, I'll pay for a new one." I told him, "I don't want a new one. That's already new. Just installed. So keep that dog of yours off it." Last summer, we had the Santa Fe Trail chuck wagons on the land here. Two of the people walking behind were English ladies. Then one of our local officials got difficult and drove them out of town, right to the fair-ground. He came on TV, calling them scroungers and scallywags. And you know what he is? He's a cross-dresser! Wears his wife's clothes – *all of them*!'

Council Grove was a significant halt on the Santa Fe Trail. It was here that a peace treaty was signed with the Osage people in 1825, guaranteeing traders and settlers safe passage across their lands. It was here too that the final wagon-trains were formed. Many of the settlers who had started out from Independence had turned off along the Oregon Trail, while there were new arrivals who had cut across country from small townships like Fort Leavenworth to the north. In Council Grove, equipment was given its final check and there were meetings to plan the convoy's daily stages, fresh water being the main requirement at every halt.

In 1847, the first settler, Seth Hays, a great-grandson of the legendary Daniel Boone, built a log trading post beside the trail. Other traders followed, and soon Council Grove became a flourishing market, where the last provisions were taken on board before the wagons moved off into unsettled territory. The Last Chance Store, built by Tom Hill in 1857, still stands at the end of Main Street, not far from 'Post Office Oak'. This giant tree, whose gnarled trunk dwarfs the building behind it, has a very convenient hollow down near its roots, where travellers along the trail would leave messages for one another, or letters to be carried back home by any kind person returning east to the Missouri.

The Daughters of the American Revolution have erected historic markers at all the key sites along the Santa Fe Trail. It was on the gravel surrounds of their Edgerton marker that I got my puncture. The Council Grove marker about the treaty with the Osage stood, I was pleased to see, in a smoothly paved area, where the stump of the tree under which the treaty was signed is now protected by roofing in an area of picnic benches. Another marker stands by the Neosho River Crossing, just north of the town, where the grassy fields still bear the indentations made by the wheels of the ponderous wagons which lumbered along four or five abreast. I'm no expert on the subject, but I read that the simple country chuck-wagons were soon replaced by 'Pittsburgs', a variation on the old Conestogas, and later by specially constructed juggernauts with wheels seven feet high and rims eight inches wide, capable of carrying two to three tonnes of freight.

I cycled along Main Street, past the Madonna of the Trail, a modern statue honouring the Pioneer Mothers. Then came The Little Shoppe on the Prairie, Santa Fe T's & Gifts, Santa Fe Liquor and KJ's Fitness Fun-At-Its, all catering for a different type of traveller on the trail. Council Grove was doing a brisk tourist trade that sunny Saturday morning.

Highway 56 more or less follows the Santa Fe Trail. By Council Grove, it had left the painful Missouri sugarloaf hills behind and was running through pleasant rolling country. I was so used to built-up areas that I was caught out on the way to Delavan. I was not carrying much water, as I was counting on being able to buy drinks in shops and filling stations. But I passed not a single one, so I had to screw up my courage and approach two very rough-looking teenagers, tattooed and naked to the waist, who were tinkering with a car, and ask if I could fill my water-bottle at their tap. They led me into their tip of a wooden shack, with dirty dishes piled high in the kitchen and eight dogs in the yard. They didn't breed them: they just liked them.

Despite appearances, the two boys were very affable and extremely polite, apologising for not shaking hands, as they were covered in grease. They volunteered the information that they were still at school and went by school bus to Council Grove, which was further than Herington, but less expensive, as Herington was in the next county. With that lack of reticence which is so refreshing and so typically American, they told me they were brothers, and shared with me their hopes of training as motor mechanics, if they could get apprenticeships, and eventually owning their own garage. For my part, I told them a bit about my journey, but stopped short of my life history and my aspirations. We Europeans are so secretive by comparison. We rarely lay bare our souls.

In Herington, I stopped at the Dairy Queen for a chicken sandwich, which turned out to be a large chicken escalope, fried in breadcrumbs and served in a burger bun with salad and ersatz mayonnaise. I scraped off the mayo and left the bottom half of the bun.

'Is there a motel here in Herington?'

'There is,' said Mr Dairy Queen. 'But I can't recommend it.'

'Well, cyclists can't be picky – and I don't think I can get as far as McPherson today.'

He made me a present of a new map, which was much more detailed than the Rand McNally I was carrying, and tried to refuse payment for the chicken. As I went out of the café, his parting shot was, 'I hope you get one of the clean rooms! There's a bar next door to the motel, in case you're desperate.'

In fact, the motel was fine. It was run by another retired man in blue overalls, check shirt and baseball cap, who was very deaf. There was a notice in my room, apologising for the fact that the sheets were not ironed. IRONING IS TOO EXPENSIVE. BUT I CAN ASSURE OUR GUESTS THAT THE SHEETS ARE CHANGED AFTER EVERY USE. That was a comfort.

Another greasy fried escalope in the Dairy Queen was more than I could face, and I had no lights to venture out to the Pizza Hut on Highway 77. So I shopped in the supermarket for a supper of ham, cheese, Triskets and tomatoes, a packet of Doritos to go with my whisky, a cinnamon roll for my breakfast, and bananas and Gatorade for the next day's ride. The old lady behind me at the check-out tried to pay for these groceries as well as her own, but I fought her off. Wherever I went, I was overwhelmed by Kansas generosity, by people wanting to pay for me and give me freebies. It was understandable when I was riding my bike, for they obviously thought I was a pauper in a country where everyone drives a car. But I had gone to the supermarket on foot, having changed into normal, non-cycling clothes, so that couldn't be the explanation there. I gave up trying to work it out. Why not just accept that everyone was amazingly kind and enjoy all the attention? I was having a wonderful time.

DAY 7

This was the day when the prairie really began. I cycled 59 miles and, apart from the small town of Hillsboro, there was nothing and nobody on the road between Herington and my destination, McPherson. There were bands of wintery grass, then wheat stubble across the flat acres as far as the eye could see. I once rode a Greyhound bus across Kansas in the height of summer, when an ocean of ripe, golden corn glowed in the sunshine. I fell asleep on the bus, travelled through the night and woke at dawn to exactly the same luxuriant yellow landscape, with the rising sun ahead of me on one horizon and the setting moon behind me on the other. There was enough grain there to feed the world. Now, in November, I was cycling across that same boundless prairie, shorn down to stubble and a few crackling cornstalks. I detoured round dead animals on the road – a full-grown stag with really serious antlers, a silver fox, a skunk and one or two other furry things I didn't recognise – but I saw no live creatures grazing.

I had made my calculations before I started. I had about eight hours of daylight to cover my target distance, an easy average of

7 mph, including refreshment stops, but there was a fierce headwind and I found even that modest speed quite difficult to maintain. I went back to the routine which had carried me through my emptiest days in the Australian Outback. I cycled for exactly seven miles, then stopped by the roadside and rewarded myself with a drink and a small snack – a banana, an apple, a granola bar, or a few dried apricots. When the wind was particularly brutal, thinking about the next snack and deciding what it should be kept my spirits from plummeting. During the morning, it took a great deal of effort to cover my seven miles in an hour, but the wind gradually lessened in the afternoon, until I was managing the distance in about 45 minutes. These little checks and calculations may seem a trifle nerdish, but they are better than going brain-dead. And it's amazing how exciting the prospect of a banana can be in a desert of featureless winter farmland.

DAY 8

Every morning, as soon as my first mug of Nescafé was ready, I switched on my TV to look at the Weather Channel. It was compulsory viewing in such a fickle climate. The great North American continent was experiencing weather which ranged from sub-zero temperatures and house-high snow in Alaska to the almost tropical sunshine of Florida, so it was a fascinating channel, with snow reports for skiers, sea temperatures for bathers, and fog and ice reports for the commuters of New York, Chicago and Los Angeles.

After the hourly nation-wide section, the channel homed in on individual states, which was where it became really interesting. I was still enjoying pretty good cycling weather. There was hoar frost every morning now, but it soon melted away in the strong sunshine. My problem was the wind, as I'd known it would be when I masochistically chose to cycle from east to west. I didn't regret my decision. I just needed to know the direction and velocity of the enemy. So far, it had never been kind enough to blow from the east; it took its pick from the other points of the compass with seeming frivolity, swinging round gaily and bringing significant changes in temperature. One day it would blow from the northwest and I would need all my layers of clothing, from my woolly hat and balaclava down to my silk long johns. Then the next day it would swing to the southwest and I would have to strip down to my short sleeves. What was constant was the western element. Northwest and southwest, I was buffeted from the side; due west, I was cycling into the teeth of the gale. What varied was the velocity – and this was where the forecast became really gripping, particularly at the very end of the state section. At this point, the forecasters with their film sequences and charts disappeared from the screen, to be replaced by a written forecast for my very own district. I could read exactly what weather was waiting to attack me, and dress accordingly. If winds of 5 mph were forecast, I would celebrate. Above 10 mph, gloom would begin to settle.

That morning in McPherson, there were deafening bolts of thunder, so close overhead that I cowered in my hotel room, expecting the roof to come crashing down about my ears at any moment. I looked uneasily at the two notices on my door. One was the usual floor plan, showing the nearest exit in case of fire. The other was a notice detailing the safest places to hide in a tornado. I was suddenly back in the cinema, watching with a child's amazed eyes as a tornado lifted Judy Garland's house and whirled it right up into the sky. There was obviously some freakish weather in these parts. When the rain intensified and turned to hail, I was glad I had picked Day 8 as my first rest day.

I dodged the downpours to cycle into the town centre for provisions. I needed to stock up now, to set off each day with enough snacks and drinks to carry me through. The prairies were not desert like the Gobi or the Australian Outback, where lack of water could be fatal, but they were empty enough to need treating with a certain amount of caution.

Downtown McPherson amazed me. It had a few shops, a couple of filling stations and a mind-boggling array of religious affiliations. I passed the following churches: Calvary Southern Baptist, Church of Christ, Church of the Brethren, Church of the Nazarene, Countryside Covenant, First Assembly of God, First Baptist, First Congregational, First Mennonite, First United Methodist, Four-square Gospel, Free Methodist, Grace Bible Church, Grace Evangelical Lutheran, Jehovah's Witness, First Christian, Presbyterian Church, Morning Star Missionary Baptist Church, St Anne's Episcopal Church, St Joseph's Catholic Church, Seventh Day Adventist Church, Trinity Lutheran and Word of Faith Fellowship.

All in a small town of 15,000 inhabitants at the very most! Talleyrand, with the snobbery so typical of a French gourmet, once remarked, 'The United States has thirty-two religions and only one dish.' In fact, he underrated the Americans. They have no fewer than five different dishes; and their Christian sects are numberless, not to mention the traditional beliefs of the Native Americans and all the other faiths imported by more recent waves of immigrants.

So how on earth does a prospective believer choose? Leaving aside all the other religions on offer, it would take a year of Sundays to attend just one service in every Christian church. Of course, most of the Christians in McPherson had no choice to make. They were born into families with deeply held religious views, who had settled in Kansas in the first place to find the freedom to worship as their own particular sect demanded. The Protestant Reformation, which Martin Luther launched in 1517, was followed a century later by the Catholic backlash of the Counter-Reformation. These two movements swept across Europe like wildfire, igniting passions and bringing hitherto peaceful nations to war. Christians on both sides of the major divide were willing to die for their own particular brand of the faith. Either that, or they migrated, many of them to the new colonies on the east coast of America. English Puritans, French Huguenots, German Catholics, Protestants from the Austro-Hungarian Empire – there was room for them all across the Atlantic. There they could live and worship unmolested, however extreme their own particular creed.

Protestant Germany was one of the hardest hit, because the Germans approached their faith with characteristic rigour and were the least prepared to compromise for a quiet life. German Catholics raged against the Reformation, while the stricter Protestant sects, such as the Amish and the Mennonites, denounced it for not going far enough. Many of these rigid German Protestants moved to Russia, at the invitation of Catherine the Great, who was herself a German and saw the benefit of granting farmland to such industrious, righteous families. When they fell out with the Russians over compulsory military service, they were ripe for the picking by American recruitment agents. In fact, they were such desirable immigrants, such useful stabilisers of the land beside the tracks, that the railroad companies in Kansas and Nebraska engaged in a bidding war for them, vying with one another in their offers of free passages, farms and farmhouses.

Most of the Mennonites who migrated, about 10,000 of them, opted for central Kansas, simply because they liked the agent, a German-speaking charmer called Schmidt. They arrived in the 1870s, bringing not only their industriousness, but an even more significant gift – a variety of wheat called 'Turkey Red', which did well on the steppes of Russia and turned the similarly dry and windy tablelands of Kansas into one of the world's richest bread baskets. These Mennonites settled chiefly around Hillsboro, which I had cycled through the previous day, with an overspill in the McPherson area. That explained all the Mennonite churches in those two towns, as well as the range of Lutheran establishments. I had moved into German Protestant country, devout and evangelical.

I spent my afternoon off enjoying the facilities of my Best Western Holiday Manor, which was a cut above the places I usually stayed in. It was a proper hotel, with an indoor pool and a sauna. But my biggest treats were having a real bath in my bathroom and a big, squashy armchair to read in. After a week on the road, staying wherever I could find a bed, I revelled in those small comforts which, at home, I take for granted. Travel always sharpens my appreciation of my good fortune.

DAY 9

I tuned in to a dire weather forecast, so I dressed in my anorak and waterproof trousers. They crackled and snapped in the northwest wind, which sprayed icy rain in my face. Even when the skies cleared, I kept on my waterproof layer for warmth. There were no towns, no filling stations, no trees, nothing to shelter me from the fierce wind. It was a flat, straight road, with a good surface, but even so, my strength ebbed and my speed gradually dwindled down to 5 mph. So I gave up in Lyons, only 32 miles along my way. I had learned in the Gobi desert, where the winds are notorious, that it was pointless to fight them. Why battle all day to cycle my 50 miles, when the fickle wind could drop in the night and I might well be able to cover the distance next morning in a fraction of the time?

DAY 10

I did the right thing. The morning dawned frosty, but calm as a summer's afternoon. I waited for the sun to thaw the ice on the road, then flew along like the winged creatures who kept me company. The ominous shadow of a hawk tracked me for a few miles, gliding parallel with my front wheel, until the great bird swooped ahead and perched on a telegraph pole to eye me suspiciously. Overhead, a cloud of a thousand songbirds swirled in the sky, blacking out the sun and chirruping excitedly as they wheeled around, flocking for their annual migration. And swarms of yellow butterflies settled on my handlebars and fluttered in and out of my spokes. It was a morning to remember, one of those calm, blissful occasions when I know why I love cycling, despite its occasional discomforts.

When I was still at school, and popular songs were more innocent than today's *Top of the Pops*, we used to turn on the radio and hear our favourite stars singing 'On the Atchison, Topeka, boy, and Santa Fe'. It was a catchy song about riding the Santa Fe Railroad, and I never dreamed, in those distant days, that I should live to cycle beside this legendary track. For most of my journey, it ran in tandem with the road, both of them taking the line of least resistance across the seemingly endless landscape. Sometimes a train crawled past me, its engine struggling to move two hundred bogeys of freight (I know exactly how many bogeys there were, because I always counted them, for something to do!). The driver would spot me in the distance and the train would emit a long 'woo-oo-oo' in greeting. In that empty prairie, the driver and I were the only living human beings, and we both waved enthusiastically to each other. There were so few people around that no one bothered to raise barriers at level crossings, even less to put up red lights. When a dirt road branched off from Highway 56 and crossed the railway track, there was just a weather-beaten pole with a wooden saltire nailed on to it: RAILROAD CROSSING. LOOK OUT FOR THE CARS. But the old-fashioned features which astonished me most were the wooden railway bridges and supports over gulleys. They looked like the originals, built in the 1870s, when the railroad was first driven out west. It was a miracle that they still supported these mammoth trains.

I reached Great Bend in double-quick time. For me, it was a stop like any other, except that the town had a wider choice of motels than most. But for the traders and settlers along the old Santa Fe Trail, arriving safely at Great Bend was a cause for celebration. They had crossed their first wide plain, waterless except for the odd seasonal stream, and arrived at the Arkansas river. From Great Bend, they could follow the north bank of the river, if they chose, as far as La Junta in Colorado, and their water supply would be assured.

I had a lot of shopping to do in Great Bend. It was the eve of Thanksgiving, and I was not sure if any restaurants would be open over the public holiday. Better to play safe and stock up on ham, cheese and fruit. In the supermarket, I was surprised to see some lone, skinny old men doing their shopping. Presumably, they had led healthy outdoor lives as farmers and survived to be widowers. But they were the exception. Everyone else was enormously fat, some even cruising the supermarket aisles in electric invalid chairs because they were too fat to walk. With a burger or a Hershey bar in one hand and a monster cardboard cup of Coca Cola (usually Diet Coca Cola to help them slim!) in the other, the shoppers were gazing in an agony of gluttony and indecision at the five thousand varieties of biscuits, confectionery and packaged cereals on display. Every grain that could be corned or puffed was frosted with sugar. Even the so-called 'health' products were bursting with chocolate chips, marshmallow pieces, jelly and fudge. The eyes of the shoppers gleamed in anticipation as they stacked their groaning trolleys. Travelling the Santa Fe Trail used to be called 'seeing the elephant'. You saw the elephant when the magnitude of the dangers and hardships on the trail really sank in. I 'saw the elephants' every day, but mine were peaceable grazers, waddling purposefully from their cars into the nearest McDonald's, Kentucky Fried Chicken or Dunkin'Donuts.

DAY 11

Thanksgiving Day, 25 November. I usually had to make my own breakfast in motels, which I never minded, because I could watch the Weather Channel over my Nescafé and buns (I never travel without my water-boiler and mug). But in Great Bend, we were offered a complimentary breakfast.

'Are you from New Zealand?' asked a fellow guest at the coffee machine.

'No. I'm from England.'

'Nearly there.'

So much for American geography!

The motel manager was a delightful young woman named Debbie, an all-American girl with blonde hair, a fringed skirt and knee-high cowboy boots. She didn't look much like a Mennonite, though her surname suggested that she might well have been descended from one. She was full of amazement, because I was the first customer who had ever arrived on a bicycle – and I had cycled all the way from Independence, an unimaginable distance! She sat at my table and quizzed me so much that I could scarcely chew my delicious brown toast and jam. Debbie had three young children. She got out her photograph album and proudly showed me pictures of her son, sitting in the middle of his football team, and her junior cheer-leader daughter.

'What about the little one?' I asked. 'Do you have any pictures of him?'

'No. He's not in a team yet.'

Until he made one of the school teams, he obviously didn't qualify.

Thanksgiving was the start of the hunting season and central Kansas was the place to come for deer, so Debbie was worried that I might not get into a motel. As it happened, I finished cycling early that day and had no trouble finding a room. A southwest wind had risen in the night. It freshened through the morning and by Pawnee Rock, the halfway point on the Santa Fe Trail, it was blowing a gale. I stopped to read the historic marker, which was all that was left of the once famous landmark, as the Santa Fe Railroad Company had hacked it away when they were laying the track. Then I tried to get back on my bike, but the wind was so strong that I could scarcely turn the pedals. I was buffeted from the side, dust blew in my eyes and I nearly toppled over. Enough was enough. I gave up the uneven struggle in Larned, 30 miles short of my target distance.

I had shopped in advance for my Thanksgiving Day dinner, but I needn't have bothered. I might have known that hospitable Kansas would look after me. I checked in to my motel just as the manageress was taking a giant Thanksgiving turkey out of the oven. Her family had all travelled home for the holiday, and I caught a glimpse of them assembled round the table. A few moments later, she came along to my cabin with a groaning tray.

'We didn't like to think of you sitting on your own at Thanksgiving without your share of the turkey.'

DAY 12

Today was as calm as Thanksgiving Day was windy. An occasional puff of breeze ruffled the stillness, but it came up, very obligingly, from the Gulf of Mexico. By midday, the temperature was up in the high 60s F. I cycled with no effort at all across the flat, empty landscape, with long views down the Arkansas river. Coming from England, with its banks of green willow, I found it strange to be riding along beside a river which was totally bare of trees.

At the entrance to Kinsley stood a magnificent, long black beast of an engine, with a cow-catcher on the front and a gleaming brass bell on top. Its white lettering introduced it as Engine 3424 of the AT & SF: the fabled Atchison, Topeka and Santa Fe. There was no one around to take a photograph of me, so I did what I usually do. I propped up Condor against one of the mighty wheels and snapped. The two of them make a fine picture, both equally well designed and suited to their purpose. A little further on I passed a signpost: KINSLEY, KANSAS. MIDWAY USA. NEW YORK 1561. SAN FRANCISCO 1561. I had reached the very heart of America.

As a reward, I got my second puncture of the trip, caused by a needle-thin burr. Punctures are such unpredictable things. I cycled through the whole of the Indian subcontinent, from Kathmandu in Nepal to Kandy in Sri Lanka, along roads which were often rough and potholed beyond the imagination of spoilt Europeans, and I had not one single puncture. Then I came to America. My bike was sporting new tyres and inner tubes, the road surfaces were splendid – and I got two punctures in the space of one week. But my luck held. My back tyre deflated just as I was cruising into Kinsley's motel.

The manageress there put me in mind of my friend Brigid. Tall and willowy, she wore long droopy skirts and long dangly earrings, and gazed at the world through dreamy eyes. But this fey, faraway look disguised an efficient operator. We took to each other immediately.

'Brigid' was obviously in a different league from the other motel keepers I had met, and I was not a bit surprised to learn that she came from Chesapeake, on the east coast. She was divorced, with two young sons, and one day she piled them into an old RV, along with the dogs and cats and the few bits and pieces of possessions she really cared about, and set off to make a home in Montana, because she's crazy about mountains.

'The RV was second-hand,' she said, 'and it wasn't really up to such a long journey. It had only got as far as Kinsley when it broke down. It needed new parts, which the garage didn't stock, so they had to send off for them and there was a long wait. Meanwhile, I heard that the motel needed a new manager. I didn't know the first thing about running a motel, but I guessed it couldn't be all that difficult, so I volunteered to tide them over until they could find someone permanent. The motel has good family accommodation, and it was a hundred times better than being squashed together with the dogs and cats in the RV. I put the kids in the local school, where they were in small classes. They started to do well academically and they're really happy there. So I guess I'll stay on till the boys graduate from high school. The pay's not brilliant, but we're comfortable. I haven't given up on Montana. I'm still longing to settle there, but I can wait.'

She and the boys were cyclists, so she knew where I could take Condor to get the puncture repaired. I pushed him along to Western Autos, where a shop selling china and knick-knacks was attached to the garage. It was staffed by an old lady, who said that her husband was really under the weather these days and had stopped doing cycle repairs. When she heard that I came from London, she beamed delightedly.

'I'm from Croydon. I was a GI bride.' We settled down to a good natter about the Old Country, and then she rang round with great persistence until she persuaded another garage, the Halfway Bodyshop, to deal with my puncture. They promised to collect the bike and have it ready by 10 o'clock the next morning.

When I got back to the motel, 'Brigid' had prepared me a generous plate of cold turkey, with home-made cranberry sauce and corn bread.

'I can't do with the shop stuff. It's just like jam. I like real berries in my cranberry sauce. Of course, the food out here's a bit different. It's all meat and potatoes. I love my veggies and fruit, but the kids have caught the Kansas disease and won't touch any of it.

They won't even eat rice for a change. It's got to be potatoes. But last night, I tricked them. I cooked broccoli to go with the Thanksgiving turkey and smothered it in oyster sauce. Then I turned the lights out – just to create atmosphere, you understand. They gobbled it all up and said how brilliant the oyster sauce was. Well, when I turned on the lights, you should have seen their faces! They were horrified that they'd eaten a stack of broccoli.' And she performed a wonderful pantomime, shaking with horror, her eyes wide-open and terrified.

I left her concocting a supper without vegetables for her children and took my delicious plate along to my room, followed by an optimistic kitten.

'Don't give her any turkey! She's already eaten two mice today, as well as her Whiskas. Her name's "Mouse", but I shall obviously have to change it to "Mouser". I've never had a cat like her. I get mouse offerings on the mat every day – and she's only three months old.'

DAY 13

As I was paying my bill, a slick-haired Mexican in blue overalls dropped into the motel office to show off his gleaming new off-white alligator shoes, which had cost him $600.

'And you wear those for work?' asked 'Brigid', amazed. 'Not the brightest crayon in the box!' she muttered as he swaggered out of the door.

I went off to collect my bike, stopping at the post office on the way.

'Are you a friend of Dorothy's?' asked the man behind me in the queue.

'Who's Dorothy?'

'Why, she's our GI bride. She's a lovely lady. I heard that wonderful English accent of yours and I thought you must be her friend.'

When I told him I was just passing through, following the Santa Fe Trail, he immediately invited me to go as his guest to Monday's Rotary lunch. I was tempted, because Kinsley was such a welcoming little town, but it would have meant staying there another three days and I had to keep on moving. So far, I had been lucky with the weather, but it was the end of November and I still had the Raton Pass to climb. At 7,834 feet, it would be impossible on a bicycle once the winter snows arrived.

For the first time that morning, the wind was directly behind me and it was wild. It gathered me up and hurled me out of Kinsley. I flew along, a force of nature, invincible, ageless. With no effort at all, I topped 20 mph, even on the uphill gradients. I was no longer last week's tortoise, straining to average 5 mph. I was the hare, or better still, the powerful, swooping eagle, America's king of the birds. I felt omnipotent. Ecstasy is a speeding bike on an open, traffic-free road.

The silhouettes of ten cowboys, nine of them mounted, dominated the skyline on the approach to Dodge City. They were bronze – or perhaps just rusted metal – and their horses pawed a mighty block of rough-hewn stone by the roadside. It was my welcome to the place variously known as The Queen of the Cowtowns, Cowboy Capital, The Wickedest City in America, The Beautiful, Bibulous Babylon of the Frontier and The Athens of the Cow Trade. This wildest of all the 'Wild West' frontier towns owed its fame to the Santa Fe Railroad. At first, it was the railhead for the transport east of millions of buffalo hides and buffalo tongues, considered to be a great delicacy. But when the trappers and railroad workers had done their worst, and the plains buffalo were virtually exterminated, Dodge City found a new source of wealth. It became the terminus of the great cattle drives from Texas. Huge herds of Texas longhorns were driven along the dusty Chisholm Trail and into the cattle trucks of the AT & SF Railroad. Then the cowboys rode into town, with their wages jingling in their pockets and a thirst for whisky, gambling and women. There were gunfights in the saloons and shoot-outs on Front Street. Legendary lawmen, such as Wyatt Earp, tried to keep the lid on the lawlessness, but the undertakers were still kept busy in the Boot Hill Cemetery.

On the corner of Wyatt Earp Drive and Second Street stands a monument to the glory days of the cattle drives – a mighty bronze longhorn bull, named 'El Capitan', which glares southwards down the trail in the direction of Texas. But Dodge City has a bovine heroine too, who perhaps never had a name to match her Wild West fame. She was simply known as 'Deacon' Cox's swimming cow and she was invaluable. When the cowboys arrived in town, they had to drive their cattle across the Arkansas river, which was wider then than it is today. This was no easy matter. They often spent three or four days trying to coax the recalcitrant creatures into swimming across. But 'Deacon' Cox's cow was fearless. She would jump boldly into the river and strike out for the opposite bank, whereupon the longhorns would follow. 'Deacon' Cox, who ran a hotel, hired her out to the trail bosses as a very profitable sideline.

Dodge City is now enjoying a third boom, tourism, thanks to its famous appearances in 1930s westerns and more recently on television. *My Darling Clementine*, the eponymous *Dodge City* and the TV series *Gunsmoke* spring to mind. When I cycled along the six miles of Wyatt Earp Drive, I had to make my way cautiously past a stream of tourist cars, even in November. With Christmas approaching, the decorations were up and the town was tamely festive rather than lawless. The Great Western Hotel, now the museum, sported swags of dark-green streamers with little red bows, as did all the shops in Front Street. These establishments were fun. They were mostly authentic nineteenth-century stores, collected from towns all over the West and reassembled in 1958 to form a typical 'Wild West' street. There was a Dry Goods and Clothing Store, a Tonsorial Parlour, a Funeral Parlour, E C Zimmerman's Lumber, G M Hoover's Cigars, a Liquor Store, a Town Drug Store and, of course, the Saratoga and Long Branch Saloons, where I could have paid to watch a display of can-can dancing, gunfights and general raucousness, had I chosen to spend the night in town. But the following wind was too good to waste and I decided to abandon what was, after all, just a safe and sanitised Wild West theme park, and press on to Cimarron.

At Dodge City, I officially entered the Great Plains, which stretch, north to south, from southern Alberta and Saskatchewan in Canada all the way down to Texas, a distance of some 2,500 miles. East to west, they cover a mere 600 miles – though that seems far enough on a bicycle, and must have seemed even further in a chuck-wagon, in the days before roads. In the west, they begin where the Rockies end, but their eastern boundary is more difficult to determine. For convenience, the geographers and botanists have placed it on the hundredth meridian, at 100 degrees west. This is the approximate limit of the 20 inches rainfall necessary to support crops, cattle and European-style agriculture in general. Where the rain ends, the scant brown grazing begins, as the short prairie grasses take over from the wheatfields and the long, lush grass of the east. Under 20 inches, the subsoil contains insufficient moisture for trees to flourish, so the sandy earth is unstable. Dust blows and the tumbleweed tumbles. As rainfall varies from year to year, so does the eastern boundary. At its worst, the drought can extend right across Kansas, as far as the Missouri river, a full five degrees further east. But the hundredth meridian, which I was now crossing near Dodge City, has served as a convenient marker.

It was particularly convenient for the banks and insurance companies in the great days of American expansion west. Sadly for the migrants, the financial institutions took it as the line beyond which they were not prepared to advance loans or insure property. Life was hard enough for the settlers without this additional problem. Spurred on by the vision of extending America 'from sea to shining sea', the politicians passed the Homestead Act in 1862, which gave all citizens or intending citizens the right to fence off 160 acres of surveyed, but unclaimed, land out west. If they lived on this acreage and improved it for five years, they could own it outright. All they needed was a filing fee and the resources to support themselves until their farms became profitable.

Walt Whitman, the poet of the great outdoors, who rarely left New York and the cities of the eastern seaboard, rhapsodised over 'the newest garden of creation', and immigration agents were sent to Europe to recruit volunteers in their thousands. The American West would flower through the honest endeavours of legions of small farmers. Unfortunately, the Great Plains were ill suited to such a scheme. Small-scale arable and livestock farming on European lines was impossible on that arid prairie, epecially as the government had given the most fertile land along the rivers to the railroad companies, to help them finance construction. To prosper, a farmer would need at least ten times the allotted 160 acres. He needed enough land for the rough grazing of great herds – but great herds of cattle were beyond the means of the migrants. To buy those, they needed loans, and loans were not forthcoming. After years of trying to scratch a living on land that was no more than a dust-bowl in bad seasons, many of the disillusioned settlers in western Kansas lost everything they had, their savings as well as their dreams.

No one in Dodge City could tell me whether or not there was a motel in Cimarron, though it was only 18 miles away, until I came to a cycle shop on the outskirts. The mechanic there knew exactly where to find the Cimarron Motel and we had a fine time together, indulging in one of those self-righteous moans that cyclists love – about the blindness of motorists, who zoom across the countryside and see nothing.

The cyclist was right about the location, but what he didn't know was that the motel had closed down. I pressed on. The sun was setting and I could get no reply from a rather smart bed and breakfast further down the road. So I went into a café to discuss my plight over a reviving mug of coffee. Again, kindly Kansas came to my rescue. The overworked, motherly woman who was grilling hamburgers behind the counter told me not to worry. 'If Joan at that B and B doesn't turn up soon, you can come and stay with us. We've got plenty of room in our house.' Meanwhile, she kept on phoning and finally made contact.

I regretted this as soon as I set foot inside the door. Though I beat Joan down considerably on price, I still had to pay forty-two dollars (a small fortune for a bed and breakfast in rural Kansas) for a stuffy little room, crowded with knick-knacks. The bed was a sea of white linen and lace, with fancy lace-trimmed, heart-shaped cushions. There were lace-edged, silk-tasselled chintz curtains of overpowering thickness and ghastliness; and my large television set was housed in a fashionably 'distressed' lime-green cupboard, with panels of yet more lace. It was the room's only amenity. There was no comfortable chair, no table, no electric socket for my kettle, and the bathroom was a route-march away at the end of a long corridor. I consoled myself with a quick snifter of whisky, then went back to the café for a tough steak and a jacket potato the size and shape of a rugby football. My kind friend had gone off duty, so there was no escape from Joan's expensive brand of suffocation.

DAY 14

I had to present myself for breakfast at 8 o'clock sharp, so that Joan and her husband Gerald could leave at 8.30 for Mass at St Stanislaus, the Catholic Church in Ingalls. It was a heavy breakfast in both senses of the word. I am never at my scintillating best first thing in the morning, and Gerald, who was an overweight and boring accountant, would have taxed the conversational gifts of even the blithest skylark. I stumbled from topic to topic, getting monosyllables in return, except on the subject of the Mennonites. Gerald, being at the opposite end of the Christian spectrum, clearly had little time for Anabaptists, though his comments were innocuous. He actually produced four sentences: 'The women still wear those long grey home-made dresses and little caps. The men go in for beards, but otherwise they look pretty normal. They're all out in the country, off the highways. We don't see much of them.' The Amish of Pennsylvania have become a tourist attraction, but the Kansas Mennonites are invisible. Opposed to technological advance, military service, the swearing of oaths and the holding of public office, they tend their farms as their forefathers did, without mechanical aids, and they study their Bibles instead of watching TV. They are friendly, but a mystery to their comfort-loving neighbours.

The previous evening, when we were haggling over the price of the room, Joan said, 'You won't regret those forty-two dollars, honey, when you taste my breakfast!' It was certainly a substantial fry-up, but she told me the bread was home-made, when I could see the supermarket wrapper quite clearly through the kitchen door. Small and active, in contrast to her ponderous husband, she kept nipping in and out from the kitchen, urging me to consume more rashers of bacon, more sausages and more toast, all at breakneck speed, so that she could clear the table before she went to church. The result was a morning of indigestion, when I snacked on nothing but Rennies.

It was foggy out on the road, the sort of morning when I would normally have stayed in bed late and made a leisurely breakfast in my motel room. But my compulsory early start meant that I had to sit around in that cluttered house for almost two hours, kicking my heels and nursing my unhappy stomach. I escaped just before the churchgoers were due home and had a calm run to Garden City, presumably named after Walt Whitman's 'newest garden of creation'. On the way, I passed a field with deep parallel striations, eight or ten abreast, ploughing into the short prairie grass as far as the southern horizon. They were the scars of wagon wheels, which still mark the start of the Cimarron Cutoff.

The original Santa Fe Trail took what is now called the Mountain Route, which I planned to follow myself. It was well watered, since it ran along beside the Arkansas River as far as La Junta in Colorado; it provided convenient depots for the trappers, who brought their furs down from the Rockies for despatch to the cities of the east; and it was relatively easy to defend from attack. But the Mountain Route had its disadvantages too, chief of them being the Raton Pass over the Sangre de Cristo range. At an altitude of 7,834 feet, it was impassable once the winter set in and an ordeal, even in the best of weather, for the lumbering wagon-trains. Then there was the loopiness of the Arkansas River, which wandered around like an idle sightseer, but always in a general northwesterly direction, up into the Rocky Mountains and away from Santa Fe. When the wagon-trains averaged just twelve to fourteen miles a day, these meanderings were a trial to the teamsters' patience; so a shorter, less mountainous route, the Cimarron Cutoff, was prospected.

At the Middle Crossings near Cimarron, wagon-trains could ford the Arkansas and head off directly to the southwest. By avoiding that tiresome detour beside the river, they could save themselves about a hundred miles. But the route was far from easy. First, they had to struggle over miles of sandhills, where their heavy wagons sank up to the axles. Then, when the mules and oxen had laboured across those, they came to the most terrible part of the route, a sixty-mile stretch without water or firewood. Once they reached the Cimarron River, life became easier. They could follow its course across the present Oklahoma Panhandle, passing the Lower, Middle and Upper Springs, to enter New Mexico just before McNees Crossing. Towards the Canadian river, the Cutoff Route became more mountainous, but there were no passes approaching the Raton in altitude. Finally, a good stretch of open grassland cut across behind Wagon Mount to join up with the Mountain Route at Watrous.

There is no road along this branch of the Santa Fe Trail, though I could have continued along Route 56 from Dodge City and cycled roughly parallel to it through Santanta, Hugoton and Elkhart. But even today, there are long stretches of empty grassland along that road, and I thought it would be safer to stick to the Mountain Route alongside the Santa Fe Railroad. There were more towns, within reasonable cycling distance of one another; and if I were caught in a dangerous winter storm, I could always hop on to a train. Anyway, I'm usually a mug for a historical connection, and the Mountain Route was the original trail.

I never knew what to expect when I arrived in a town, because none of the guidebooks had much to say about Kansas. *The Rough Guide to the USA*, for instance, devoted just six pages out of its 1,384-page tome to the entire state! Yet it was a wonderful, welcoming place to travel. What Kansas lacked in famous landmarks and buildings of architectural beauty, it made up for in the wagon-loads of open, talkative characters, always ready to stop for a chat and refreshingly free of political correctness. We may have caught that disease from the Americans, but the citizens of Kansas had never heard of it. Working from my notes of some of their conversations, I have had a struggle to give their flavour, while toning them down enough to make them publishable! If you want to know what real Americans in the American heartland are thinking, ignore the media and spend a week or two in rural Kansas.

Garden City was not mentioned in the guidebooks, so I had no useful list of motels. But I picked at random and struck so lucky that I decided to take my second day off there. After last night's claustrophobic bed and breakfast, it was a great relief to have some privacy again, in a spacious room with a writing-desk and armchairs. In England, Indians from the subcontinent run restaurants and corner shops, when they are not successful accountants or technocrats. But in America, there is no scope for Indian restaurants outside New York and San Francisco – steaks, pork chops, fried chicken, pizzas and hamburgers, all served with French fries and ketchup, being the staples of local menus. So in the USA, non-professional Indians go in for managing motels. The owner of mine in Garden City came from Bombay. He told me that his brother had spent four years in London, working on a higher degree, then emigrated to the States, via Canada. When he was settled in Kansas, he sent for one brother at a time. Now, with children and grandchildren, there were over a hundred members of the family in the USA.

Knowing the usual menus by heart, I'd already decided on pork chops long before I went out to dinner. They go down well with red wine, so I bought a bottle of very nice Californian Cabernet Sauvignon from the liquor store and decanted half of it into a

Gatorade bottle. I love wine with my dinner, but Kansas, with all its Mennonites and Evangelicals, regards drinking as a sinful activity, performed surreptitiously by low men (and the occasional sleazy woman) in dark, smoke-filled bars. I had not been offered the demon wine with my meal since my first evening in the Kansas City Hilton.

For the first few days, I had no idea how to deal with this problem. Then I discovered the Ruby Punch flavour of the high-energy drink Gatorade, which was a beautiful deep crimson, exactly the colour of a full-bodied red wine. That was my answer. I went out in the evenings, clutching my half-bottle of liquor-store wine in its Ruby Punch Gatorade bottle. When the waitress asked me what I wanted to drink with my meal, reeling off all the unattractive options, 'Coke, Fanta, Sprite, Dr Pepper, coffee?' I would say wearily, 'I've just cycled fifty miles. I'm riding the Santa Fe Trail and it's been uphill/I've had the wind against me/It's been raining/I've had a puncture . . . I feel absolutely done in. I really need my energy drink tonight.' And I would wave my Gatorade bottle before her sympathetic eyes.

'Fifty miles? On a bike? You must be dying for that Gatorade. I'll get you a glass for it, honey.'

I was soon the heroine of every restaurant. I had cycled an unimaginable distance and everyone clucked over me, while I settled down to enjoy my health-restoring drink. I might have been a bit of a cheat, but I had not told a single lie. I had, after all, cycled the fifty miles which so amazed the car-driving Kansans, and I had not actually lied, in so many words, about the contents of my Gatorade bottle. I had just practised a little harmless deception.

DAY 15

A day for reading, letter-writing, laundry and picnics in my room. I've come to prefer motels to hotels, as I like to provide my own breakfast, eating exactly what I want, when I want it. And motels certainly simplify life with a bicycle. In hotels, I have to plead for some corner where I can chain up Condor in safety, out of the wind and weather. Then I have to remove every single bit of baggage and equipment, and haul it up to my bedroom. In motels, I simply wheel my bike into my room – and I don't even need to unload it. I just unbuckle the panniers and delve. Many motels in

America advertise 'Discounts for Seniors', and I have had some amusing exchanges at reception. On one occasion, in a two-storey motel, I asked if I could have a room on the ground floor.

'Of course you can, honey. We like to put our Seniors on the ground floor. So many of them have difficulty with the stairs.'

'It's not the stairs I'm worried about. I need a ground-floor room so that I can wheel my bike into it.'

'Your bike? You're on a push-bike? Holy smoke!'

DAY 16

Around Garden City, Stetsons and high-heeled Mexican boots began to replace the eastern uniform of baseball caps and trainers. The men swaggered more, trying to project the macho image of the gun-slinging cowboy West, even if they went to an office every day to add up figures. The small towns looked much the same as before, but the richer tilth of central Kansas had turned to sand, with spiky reed-like grass and low succulents.

A buffalo reserve outside Garden City held a few sad survivors of the seventy million buffalo who are thought to have roamed the prairie, before the hunters decimated them for their hides and tongues and the railway workers finished them off for meat. There were none to be seen in the wild. In fact, there were scarcely any animals at all. The Great Plains were so empty that the occasional lonely horse or donkey would trot to the roadside fence as I cycled past, hoping for some contact with another living creature. I felt sorry for them and often pushed my bike over for a chat. Talking to horses! I thought. What next?

I was reading American poets on this ride, and these unhappy quadrupeds brought to mind some verses of that old fraud, Walt Whitman. In his 'Song of Myself', he enthuses over animals:

I think I could turn and live with animals, they are so placid
    and self-contain'd,
I stand and look at them long and long.
They do not sweat and whine about their condition,
They do not lie awake in the dark and weep for their sins,
They do not make me sick discussing their duty to God,
Not one is dissatisfied, not one is demented with the mania of
    owning things,

Not one kneels to another, nor to his kind that lived
  thousands of years ago,
Not one is respectable or unhappy over the whole earth.

Without wishing to anthropomorphise non-humans or endow
them with emotions they cannot feel, my meetings with those
lonely horses and donkeys was enough to convince me that
Whitman had no idea what he was talking about. Animals might
not be capable of discussing their duty to God or weeping over
their sins, but they can certainly be unhappy when they are caged
or ill-treated, or even when their social needs are neglected.
Animals of most species hate being alone. And they *do* kneel to one
another, not literally, but with their own kind of animal deference.
There is always a top dog, whom the other members of the pack
or herd are very careful not to cross; and there is a pecking order
between species. On my ride across the Great Plains, I saw two
mixed herds of llamas and sheep, and was amused to see their
interaction. The llamas, long-necked and conceited-looking, like all
camelids, obviously inspired awe in the lowly sheep. When I cycled
past their enclosures, the llamas strolled up to the wire fence with
the boldness of born leaders to look down their noses at me, while
their ovine subjects scuttled timidly away.

An empty road on a glorious sunny day, with a warm southwest
breeze, just strong enough to freshen the air. It was 'real conducive
to cycling', as the shop-boy said when I stopped for a Gatorade.
The road was noticeably rising now, but I had my cycling legs and
was riding with ease. I checked my map and saw that I had started
at 1,000 feet in Overland Park, beside the Missouri river. Council
Grove stood at 1,250, Lyons at 1,690, Kinsley at 2,160, Dodge City
at 2,500, Garden City at 2,950, and by the time I reached Syracuse
that evening I would have climbed to 3,230 feet. The land had
been sloping upwards the whole way, but so gently that I had been
aware of it only when a strong west wind was slowing me down.
Colorado and New Mexico were likely to be more challenging.

At Kendall, I crossed into Mountain Standard Time, so I gained
an extra hour's televiewing in Syracuse. Still on the subject of
animals, I watched a programme about cats, who were described
as 'our partners', and another on the training of drug-sniffing dogs.
The drug-recognition course is so demanding that only one dog in

twenty-five actually manages to 'graduate'. One cheering fact was that the Police and Drug Squads take many of their 'recruits' from animal refuges, because the hyper-active behaviour which makes some dogs impossible to handle in a domestic situation equips them perfectly for the demands of drug and mountain-rescue work. They like to be kept busy.

COLORADO

I think heroic deeds were all conceiv'd in the open air and all free poems also,
I think I could stop here myself and do miracles,
I think whatever I shall meet on the road I shall like, and whoever beholds me shall like me.

Walt Whitman

DAY 17

The motel owner in Syracuse told me there were no hills on the way to Lamar. In fact, there was just one hill – all the way! Car drivers never notice hills unless they're as steep as the north face of the Eiger. Despite the ascent, I covered my 50 miles quite comfortably in a warm, gentle breeze under an overcast sky. Halfway between Coolidge and Holly, I crossed the state border and exchanged the perfect tarmac of Kansas for the rougher surface of the Colorado roads.

I went for a coffee in Lamar's Best Western, the Cow Palace Inn, to pick up one of their complimentary Colorado maps, which showed the distances between towns. The forecasters were predicting unsettled weather in the mountains, so I needed to review my options. I had not taken the Cimarron Cutoff from Dodge City, but I could still join it from Lamar, cycling due south into Oklahoma through Springfield to pick it up in Boise City. But that run looked even more deserted than Route 56 from Dodge City. As the weather was still mild for December, I decided to stick to the Mountain Route and take my chance on the Raton Pass.

I liked the Cow Palace Inn so much that I went back for dinner. Along with most other buildings in Lamar, it was already decked out with Christmas lights, and my stroll there along the main street was magical. Our own much-vaunted lights in Regent Street, and even the famous Blackpool Illuminations, were positively dowdy by comparison. Every house and public building in Lamar was outlined in lights, its roof, gables, doors and window-frames picked out with strings of white bulbs. There were illuminated, life-sized Santas, sleds and reindeer in the front gardens, illuminated Christmas trees with multicoloured presents and baubles, and illuminated Nativities, complete with sparkling wise men, camels, shepherds and sheep, outside the churches. Everyone was trying to outdo the neighbours in fantasy, and there were prizes for the brightest, most imaginative displays. I wandered round town in a shock of childish delight, trying to take in every detail. I thought the exuberance was peculiar to Lamar, that it was somehow 'Christmas City'; but Lamar's decorations turned out to be quite ordinary compared with the extravaganzas which awaited me elsewhere.

An illuminated archway led me through to a glittering Aladdin's cave, which was the vestibule of the Cow Palace Inn, and swags of lights festooned the buffet bar, where dinner was served. It was the size of a sports hall, and would have seemed a barn of a place had it not twinkled with thousands of fairy lights and candles. To add to my delight at the spectacle, I saw wine-glasses on the tables. I was out of strait-laced Kansas!

'May I see the wine list, please?'

'There isn't one,' said the waiter.

His Nike trainers contrasted oddly with his formal black trousers, braces and white shirt, but at least he wasn't dressed as a cowboy or Santa Claus.

'If you want red, we've got Cabernet, Merlot, Claret, Pinot Noir, you name it.'

'Are they Californian?'

'Don't ask me! They're good.'

It was a novelty to have wines offered by their grape variety, rather than their origin and year, but I was to learn that it was common practice in the States.

DAY 18

Colorado fares better in the guidebooks than Kansas, but my particular corner of the state goes unmentioned. Colorado, for tourists, is synonymous with the Rockies and mile-high Denver. It's where they go for skiing, climbing, white-water rafting and mountain-biking, none of which were available along my south-western route. Though my road was rising gently, it would have seemed pancake-flat to a motorist – and boring, as most roads are when you rush along them. The Great Plains may lack the drama of jagged mountain peaks, yet those flatlands, which stretch to infinity under a boundless sweep of cloud-smoked azure, bring their own brand of exhilaration.

Oscar Wilde once said that nature imitates art, and I realised how true that was. First the nineteenth-century Romantic painters taught us to admire dramatic landscapes, with towering crags, raging seas and stormy sunsets. Then the Impressionists charmed us with parasols on the beaches of Normandy and merry, buxom dancers under the summer lanterns of Argenteuil. Our eyes have become so accustomed to these paintings that we have lost the capacity to interpret scenes for ourselves. We rush across spectacular plains, dismissing them because they have never been painted and we are uncertain how to respond. In their day, the landscape artists we so admire were revolutionaries, who aimed to shock us into a new view of the world. A century or so later, they have turned against their will into artistic commissars, buckling us into the very straitjackets from which they once struggled to free us. Few people actually look at the Great Plains. They don't photograph well, so travellers tune in to the car radio or the aircraft video and dismiss them, yawning with boredom until they wake up in the mountains, which they have been trained to admire.

Yet these vast expanses of grassland have their own fascination, just like deserts, and I had never felt so happy on a ride. My happiness rolled on and on in a tidal wave, sweeping over the endless prairie. Travelling slowly on a bicycle, I was aware of the texture and colour of the sand, of small changes in the vegetation, of shy creatures hiding in the scrub and, above all, of the weather. The wind rose, dropped and veered from one direction to another, changing the cloud formations from towering castles to flying wisps of white. And I was in tune with all of these changes. They affected me personally, exposed as I was on the open road – just as they would once have affected the travellers on the Santa Fe Trail. We were all at the mercy of the elements. It seemed as if my sheltered life in London had never existed. I was free in the sharp, invigorating air, at one with the landscape. Like Whitman, I felt as if I could perform miracles.

There is diminishing rainfall these days on the Great Plains. Saltpans sparkled in the sun, where once there had been pools of water, and the earth was so dry that I sometimes cycled through miles of blazing stubble fire caused by some cigarette end, carelessly thrown from a car window. The once tumultuous Arkansas river was no more than a narrow stream, with sandbanks in its course and a fringe of spiky grass. I followed it into the neat little town of Las Animas, where I saw two fellow cyclists and an old man on a tricycle, who gave me a cheery wave. Even more remarkable, I saw a bus in the town centre – my first since Kansas City!

Las Animas was significant, because what is now a suburb with the unlovely name of Boggsville was the first undefended settlement to be established along the Santa Fe Trail. I cycled along and took a photograph of its red-brick and sandstone-trimmed town hall, an imposing Victorian structure with tall church-like windows and a strange kind of oriental minaret projecting from each corner. Before the founding of Boggsville in the 1860s, settlements along the American trails were fortified enclosures, manned by the US Dragoons, an elite cavalry corps originally raised by President Jackson in 1833 to defend the frontier territories from the Mexicans. But their main role soon became the protection of the chuck-wagons. The Native Americans regarded the prairies as their ancestral home, so it was inevitable that the occasional lightning raid on a wagon-train would escalate sooner or later into all-out war. And the native tribesmen were no mean warriors.

In 1540, the Spanish governor of what was then the Province of New Galicia in New Spain, now known as Mexico, set out from Mexico City in search of the legendary riches of the Seven Cities of Cibola and the fantastical Empire of Quivira. The Spaniards were always hungry for gold and Don Francisco Vasquez de Coronado was no exception. The Seven Cities turned out to be nothing more spectacular than the Indian pueblos of what is now the state of New Mexico. Disappointed, Coronado ventured further north and east, as far as central Kansas. He scoured the Great Plains for 25 days, but still found no gold or gemstones. Two-thirds of his expeditionary force of 300 men died or were killed on the mission, and Don Francisco was stripped of his rank when he returned, empty-handed, to Mexico.

But Coronado's expedition, which was such a disaster for himself and his followers, transformed the lives of the Plains Indians. In their skirmishes with the Spaniards, the Apaches and Navajos captured a number of horses, creatures they had never seen before. At first, they ate them. Then they realised that horses could be put to better use. They took to horsemanship with astonishing rapidity and skill. By the late 1700s, the use of horses had spread across the prairies from the warlike Apaches and Navajos to nomadic buffalo-hunters, such as the Kiowa, and even to more settled agricultural peoples, like the Pawnees, who now rode out on occasional buffalo-hunting sorties. So the native peoples, who had previously been subsistence farmers or nomads within a limited seasonal round, became lords of the plains, dominating them from the backs of their swift Spanish horses. The seeds were sown for the great flowering of indigenous plains culture. A Navajo song in praise of the horse runs:

> He stands on the upper circle of the rainbow
> The sunbeam is in his mouth for a bridle
> He circles round all the people of the earth
> Today he is on my side
> And I shall win with him.

The clash of civilisations was bound to come. At first, there were treaties with the Kansas and Osage peoples, at the eastern end of the Santa Fe Trail. The one signed in 1827 at Council Grove, for example, allowed the traders unmolested passage across Osage territory. But the tribes to the west, the Apache, Comanche, Navajo, Kiowa and Pawnee, were more of a problem, and serious trouble broke out in that same year, when the Pawnees attacked a caravan of returning traders and made off with a hundred head of mules and cattle. The following year, a small party of Indian braves crept up on sleeping traders near the Mexican border, seized their guns and shot two of them. When a group of curious Indians appeared next morning on the opposite bank of the creek, the enraged traders shot them all, not caring whether they were the murderers or not. The traders got themselves safely back to the Missouri river, but the Indians attacked them relentlessly on the way and seized a thousand horses and mules. This was the kind of incident which led to bitter feuding, as the Native Americans struggled to protect their lands and their way of life. They were to fight for two generations, until they were finally suppressed and rounded up into reservations.

There was trouble with the Mexicans, too. The Republic of Texas became a State of the Union in 1845, so the American nation inherited the Texan claim to the Rio Grande boundary, which the

Mexicans were disputing. There was also competition along the Santa Fe Trail from Mexican traders. In 1846, when American trade along the trail topped the million-dollar mark for the first time, Congress declared war on the Mexicans. General Kearny led his troops along the Mountain Route into New Mexico, finding little resistance. On 19 August, he entered Santa Fe without a shot being fired and claimed New Mexico for the United States. The campaign had lasted just three months, though the Mexican War did not end officially until 1848, with the signing of the Treaty of Guadalupe Hidalgo. Throughout this period, there was a tremendous build-up of traffic along the Santa Fe Trail, as traders carried supplies and reinforcements to the army. More forts had to be built to house the troops and protect the trade. A continuous line of them soon stretched from Fort Leavenworth, the main army base in the east, to Fort Marcy in Santa Fe itself. Most of these western forts remained active until about 1886, when the Apaches, the last tribe to resist the American thrust to the west, were finally subdued.

So the town hall I photographed in Boggsville, which was built around 1862, marked a significant step forward in the American colonisation of the west. Standing proud and undefended on the Santa Fe Trail, it proved to the world that the bitterest phase of conflict was nearing its end. The Mexicans were defeated and the suppressing of the native peoples was progressing satisfactorily. Peaceful settlement could begin.

There was a museum in Las Animas dedicated to that great mountain man, Kit Carson. When I look back on my travels, I have one particularly vivid memory. I can still picture myself standing alone at daybreak on the Kit Carson Pass over California's Sierra Nevada, my feet in the snow and my head in the heavens. Exhilarated as I always am on achieving the summit of a climb, on that occasion I was completely bowled over by the majesty of the surrounding peaks. They had a snowy perfection, a sublimity which I had never seen before in any other mountain range. It was my birthday, my best birthday ever, and the world sparkled.

So I had to go and see this Kit Carson Museum. I walked to the edge of town, across the railroad tracks, past the 'County Correctional Facility', only to find that the museum was closed for the winter. A woman pulled up in a van.

'Can I give you a lift somewhere? Have you broken down?'

'No. I'm just walking, thank you.'

'Walking'? she shrieked in amazement. 'Nobody walks!'

DAY 19

A chill wind was gusting from the north, which suited me quite well, as the Arkansas River curved to the southwest, with my road to La Junta beside it. I sped along, breaking my run to explore the site of Bents' Fort, the first along the Santa Fe Trail, though there was not much to be seen there.

The fort was an entrepreneurial gamble by two brothers, Charles and William Bent, at the time when the fur trade was reaching its early peak, around 1833. More and more trappers were heading every year into the southern Rocky Mountains to bring out bundles of pelts. These valuable furs needed safe warehousing and an organised market, so the Bents constructed a fort on the Upper Arkansas river. With its massive adobe walls, it immediately became a landmark on the trail, invaluable as a depot for the fur trappers and then as a base for the newly formed US Dragoons. It was a short-lived enterprise, as the fur trade began to dwindle and the traders in other commodities increasingly preferred the Cimarron Cutoff. So William Bent burned down the fort and established another one, further east, on a busier stretch of the Arkansas.

The original Bents' Fort may not have lasted long, but it was a pioneering venture, the first of the great string of forts built to protect the growing traffic along the Santa Fe Trail. These forts themselves needed a flood of supplies, especially after the Mexican War, when the supply line for the garrisons was extended to Santa Fe. So rich government contracts were signed with the big companies for trains of a hundred juggernauts, regular stagecoach routes and postal services. The nature of commerce on the trail changed. It became more professional, squeezing out the little man with his solitary wagon or string of mules. The Civil War brought yet more traffic and the throng of traders continued to grow, swelled by families of settlers and lone miners, 'Forty-niners', off to seek their fortunes in the California Gold Rush and the Colorado Gold Rush of 1858. Figures available for 1859 show that the trade that year was worth $10 million. By 1862, a staggering 3,000 wagons were rolling across the Great Plains and there was $40 million of trade.

Thanks to the following wind, I covered the 21 miles to La Junta in less than two hours and ate my picnic lunch outside, enjoying the sunshine in the sheltered porch of my motel cabin. That was at 1 o'clock. By 3 o'clock it was snowing. The temperature had plummeted and autumn had suddenly turned to winter, all in the space of two hours. I switched on the Weather Channel. A blizzard was expected in Trinidad, my next stop, and the Raton Pass might have to be closed. That was it, then. The swift leap into winter, which I had been fearing since Kansas City, had finally happened. But I had been very lucky. In such a violent, unpredictable climate, I had been blessed with decent weather all the way along the trail so far. It could easily have turned against me three weeks ago.

Once over the Raton Pass, I might be able to cycle again, but I obviously needed transport over the top. I went along to La Junta's bus office. An old man in an anorak and baseball cap was crouching over a one-bar electric fire behind the counter. He was whiling away his afternoon with a piece of crochet, some kind of white doily. Scowling with effort, he plied his hook and took not the slightest notice of me. So I coughed and broke his concentration with my enquiry about a bus to Trinidad. He was obviously the sort of grouch who delights in bad news.

'Well, you *can* take a bus as far as Trinidad, but the road's in such a terrible state, it can't go direct,' he said triumphantly. 'You'll have to go by Pueblo. It'll take you all day – even supposing the bus is running at all in this weather. And you can't take that bike with you, unless you box it. You can buy a box from Joey's Bikes. Boxes cost $25.'

'Why do I need a box on a bus?'

'Because we've had so many complaints about damage to bikes that it's the rule now. They used to dump their old, scratched things in the bus, then claim damages from the company. So no box, no bike,' he concluded, almost crowing with satisfaction. I left the old buzzard to his crochet and went to see what Amtrak could do for me.

There, I was greeted by another strange character, an alarming prize-fighter of a man with a shaven skull but, contrary to first impressions, he could not have been more helpful. When I told him I didn't have a box for my bike, he pursed his lips and sucked his teeth, thinking the matter over.

'Well, you could get a box from Joey's, I suppose, but it would cost you – and it seems a bit of a waste, just for that short ride. Of course, if you were going to Los Angeles or Chicago, that would be a different matter. So I tell you what. You turn up here with your bike at eight-thirty tomorrow morning. There's no need to buy a box, or take the pedals off, or anything like that. I'll see you on to the train, then you won't have a problem. And if I were you, I wouldn't get off at Trinidad. I'd go straight over the top to Raton. It's only another twenty-one miles and the ticket costs the same. It's going to get milder in a day or two, or so they say. The long-term forecast's quite good. So go on to Raton and stay in a hotel up there till the snow melts. I'll give you the name of one that's real cheap – and good.'

DAY 20

I skidded along to La Junta Station through an inch or two of slush, congratulating myself on the happy turn of events. Had the weather been fine, I would have cycled over the Raton Pass. As it was, the snow had given me the excuse to ride up there on the legendary Atchison, Topeka and Santa Fe Railroad. Another clerk was on duty.

'You can't take that bike on the train. It's not boxed.'

'Your colleague yesterday said that it was allowed without a box on a short ride,' I said firmly, looking him straight in the eye. Never appear uncertain.

'Well, that's a new one on me. I'm sure it should be boxed.'

'Not if you're only going to Raton.' I held my breath.

'OK then.'

He issued my ticket and wheeled Condor out to the train.

'You can't put that bike on here without a box,' said the conductor.

'You can as far as Raton,' said the clerk.

'You can? It's the first I've heard of it.' But he accepted the bike all the same. I had established a new Amtrak rule. Bikes could travel from La Junta without boxes, provided they only went as far as Raton. With Condor safely installed, I climbed up into the warmth and comfort of my double-decker Amtrak train. There were very smart sleeping cars, but even the normal daytime travellers had reclining seats, leg-rests, foot-rests and pillows. I wallowed in luxury.

A light snow was falling as we pulled out of La Junta. It thickened across the Comanche National Grassland, until only a few green spikes of cactus were poking through the blanket of white. When we crept into Trinidad, the sky was white as well as the falling snow, an opaque lens through which I could scarcely see the Purgatorio river, frozen beneath its bridges. The Eskimo are said to have hundreds of words for snow – nouns, adjectives and verbs, which describe every nuance of its quality. We have snow, sleet, slush, snowfall, snowstorm and blizzard, and just one adjective, white; which makes it very difficult to convey the excitement I felt as the train climbed the mountain pass, and we graduated from a mere snowstorm to a raging blizzard. We were travelling through a white world, which I can only describe as growing whiter, pathetically inadequate as that may seem. The train snaked up the mountain. It was so long that I could see its three toiling engines rounding the bends ahead. Trucks were crawling through the blizzard on the road beside us. It was not yet closed to traffic, but snow lay so thick on the tarmac that cycling would have been impossible. When we neared the summit, we crept along the edge of a dramatic canyon until a railway tunnel swallowed us up, taking us under the highest point of the Raton Pass at 7,834 feet. There the engines took heart. They cleared the tunnel, accelerated and whistled their cheerful way down to Raton town, a thousand feet below. The blizzard was so blinding that I could scarcely see my way across the platform into the station buildings.

I found the station-master on the phone, trying to make alternative arrangements for a group of Amtrak passengers. They were booked to travel on to Colorado Springs, but couldn't be bussed there because the road was closed.

'What are you doing here on a bicycle in December? Anyone who comes up here after Hallowe'en must be nuts!'

He gave me a mug of coffee and volunteered to take care of my bike and panniers while I went out in search of a hotel. He recommended El Portal, because it was nearest to the station. Looking back on that day, I still don't know how I got there. The blizzard was sweeping across Raton, piling the snow into huge drifts. I put on my cycling waterproofs, but I had no boots to tuck the trousers in, so my socks and fleecy-lined jogging pants were soon saturated. The snowdrifts outside the station were waist-deep.

I laboured across the concourse and down the station road, every step a monumental effort. A few times, I overbalanced, collapsing exhausted on my face in a drift, with one leg encased to the top of my thigh in the snow. I have never seen the attraction of polar exploration! It took me almost two hours to cover the short distance to the main street, where the snow-ploughs had been out and I was able to walk in the middle of the cleared road. Needless to say, there was not a car to be seen. I staggered into El Portal in such a state of cold and exhaustion that I was rushed straight into the warm kitchen, seated beside the stove and revived with a bowl of soup. But worse was to come. I needed my gear, especially my dry clothes, so I had to go back to the station in the afternoon to collect my bike; and I had to do it on foot, because there were no taxis running. Fortunately, the snow had ceased by then and the concourse had been cleared, but manhandling my bike and its heavy panniers along the station road through thigh-deep snow-drifts was an ordeal I shall not forget in a hurry.

NEW MEXICO

Stars scribble on our eyes the frosty sagas,
The gleaming cantos of unvanquished space.

Hart Crane

DAY 21

'I was on the train, heading for California,' said Jay, 'when it stopped at Raton Station and I thought, Hey, this looks a neat little place! So I got off, on a whim, and I've been here ever since.'

It was snowing again, and we were sitting companionably in front of a wonderful log fire. The El Portal was a proper hotel, with a lounge full of squashy armchairs, a tall Christmas tree twinkling in the corner and a snowy Nativity scene lovingly arranged on a side table. Much as I had enjoyed the convenience of motels, it made a pleasant change to be inside one self-contained building, where there were public rooms to sit in, and the bedrooms led off warm internal corridors. Those individual boxes which constitute motels would have been far less comfortable in Raton's extreme weather. The El Portal was the perfect place to sit out a cold snap.

In no time at all, as is the way with Americans, I had heard Jay's life story. He was a handsome young ex-Marine, an electronics engineer, who had left the services to join IBM.

'But I couldn't stand it. These huge corporations have such a cut-throat style. So I packed it in and decided to try my luck out west. And do you know, I found the perfect job here in Raton, the very day after I jumped out of the train! It wasn't at all where I intended to work, but things just fell into place. It must have been meant.'

'What sort of work is there in a small place like this?'

'I'm working for a highly specialised electronics firm. We sink sensors into the earth, so that geologists can take computer readings of the composition of the rock. We work mostly for the mining companies, of course, but we get military contracts too, locating bombs and land-mines for clearance. We're a small firm and we work in small specialist teams. I find that much more rewarding than my old job at IBM, where I was lost in the crowd. And the wonderful thing is that I'm on the same salary, in a nice little place where the living costs are substantially lower. I can't believe my good luck! Next week, I'm driving to San Diego and being paid for it! Just imagine!'

The El Portal Hotel was an imposing, butter-coloured building, covering a whole block and now mostly converted into flats. It was opened towards the end of the 1800s as the Seaburg Hotel at Willow Springs, the first watering place after the Raton Pass. A local mountain man, Uncle Dick Wootton, had dynamited a toll road to widen the Indian track through the pass. This had eased the most difficult stretch of the Santa Fe Trail. Between 1866 and 1879, a new breed of people called 'tourists' began to swell the number of travellers out west, and the Seaburg Hotel prospered. Then Uncle Dick sold his toll road through the Raton Pass to the Atchison, Topeka and Santa Fe Railroad. The company laid its tracks along his road-bed and the first engine steamed into Willow Springs, now called Raton, on 9 February 1880. That was the start of Raton's boom time. Demand for rooms at the Seaburg Hotel became so great that the old adobe livery stables had to be annexed in 1904, and the hotel expanded to form the grandly named Seaburg European Hotel. It was the biggest, most magnificent hotel in New Mexico.

Jay lived there, and I was the only guest. The new owners were a delightful young couple from California, who had plans to restore the hotel. Raton was in a fine situation, high in the Sangre de Cristo mountains, themselves foothills of the Rockies. Surrounded by state parks, ski resorts and wildlife refuges, its moderate elevation ensured pleasantly cool summers and tolerable winters. And there was an enviable collection of authentic early Western buildings in its historic centre, some of them decorated with 1930s New Deal murals. Mining was the town's main money-spinner, but there was no reason why Raton should not be livened up a little and promoted to tourists as an interesting historical site along the Santa Fe Trail.

The hotel had no restaurant as yet, but Lisa was a great cook and a generous soul, who invited Jay and me into the family kitchen every lunch-time. Jay said grace, then we all tucked into bowls of Lisa's substantial rice and vegetable soup with fresh, home-baked tortillas.

Raton was certainly in need of a few young entrepreneurs. I doubt if it was a lively town in the best of weathers; and on that stormy weekend, everyone had bunkered down at home. There was not a living creature in the streets, not even a stray dog. I went out in search of an evening meal, passing unlit shop windows, which was surprising in the run-up to Christmas, and very untypical of commercial America. There were few restaurants and only one of them was open. The sole customer, I took a seat by the window and gazed across the empty main street, South 2nd, at the old Shuler Theatre. It was closed that Saturday night, but there were posters outside advertising the Christmas spectacular, an all-male ballet company performing *Swan Lake*.

I ordered lasagne, salad and a small carafe of Chianti from a worried-looking waitress. There was an air of anxiety about the place and I suspected that more confidences were on the way. So I was not the least bit surprised when an older woman came over to my table.

'Is everything all right?' she asked, obviously really keen to know and not just making the standard bored enquiry. 'You see, we only opened on Wednesday and we've no experience of running a restaurant. We've hired a chef, and my daughter and I are working here full-time. Howard, that's my husband over there, has kept on his job in the post office, until we see whether the business is going to be a success or not. He comes over to help in his lunch-breaks, and delivers the take-aways in the evenings.'

While I was there, the unfortunate Howard was called out on three occasions to deliver pizzas to motels on the outskirts of Raton. He made three separate journeys, in atrocious driving conditions – two of them to the same motel, the Best Western, and the third to Motel 8, in the next street.

I assured them that the lasagne was delicious. They were closed on Sunday, but I promised to return on Monday evening. Then I skated and skidded back over the icy road to El Portal, where Jay was sitting in front of the fire, reading and sipping a glass of wine. He asked me what the food was like in The Grapevine, and again, I sensed that this was not just a polite enquiry.

'I need to know what the competition's like out there. Raton's short of really good places to eat, so Lisa and I are thinking of going into partnership. She's a fantastic cook, and I could look after the business side and work there in the evenings. We've got our eye on that vacant shop at the corner of the hotel block. It's in a good position for a restaurant.'

I wondered how he could find time to be an active partner in a restaurant, when he obviously had a busy and responsible full-time job.

'Well, there's not much else to do up here in Raton. And I'd like to get a couple of businesses up and running before I settle down. I'd like to get married, but I'm a Christian with Christian ideals, and marriage for me is a commitment for life. It's not easy to find the right girl, but I'm in no hurry. I can wait. Meanwhile, I shall get on with my career, set up a couple of businesses and get myself well established.'

We finished off his bottle of Merlot and Jay went to bed early, to be up in time for the first Sunday service. I went up to my sumptuous 'Hollywood Room', where I fell asleep surrounded by posters of old movie stars. 'Clark Gable and Jeanette Macdonald. They were born to fall in love.' If I had to be snowed up for a few nights, I could not have hit upon a more congenial place.

DAY 22

A day of brilliant sunshine. After a sub-zero start, the morning gradually warmed up and there was a slow thaw. I was invited down to the kitchen at lunch-time for one of Lisa's hearty soups, but my Sunday dinner was a problem, as Raton was a shuttered ghost town. I wrapped up well and made my laborious way through the snow out to Highway 25, where I found a Texaco service station with a shop selling the usual plastic sandwiches. It was run by a garrulous chemical engineer, a shrunken little man who had fought in Vietnam and looked considerably older than his 52 years.

'I had my first heart attack when I was thirty-eight,' he announced, as a rather surprising conversational opening. 'It was a death wish. I didn't like my life.' I paid for my sandwiches and started to inch my way to the exit, smiling nervously.

'You must be British. My ancestors came over in the *Mayflower*, but my mother was Boston Irish, first cousin to Rose Kennedy. The Kennedys! Ha! American presidents are all unnecessary – just wastes of space. I don't know what it's like where you come from, but here we've got too many tiers of government – national, federal, state, county, local – all collecting taxes and all corrupt.' In his jaunty cowboy hat and boots, he held forth about venal politicians, lazy ethnic minorities, overpopulation (out in the empty west!), lies on television and organised religion.

'I was brought up a Catholic, but as late as the nineteen-fifties, I heard our local priest telling a woman that it was her own fault if her husband beat her. She should do as she was told. The danger is here,' he concluded, pointing to his head.

I was just about to make my escape, when the first car of the afternoon pulled up and a couple walked into the shop to enquire about the state of the road over the Raton Pass. I was cheered to learn that they had driven up from Phoenix and seen no snow until they were about twenty miles outside Raton. If the thaw continued and I waited until mid-morning, I might be able to move on tomorrow.

DAY 23

There was a hard frost in the night, which turned the cleared roads to skating rinks. I walked out to the highway, but the snow-ploughs had banked the drifts into mountains of ice where the hard shoulder and pavements should have been. There was no space for a cyclist. I was stuck for at least another day, so I wandered back into town for a chat with my friend, the station-master. He had managed to get his stranded passengers into motels overnight and off his hands the next day, when the highway to Colorado Springs had been cleared. He was proud of his primrose station, with its pale-blue woodwork and Renaissance tower. It was the original AT & SF station, built when Raton was in its infancy. A little way across the concourse stood an egg-yellow structure, built in the sensuously rounded Indian adobe style. 'That there's the original Pony Express depot. With the railroad and the Pony Express, Raton was a real transport hub in the old days. Look at all those old warehouses.' I commented on the delicate colouring of his station, particularly the pale-blue doors. 'They're for luck.'

I began to notice blue all over the place, on homes as well as public buildings – blue doors, blue window-frames, sometimes even blue roof tiles. It was a colour popular with everyone, whatever their cultural tradition, and it was popular for the same reason. The Moors of North Africa had painted their doors and window-frames blue, in the belief that blue kept out the devil. When they overran Spain, the Christian Spaniards, equally superstitious, decided to play safe and adopt the Muslim practice. Even after the Reconquest, they remained addicted to blue woodwork and carried their addiction to the New World. When they arrived in New Mexico and started to splash on their blue paint, they found, to their great surprise, that it was already the favourite colour of the pueblo Indians, who had daubed it on their adobe houses for centuries. The Indians mined turquoise, and believed that both the gemstone and its colour would keep their own brand of demons at bay. So, though the shades of blue were slightly different, their prophylactic powers were believed to be the same. For once, the invading Spaniards and the subjugated native peoples were singing to their different gods from the same magical hymn-sheet.

Somewhere in New Mexico, there are petroglyphs of various unestablished dates (ranging from about AD 200 to 1600), which show an Indian flute-playing god named Kokopelli. When I first saw Kokopelli brooches in Raton, I thought immediately of Krishna, the flute-playing Hindu deity. But on closer inspection, I saw that their flutes were their only common attributes. Kokopelli is generally portrayed as a cheeky little dancing hunchback of indeterminate age, while Krishna, an avatar of Vishnu, the Great Preserver, is a dazzlingly beautiful blue-skinned young cowherd, irresistible to pastoral maidens. I never seem to have enough wallets for all the different currencies I need to carry on my travels, so I bought an extra wallet in New-Mexican blue, embroidered with a little Kokopelli. And I couldn't resist the most ridiculous souvenir of all – a silver Kokopelli on a bicycle, still playing his flute!

DAY 25

The visitor centre assured me yesterday that the highway was clear of snow just five miles out of Raton, so Howard in The Grapevine offered to drive me along the road until the hard shoulder emerged and it was safe for me to cycle. He took half an hour off from the post office and collected me from El Portal in his pick-up truck. I had made so many friends there that I felt quite sad to be leaving, yet the travelling demon urged me on. In some ways, I envied the people I had met in Raton. They were calm spirits who could settle down in an unimportant place, remote from the preoccupations, wonders and sufferings of the wider world. They seemed perfectly content with their local lives, while I was a questing nomad, always fretting to move on to the next road, the next country, the next continent.

We drove past the Whittington Centre, the famous 33,000 acres of shooting range operated by the National Rifle Association. I heard the busy crack and rattle of small arms. The centre was obviously well patronised, even on a weekday morning.

'I don't know about all the guns you have over here,' I said. 'There's been another high-school shooting. Twenty children dead, killed by one of their classmates.'

'I don't know what to think about it either,' said Howard. 'But I tell you, I'd be unhappy about giving up my gun. I'm used to keeping one by me and I wouldn't feel safe without it.' He opened the glove compartment, and there was his revolver, nestling innocently among the tissues and the chewing-gum. 'But some people are so irresponsible with their weapons. I know what I'd do with those kids, though. I'd string them up in front of the whole school! That would stop the copycats. I'm a firm believer in capital punishment. Killers don't deserve to live, even if they are only kids.' Howard was a mild, softly spoken man, a kind neighbour who was going out of his way to help me, yet his views were shockingly extreme to my European ears. More evidence that America was different. I didn't argue.

He dropped me in the sunshine at Three Mile Bridge, where the road was two endless parallel strips of snow-free tarmac, cutting through the white-sprinkled desert. For the first 25 miles, as far as Maxwell, the road was still descending from the Raton Pass. The sky was startlingly blue and the air electric. I swooped down the hill so fast that icicles started to hang from my nose and I had to put on my balaclava. Part of the exhilaration was the complete emptiness of the road. I felt like a driver in one of those ridiculous motorcar advertisements, where the latest models speed along the Riviera corniches, tackle the Great St Bernard and burn rubber along city streets, all miraculously devoid of traffic. Driving would be such fun, if only!

New Mexico is the one state in America where cyclists are allowed on the Interstate Highways. Interstate 25, which cuts a rugged path along the eastern edge of the Rockies, from Buffalo,

Wyoming, all the way down to the Mexican border, has to double up as US Road 85 through New Mexico, as there's no alternative route. The land is too sparsely populated for extra roads. I made the most of the luxury, drifting out of my usual rough hard shoulder on to the silky surface of the highway proper. On the rare occasions when a truck came along, I would hear it miles away in that silent world and return at leisure to my cramped and stony cycle path. It was blissful, carefree cycling, totally safe.

There was usually a toot and a wave from the driver's cab. At the speed he went, the land flashed by too fast to reveal its secrets. He was probably counting the miles to his next coffee stop, and I was a break in his monotony, another human being on the long, empty road he travelled every week. But at my speed, the landscape unrolled like a slow-motion art film. As my angle of vision changed, new scenes were brought into focus across the spiky yellow grass. I crossed the Red and Cimarron rivers, which were frozen solid, except for a narrow channel gurgling in their centre. The distant buttes were broken by the perfect cone of Red Peak, and beyond, the sun caught the snows of the Sangre de Cristo mountains. I paused to take in each fresh view before the kaleidoscope shifted and the sparkling colours of the high desert fell into new patterns.

But it was too good to last. A strong southerly wind blew up in the afternoon and I was glad to call it a day in Springer, once the capital of Colfax County, until the honour was transferred to Raton. The pale primrose court house, whose French château-style tower looked incongruously fancy in such a plain town, was now the Santa Fe Trail Museum. I was looking forward to my visit, because I had read that it housed a novelty, over and above the usual array of trail exhibits – the only electric chair ever used in the State of New Mexico. Sadly, the museum was closed for the winter. But culture's loss was gastronomy's gain. It turned out that the only restaurant in Springer closed its doors at 6 o'clock. Had I managed to visit the museum, I would have missed my dinner!

I was now in the land of tortillas, enchiladas, tamales, burritos, fajitas, papitas, stuffed sopaipillas, blue corn chips and salsa – all of them bursting with chilli pepper. Even breakfast eggs, *huevos rancheros*, came with a fiery finish. On my one visit to Mexico proper, my palate was burned to a cinder and my taste buds cauterised. Since then, I have steered well clear of Mexican cuisine. Indian curries use chilli, but there are variations in the heat of the dishes, and spices add subtlety to the flavours. Mexican food is just hot. I was keen to try their national speciality, dating back to the time of the Aztecs, of chicken in chocolate sauce. The chicken arrived in a coat of rich, dark brown, glistening like volcanic mud. It took the roof off my mouth. The sauce was a living fire, which had totally incinerated the flavour of chocolate. So I didn't travel through New Mexico with high expectations. I knew that I might have to sink to hamburgers, the only alternative to Mexican cuisine – and even they came with chilli, as did the salads. It was no consolation that wine was freely available in restaurants. The only drinks that could douse the flames were water or beer.

DAY 26

After Springer, the road began its steady 500 feet climb up to Wagon Mound, a huge, flat-topped outcrop which was one of the most famous landmarks on the Santa Fe Trail. When travellers along the Cimarron Cutoff caught sight of Wagon Mound, looming on the horizon in the Cornudo hills, there was a great cracking of whips and general jubilation. They were almost back on the main route. Their track wound past Rabbit Ear Camp, Round Mound and Point of Rocks, becoming rougher and stonier as they made for the Canadian river. From there, they bowled across an easy stretch of grassland to rejoin their fellow travellers west at La Junta (The Junction), now known as Watrous. They had survived their ordeal.

While the oxen on the Cimarron Cutoff were plodding along to the east of Wagon Mound, the travellers on the main trail took its western side through Rayado, Ocate Crossing and the mighty Fort Union, which was constructed in 1851 as the principal supply and staging centre for military operations in the southwest. Nearby stood the smaller Fort Barclay, a civilian depot and trading station built slightly earlier in adobe style by Alexander Barclay. He had been an employee of the Bent brothers and had modelled his own station on the original Bents' Fort.

Side roads struggled through the foothills of the Sangre de Cristo mountains to connect these spots with the main highway, and in warmer weather I might have attempted them. But in December, there was thick snow up there, so I had to stick to Highway 25, which was in fact a happy compromise, as it lay neatly between the two branches of the trail; and it passed right under the shadow of the towering Wagon Mound.

I stopped overnight in the small town of Wagon Mound, to get a closer look at the landmark. They had told me in Springer that there was accommodation at the Save-o-Mat, so I turned off the highway to look for what I imagined would be a store with a couple of rooms above it, like many of the small hotels in southern Europe or Pakistan. Instead, it turned out to be the Wagon Mound service station and it had a proper little two-cabin motel.

At this stage of my descent from Raton, I was well down below the snowline, but there was a bitter north wind – splendid while it was blowing me along on my bicycle, but less attractive once I stopped. I shopped in the service station for my evening meal of Doritos, Cheesos and chocolate-chip cookies, the only food available in town, then holed up for an afternoon of postcards.

Once in Cajamarca, high in the Cordillera Occidental of the Andes, I had wandered through streets that were literally starlit. The moon had not yet risen, but the heavens were ablaze. Galaxies raked the blackness like searchlights and the planets were my street lamps. I never thought to see such a spectacle again. But when I strolled out towards Wagon Mound in the early evening, it was further than I thought and darkness overtook me. In the middle of New Mexico, far from the sodium lighting of towns, I was blinded by the glittering planets and the swathe of galaxies so bright that they lit every pebble on my track. I stood gleaming in the frosty night, phosphorescent as a fish.

It was one of my coldest nights ever. I might have had a heater and a comfortable bed, but for glacial air, my cabin ranked with the icy room I was once grateful to be given on the Chinese border, 14,000 feet up in the Karakorams. There I put on every garment I possessed and tried to sleep on a short couch with neck-breaking wooden arms, while the wind howled through the broken window-panes of the border post. But at least I wasn't outdoors in my tent!

The Save-O-Mat's two cabins stood isolated from the rest of the premises. They were joined together, but that still left five out of the six sides of their cube exposed. There was no insulation in the wooden walls or the flat roof, and the floor was flimsy planking over the frozen earth. My paraffin heater struggled dutifully all night, with no help from the second cabin, which was unoccupied and cold. I heaped the covers from the other bed on top of my own, but I still slept fitfully. The frosty stars soon lost their magic.

DAY 27

It was a crisp, bright morning, with hoar frost on the grass but no prediction of snow – the perfect morning for an energetic cycle ride. I zoomed down from Wagon Mount, but then the road began to rise again, just as a wind got up from the southwest. For the first time since Missouri, I had to get off and push. A herd of does fled over the prairie as I approached, but horses and a field of bullocks just stood and stared, grass and hay dangling from their chops as they stopped chewing to concentrate. A hundred pairs of startled eyes told me that they didn't see many cyclists along that road.

I crossed the Mora river at Watrous, where the Mountain Route and the Cimarron Cutoff joined, stopping off to see Samuel Watrous's Home & Store, founded in 1849. I visited the nearby Fort Union National Monument, a massive ruin inside a circle of deep wagon ruts. Then I climbed the mountains against the wind to Las Vegas – the sober New Mexican version, not the glitzy magnet for gamblers in Nevada. The Nevada Strip is the preposterous boulevard running through the centre of Las Vegas, where addicts can throw away their life's savings at the blackjack tables and slot-machines of Caesar's Palace or the Luxor Casino, complete with pyramid, Cleopatra's Needle, floor shows and Egyptian theme-rides. By contrast, the Old Plaza at the heart of New Mexico's Vegas is a polite grassy park, graced with nothing more extravagant than a cluster of mature trees and a Victorian band stand. The Plaza Hotel, once one of the grand old ladies of the West, still welcomes visitors beneath its discreet classical pediment.

New Mexico's Las Vegas is definitely Hispanic. The site was occupied by Comanches until 1835, when the Mexican government gave land grants to a few families to found a city. The Santa Fe Trail, Fort Union, annexation by the United States and the arrival of the railroad all combined to produce a boom town, where the fortunes of the cattle barons lined the streets with elegant buildings. It had its share of hoodlums and gunslingers, but it was never as raucous as the likes of Dodge City. Las Vegas is a place to experience the more gracious side of the early West, unjostled by mobs of tourists. Stalls selling tribal feathers and cowboy hats are nowhere to be seen in the plaza.

After dropping down from the Raton Pass, my road had climbed quite steeply until I was almost back to the same altitude. Las Vegas, at 6,436 feet above sea-level, was typical of the old towns of New Mexico. None of them were built on the plains. When the early settlers were surrounded by Apaches, Comanches and Kiowas, some of the most warlike of the native tribes, their only safeguard was to hide themselves away, high up in the canyons.

The Spaniards claimed to be the rulers of South and Central America, and of all or part of the present-day North American states of New Mexico, Texas, California and Florida. But in fact, they had only a precarious hold over the cities they had founded there; and it took the Spanish army and the co-operation of the local peoples to protect even those. The surrounding countryside was dangerous Indian territory, rarely under their control. Missions were set up, then abandoned, because the security of the monks could not be guaranteed. The chief reason Santa Fe survived and blossomed as the capital of New Mexico was the character of the local Pueblo Indians. They were a particularly peaceful, hospitable people, who showered the arriving Spaniards with gifts. It was their way of showing friendship, though the invaders interpreted their offerings as tributes of submission, 'rendering obedience to His Majesty'. The small contingents of Spaniards usually managed to hang on to their conquests by playing off one hostile tribe against another, and drafting their Indian warrior allies into service under their own Spanish officers. Given that the Spanish adventurers and settlers who sailed out to their New World far preferred the more settled and silver-rich countries of South and Central America to the fragile agricultural economies of North America, it is a particular miracle that underpopulated New Mexico survived.

I must have looked quite fragile after my hard uphill ride to Las Vegas, because I was cosseted in my motel by the most unlikely character. Dave was a former Hell's Angel. His head was a shaven skull, to match the skull and crossbones tattooed on his brawny arms – along with the usual selection of hearts, raging fires, rings of barbed wire, bluebirds, pentacles and all manner of other esoteric symbols. He sported an earring and a nose-ring, and wore black leathers with 'Hell's Angels' patterned in studs on his back, and long black boots with chains and spurs. Had he been on duty at the check-in when I arrived, rather than his demure wife, I would have fled from the motel in terror.

'You're not travelling round America on that thing!' he said, pointing disdainfully at my beautiful Condor. 'Awesome! But it's not safe. Anything could happen to you out on the road. Are you armed? Show me your gun.' Later that afternoon, I was invited for 'English tea' in their flat. Dave produced a postcard of Las Vegas, already addressed to the motel. 'Now as soon as you get back to London, England, you send us this postcard, do you hear? Betsy and I won't rest until we know you're safe back home.'

DAY 28

Dave and Betsy were horrified that I was planning to cycle on to Santa Fe. 'You can't do that! You're mad! There's nothing on that road. Nowhere to stay. And you'll never get over the Glorieta Pass. There'll be deep snow up there.' The Glorieta, at 7,409 feet, was even higher than the Raton, so I guessed they were right about the snow. I gave up and was rescued by Will. Will and Joyce were friends of friends, who lived in Santa Fe and were expecting me to go and stay with them. When I phoned them from Las Vegas, Will immediately offered to drive over and collect me. Like Dave, he thought it would be lunacy to attempt that road on a bicycle in mid-winter.

DAY 29

First, Will gave me a conducted tour of Las Vegas, in the warmth and comfort of his car, pointing out the roof-top from which General Kearney had proclaimed the annexation of the state of New Mexico in 1846 and the Carnegie Library, a copy of President Thomas Jefferson's house in Monticello, Virginia. Then we drove along the utterly empty highway, climbed up to the snows of the Glorieta Pass, the scene of the Civil War Battle of Glorieta in 1862, and descended into La Villa Real de Santa Fe de San Francisco. The Spanish are fond of grand titles.

Today's tourists, who jet around the globe till they are jaded with wonders, are still bowled over by the beauty of Santa Fe, rising high on its desert plateau under the red steeps of the Sangre de

Cristo mountains. To travellers along the trail, weary from 900 miles of desolation, it must have seemed like paradise itself.

Santa Fe was named after that dazzling city in the Spanish Sierra Nevada, Santa Fe de Granada. On one of the greatest days in Spanish history, 2 January 1492, the Catholic monarchs, Ferdinand and Isabella, rode into Granada in triumph, having driven the last of the occupying Moors out of Spain. Two years later, the newly confident joint rulers despatched Christopher Columbus on his first voyage, and so began the Spanish connection with the New World. Occupation followed speedily, and a century later, the Spaniards had already fanned out from Mexico deep into North and South America. Santa Fe was founded in 1609 as their capital of New Mexico. By the time the Pilgrim Fathers arrived at Plymouth Rock in 1620, Santa Fe already had its Palacio Real along the northern edge of the Spanish plaza, fifty churches built by the busy Franciscans, and the broad tree-lined avenue along the river, the Alameda, without which no self-respecting Spanish city would be complete. Santa Fe is the oldest state capital in the United States of America; its Palacio Real, better known as the Palace of the Governors, is the country's oldest continuously inhabited public building; and two of its seventeenth-century Franciscan mission churches are still in use today. When traders and migrants from the basic log-cabin settlements of the east arrived along the Santa Fe Trail, they entered a wealthy, gracious capital, the likes of which they had never seen before.

DAY 30
It was icy cold up there, but festive, decked with green garlands and red poinsettia wreaths for Christmas. Politically correct signs wished us all 'Happy Holidays'. After my weeks of cycling, I was sorry not to sweep down the street signed 'Old Santa Fe Trail' and pull up in the plaza, at journey's end, on my trusty Condor. Driving in with Will was a bit of an anticlimax.

The glittering stores were thronged with frazzled Christmas shoppers, mostly American tourists, in Santa Fe for the so-called 'festive season'. Husbands, bored out of their minds and laden with parcels, trailed like docile native porters behind their avid wives, who were trawling through the Indian handicraft stalls. They poked at turquoise jewellery, Navajo rugs and Hopi pots, desperately searching for that amusing original gift. 'Honey, just look at those cute little totem poles! Don't you think Joylene would just love one for her yard?' History was the last thing on their minds. I forced a path through to the sky-blue doors of the Palace of the Governors and had the peaceful museum all to myself.

When I emerged to meet Will in the lobby of La Fonda Hotel, home from home to Hollywood stars and those equally celebrated back to 1610, it was already dusk and the spectacle took my breath away. Santa Fe's Christmas lights were not the usual garish electric baubles, but candles rooted in soil inside brown paper bags. They marched in rows along the tops of walls and picked out the roof-tops with their warm golden glow. They were perfect – the only possible Christmas lighting for the city's red-ochre adobe walls.

The Pueblo Indians knew how to construct multistorey houses out of mud, but their buildings were friable and easily washed away in heavy rains. The Spanish Franciscans used the same materials as their Indian workers, but passed on the superior building techniques which they themselves had learned from the Moors. They taught the Indians to combine the local mud with sand, charcoal and chopped straw, then mould it into bricks to be baked in the sun. After a finishing coat of wet mud, their brick buildings looked exactly the same as the traditional structures of the Pueblo Indians, but they were strong enough to survive the centuries. These red adobe buildings, with their smoothly rounded silhouettes, are the great feature of Santa Fe architecture. They give the city an attractive cohesion, which some people think is taken to extremes. It is difficult these days to get planning permission for any building not in the adobe style. Even petrol stations and multistorey car parks have to look like Franciscan churches. And much of the construction is sham. Concrete houses and hotels are given a red mud finish, and what used to be the ends of supporting beams are stuck on to the exterior, like the prickles of a porcupine, but less useful. Most have flowery courtyards at their heart, Spanish-Moroccan or Mozarab in style. I suddenly realised where Gaudi got the inspiration for those blocks of flats in Barcelona, which are as soft and rounded as melting ice-creams. They are pure adobe, in bright modern colours.

Will gave me a quick tour of the scores of art galleries in Canyon Road and showed me the Miraculous Staircase in the Loretto

Chapel. Legend has it that when the chapel was constructed, no local craftsman was skilled enough to build the staircase up to the gallery. The nuns prayed for help and a mysterious travelling carpenter arrived in town. He built a spiral staircase with no visible central support, no nails and no screws – and the next day he was gone. Was the carpenter St Joseph, or even Jesus?

I shall have to go back to Santa Fe. There was so much else to see there, and in neighbouring Taos, but Will and Joyce lived way out of town and there were no buses, so I was dependent on being driven everywhere and had no chance to poke around. That evening, we drove back early for our date with Joyce's speciality – her delicious beef in port and mushrooms – and I was glad to get away from the crowds. The cold and altitude were getting to me. Ascending swiftly by car, I had had no time to acclimatise, so I was gasping for breath and my head was drumming like a marching band. A calm house in a peaceful residential suburb was exactly what I needed. Next time, I shall travel to Santa Fe in milder weather, in my own hired car, avoiding the Christmas frenzy and the famous opera season. I shall conquer the altitude slowly and painlessly, and visit the ancient adobes of Taos Pueblo, the artists' colonies and the house where D H Lawrence stayed. I might even, if I feel brave enough, make a trip to Los Alamos on the Pajarito Plateau. 'The Poplars' on 'Baby Bird Plateau' sounds idyllic, the perfect spot for a picnic. But it has a darker purpose. It was the headquarters of the top-secret Manhattan Project, which produced the atomic bomb, and it is still America's main centre for nuclear research.

DAY 31

The Santa Fe Trail, like the other legendary trails out west, was a short-lived phenomenon. Little by little, the tracks of the Atchison, Topeka and Santa Fe Railroad were creeping westwards, and on 9 February 1880, the first train steamed into Santa Fe Station. The arduous wagon-trail across some 900 miles of blank, hostile plain was abandoned to history.

Yet, when the trail originally opened up, it was seen by the New Mexicans as a comparatively quick and easy route. The manufactured goods they so desperately needed had to travel a mere 900 miles from the Missouri. Their previous life-line, the Camino Real (the King's Road) from Mexico proper, was a clear 1,000 miles longer. Known locally as the Chihuahua Trail, the Camino Real followed the Rio Grande from Santa Fe through Albuquerque, El Paso and Chihuahua to Mexico City and on to Vera Cruz, the closest Mexican port. It was a route which was more attractive to the 'Anglo' traders from the east than it was to the New Mexicans. Demand for calico and basic household goods along its upper reaches was so high that by 1840 half the freight from the Missouri was continuing to markets along the Chihuahua Trail, where there was Mexican silver coin and Mexican mules to pay for it.

I was travelling on from Santa Fe myself, to cycle another Camino Real up the Pacific coast from San Diego to San Francisco, and I was due to stay with more friends of friends, this time in Albuquerque. Will would have given me a lift, but the weather was sparkling, so I decided to cruise down the mountains on my bike – but not along Highway 25, the Chihuahua Trail. For once, there was a parallel route, the Turquoise Trail.

Turquoise jewellery-making and the carving of turquoise fetishes is one of the traditional crafts practised by the Native Americans. Because the stone has the power to avert evil, they have mined it for centuries and valued it above all others. Gem-quality turquoise is quite rare these days, as the seams are nearing exhaustion, so the craftsmen are turning to stabilised turquoise, which is genuine but in need of chemical hardening – and the rogues are turning to dyed plastic. *Caveat emptor*!

The Turquoise Trail has no history at all. It's just a pretty name. A Turquoise Trail Association was set up in 2003 and the road was marked as a National Scenic Byway at about the same time. Its title must have been chosen with an eye to the tourists, as the towns along it have more to do with yellow and black gold than blue stones. Nearest to Santa Fe, Cerrillos was built by the AT & SF Railroad, after gold was struck there in 1897. In its heyday, it needed four hotels and twenty-one saloons to slake the miners' thirst. The next town along, Madrid, was a thriving coal-mining town from the late 1800s to about 1950. It was remarkable for producing both hard and soft coal in the same area, and its coal powered the railroad. Golden, not surprisingly, was another town founded on gold. In 1825, it saw the first gold rush in the American West, predating the more famous rushes to California and Colorado by more than twenty years.

As far as I could make out, the only one of these three towns which had any connection with turquoise was Cerrillos, but that one location was more than enough. Cerrillos holds one of the planet's greatest stores of turquoise. The local Indians hacked hundreds of tons of this treasure from the bleak surrounding rocks, using the most primitive tools, and exported it as far as Tenochtitlan, the capital of Mexico, where it was used by the Aztecs to embellish their palaces and decorate their wives and warriors. Most of the Aztec turquoise was seized by the Spaniards, when the empire fell, and travelled in their kitbags to Spain. The most precious items now form part of the Spanish crown jewels. Legend has it that there are fabulously rich lost mines, which were blocked off and buried by the Pueblo Indians, to keep their treasure safe from the greedy Spanish conquistadors.

The Americans love their cars and they are proud of their history, particularly the taming of the Wild West. Put these passions together, and you have the perfect American holiday – bundling the kids and the dog into the car and motoring along the pioneer trails. They feel bold and adventurous in their air-conditioned comfort, cushioned from motel to motel, from McDonald's to McDonald's. Not for them the tame delights of Disneyland or the Caribbean.

Along the Turquoise Trail, I was expecting three 'ghost towns', their dirt roads deserted and their wooden buildings falling apart. What I found were American families motoring and coaching along in their droves. In Cerrillos, they tumbled out of their vehicles into the Casa Grande Trading Post, Turquoise Mining Museum and Petting Zoo, a single imaginative enterprise under one roof, crammed with jewellery, sweets, soft drinks, dead rattlesnakes and live rabbits, and designed to cater for all ages and tastes. Then on to the famous 'Christmas in Madrid' celebrations, for more shopping and a mid-morning Coke and cookies in the Mine Shaft Tavern. The old miners' cottages were expensively restored and let out as painters' studios, craftsmen's workshops and antique markets. Some years ago, the ramshackle ruins along the Turquoise Trail were havens for artists, hippies and society's 'opters-out' generally, with peaceful wooden huts in the mountains, far from the frenzied capitalism of the cities. Then tourists arrived to view the curiosities, film-makers used the towns for Western scenarios, there was outdoor summer jazz, and fashion followed. Now the miners' 'ghost towns' are little more than wall-to-wall shopping opportunities. But the trail made an interesting day's run.

I ended my ride in the spacious, gracious university city of Albuquerque, which nestles comfortably in its valley between the Sandia mountains and the cottonwoods along the Rio Grande. There I enjoyed Bob and Alice's generous hospitality, sharing their spare bedroom with the ashes of their dear departed Trixie and Spot. I bought some three-ply knitting wool, no longer obtainable in England, and had it posted home. Then I travelled on by Amtrak to San Diego.

The city of Albuquerque swims occasionally into my dreams. I know that one day I have to go back there and cycle along Central Avenue. The lure is the legendary Route 66, Chicago to Los Angeles, which crosses the Camino Real in a blaze of neon hoardings right in the heart of downtown Albuquerque. But that's another story, another historic trail . . .

THE WAY OF SAINT JAMES

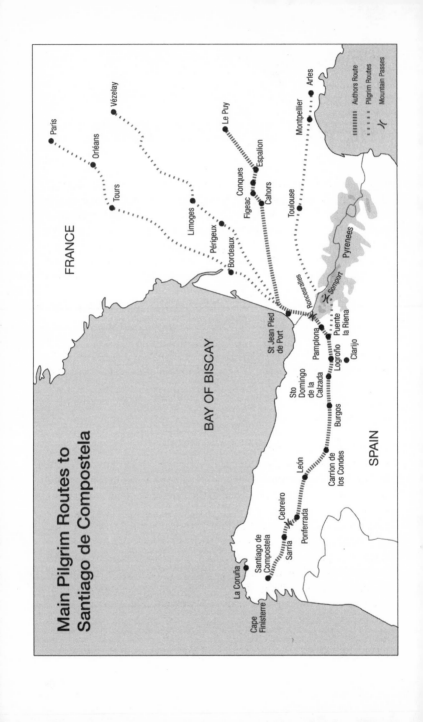

Main Pilgrim Routes to Santiago de Compostela

PRELUDE

I do assure all the world that I had rather go five times out of Englande to Rome than one to Compostelle; by water it is no payne but by land it is the greatest journey that an Englishman may go.

Andrew Boorde, physician

When Andrew Boorde decided to make his pilgrimage to Santiago de Compostela around 1535, he no doubt consulted one of the Confraternities of St James, which have existed since mediaeval times to give advice and encouragement to those undertaking this arduous journey. Almost five centuries later, that is exactly what I did. I joined the Confraternity of St James of Compostela, which has its offices and library in Southwark, and attended their annual Pilgrim Day, on that occasion in Warwick.

It was a very practical day – just what was needed. After a few words of welcome by the chairman, we were divided into two groups, walkers and cyclists. In my group, those of us who were hoping to cycle to Santiago met the Confraternity members who had already made the two-wheeled pilgrimage. We discussed everything from weather and accommodation to pannier-packing, gears and sprockets. We were a wonderfully miscellaneous gathering. United in purpose, we spanned every age, from school-leavers undertaking the pilgrimage as a gap-year project, to the very old, who wanted to accomplish something meaningful and challenging while they still had the strength to manage it. Then there was a wonderful cross-section of expertise. Doctors, clergy, musicians and teachers exchanged tips and misgivings with cycle mechanics, sports outfitters and retired army personnel, used to the long hard slog. One ex-army officer related his adventures on a bicycle named Copenhagen, after Wellington's famous horse. Motives for the pilgrimage were equally mixed. Devout Christians mingled with trail-walkers, historians, students of the Romanesque, mountain-bikers seeking a challenge, people marking a turning-point in their lives, such as retirement, and those trying to come to terms with a bereavement or simply needing some space for reflection. Such an ageless, sexless, classless gathering is all too rare. After a sociable picnic lunch, we bought copies of the Confraternity's excellent pilgrim guides and articles of pilgrim attire. I came away with a royal-blue sweatshirt, which carried the Confraternity's name around a discreet white cockleshell on the front, while a giant version of the same shell emblazoned the whole of the back. Motorists would certainly see me ahead and know what I was about.

In the great days of pilgrimage, the three holiest shrines in Christendom had their own insignia. Pilgrims who tramped or rode across Europe to Rome carried the crossed keys of St Peter. Those who went to Jerusalem were known as 'palmers', because they came home waving a palm branch to prove that they really had travelled as far as the Middle East. Pilgrims to the shrine of St James in Compostela 'took the cockle', because the cockleshell or, more accurately, its larger cousin the scallop-shell, is his emblem – of which we are all gastronomically reminded when we enjoy our 'Coquilles St Jacques'.

But why the cockleshell? The Church relates that, after the death of Christ, St James the Greater, son of Zebedee and brother of St John, carried the gospel to Spain. When he returned to Judaea in AD 44, he was beheaded by Herod and became the first of the apostles to be martyred. His followers, guided by an angel, took his body to Jaffa. There they found a miraculous stone ship, without sails or crew. This ship drifted with its precious cargo to the coast of Galicia, where it ran aground seven days later (its sailing time from the Middle East being something of a miracle in itself!) in Iria Flavia at the mouth of the Ulla river, not far from Cape Finisterre, the End of the Earth. The arrival of this weird stone ship caused such a panic on the beach that a horse plunged itself and its rider under the waves, to resurface covered in white scallop-shells. These became the symbol of St James.

Galicia at the time was ruled by a pagan, Queen Lupa, so the saint was hidden underground for protection and there he slept for eight hundred years, until he rose in all his might and glory to lead the Spanish armies to victory over the Moors. 'Santiago', as he is known in Spain, became the country's patron saint, and the Spaniards littered the New World with Santiagos – cities in Mexico, Cuba, Argentina, Paraguay and Santo Domingo, as well as the best-known and loveliest of all, the capital of Chile. But more of St James later.

Mediaeval pilgrims to his shrine at Santiago de Compostela wore an easily recognisable uniform, consisting of a long home-spun tunic, a broad-brimmed hat, often pinned back with a silver shell brooch, and a scrip, or wallet, for their money and papers. A gourd for drinking-water, a staff and a scallop-shell completed their luggage. The shell was particularly useful, as it could serve as plate, drinking saucer and alms bowl for begging.

I pride myself on travelling light, but the ample contents of my two panniers would have shocked my predecessors along the way, as would my cool and comfortable cotton trousers, baggy shirt and baseball cap. My only claim to authenticity, when I boarded the European Bike Bus to Lyon, was the scallop-shell on my handlebar bag.

From the Gare de Perrache in Lyon, I took a lazy little local train to the starting-point of my pilgrimage, Le Puy. Condor rode peacefully in the driver's cab, while I was deafened in my carriage by a horde of young football fans returning from a French triumph. Their faces were painted in red, white and blue stripes and one of them carried a traffic-cone, which he was using as a megaphone. They set up a non-stop rhythmic victory chant: *'On est, on est champion! On est, on est champion!'* After three or four stations, my ears could stand it no longer, but I was nervous of moving. An unpleasant experience on a train with a mob of drunken English football supporters had taught me extreme caution. So I debated within myself. Should I sit there and endure the racket, or should I draw unwelcome attention to myself by moving? I eventually screwed up my courage and tried to slip unnoticed to the far end of the compartment. At this, the rhythmic chanting changed to: *'Au'voir, au revoir madame! Au'voir, au revoir madame!'*

They got out a few stations before I did, and when they passed my window, the boy with the traffic cone came right up to the glass and yelled, *'Au'voir, au revoir madame!'* one last time, to the great mirth of his comrades. They enjoyed teasing me, but I never felt threatened. There was not a beer can in sight, and the boys were in high good humour. I wondered if this was because the south of France is wine-drinking country? Soccer hooligans are usually lager-swillers, from beer-drinking societies like England, Holland, Denmark and Germany. Beer, being a long drink, can be drunk throughout the entire day of a match and well on into the night, revving up the testosterone and fuelling the animal aggression. But a bottle of wine makes one mellow, and even lulls the drinker to sleep. Burgundy and Chablis are rarely seen on the terraces. Perhaps that explains the spontaneous gaiety of those French football fans. They had not drunk themselves into a xenophobic rage.

THE RIVERS OF FRANCE

Give me my scallop-shell of quiet,
My staff of Faith to walk upon,
My scrip of joy, immortal diet,
My bottle of salvation,
My gown of glory, hope's true gage,
And thus I'll take my pilgrimage.

Sir Walter Raleigh

These days, most pilgrims to the shrine of St James begin their overland journey at St Jean-Pied-de-Port, the Basque stronghold on the French side of the Pyrenees. But there are four other starting-points, well documented in history. There is the route from Paris, the Via Turonicensis, which set out from the Royal Abbey of St Denis and passed through Orléans, Tours, Poitiers and Bordeaux; the route from the Benedictine abbey church of La Madelaine on its hilltop in Vézelay, the Via Lemovicensis, which ran through Neuvy St Sepulcre and Limoges; the route from the splendid Romanesque ex-cathedral of St Trophîme in Arles, the Via Tolosana, through Montpellier, Toulouse and Pau; and the oldest recorded route of all, from the Cathedral of Le Puy en Velay, the Via Podensis, which crossed the gorges of the Massif Central to Figeac, Cahors and Les Landes. All of these starting-points were pilgrimage destinations in their own right, and the four main overland routes took in as many important sanctuaries as possible. I shall try to avoid turning my account into a catalogue of Romanesque churches and monasteries!

The pilgrim paths from Paris, Vézelay and Le Puy merged at the hamlet of Ostabat, just off the present D 933 between St Palais and St Jean-Pied-de-Port, to flow together over the Pyrenees by the Pass of Roncesvalles. Pilgrims from Provence and Italy, who gathered in Arles, took the higher Somport Pass (which some scholars claim to be the pass famously used by Hannibal and his elephants), to join the other three contingents at Puente la Reina in the kingdom of Navarra. From that point onwards, the great tide of walkers and horsemen struggled together across the burning plains of La Rioja, Castile and León, to reach the cooler shores of Galicia in time for the Feast of St James on 25 July.

I had cycled the gentler routes from Vézelay and Arles, but I felt particularly drawn towards the Way of St James from Le Puy. The shrine of the Black Virgin in the cathedral there is the earliest recorded starting-point for Compostela, a fact which appealed to my antiquarian tastes. And then the actual route across some of the wildest, remotest parts of France promised to be spectacular, if a little gruelling.

Le Puy itself is geologically astonishing. The city stands in a depression between huge basalt plateaux, its green and fertile plain pierced with the most extraordinary volcanic chimneys, like church spires. On top of one 80 m vertical outcrop, a climb of 267 steps leads breathlessly up to a little gem of a Romanesque church, St Michel-d'Aiguilhe (St Michael of the Needle), whose soaring eleventh-century bell-tower with its pointed apex adds vertigo to an already dizzying vision. The pinnacle of another volcanic shaft, the Rocher Corneille, is topped with a gigantic statue of Notre Dame de France, cast from the iron of no fewer than 213 cannon captured at the Battle of Sebastopol. By comparison, the Cathedral of Notre Dame du Puy, poised on its own steep hill, seems distinctly squat, a shrine for the vertically challenged.

I arrived in Le Puy on 14 July, Bastille Day, and joined the crowds of French holidaymakers visiting the main tourist sites. I was profoundly moved by the simplicity of St Michel-l'Aiguilhe with its plain oval ambulatory and interested, as a classicist, to learn that the rock was previously home to a temple of the Roman god Mercury. Mercury (Greek Hermes) often became St Michael when his worshippers were converted to Christianity. He was the ancient 'psychopompos', the god who escorted the souls of the dead to the underworld, protecting them on their dark journey. St Michael adopted this role, substituting his sword for Mercury's less warlike staff. In St Michel-d'Aiguilhe I found a beautiful prayer which confirmed this identity: '*Défendez mon âme contre tous ses ennemis, et lorsque viendra pour moi l'heure de quitter ce monde, venez alors, Prince très glorieux, me soutenir dans la lutte finale: que votre glaive étincelant repousse au loin, dans les abîmes de la mort et de l'enfer, l'ange prévaricateur dont vous avez vaincu l'orgueil.*' (Defend my soul from its enemies, and when the time comes for me to leave this world, come, most glorious Prince, to support me in my final struggle: may your gleaming sword banish into the abysses of death and hell that fallen angel, whose pride you have conquered.)

St Michael provided a suitably uplifting start to a Christian pilgrimage. Reflecting on the transience of human life and other such spiritual matters, I made my way to the cathedral, to come down to earth with a bump. As usually happens when I particularly want to see a building, I found it heavily under repair. Its dim nave and organ were completely blocked off by scaffolding, and I had no view of the miracle-working Black Madonna. But I did manage to get my new pilgrim's record stamped with her image by a benign old lady in the sacristy. The Confraternity of St James had provided the record folder as proof of my pilgrim status, with instructions to get it stamped at churches and monasteries along the way. These stamps would be evidence, when I arrived at the cathedral in Santiago, that I had in fact made the pilgrimage. Then, if my motivation were judged acceptable by the cathedral administration, I might be presented with a 'Compostela', a signed certificate recognising my achievement.

The sacristy lady asked if I was making the pilgrimage on foot.

'No. I'm travelling there on my bicycle.'

'*A vélo! Mais vous êtes d'un âge discret!*' (a polite French term for 'old').

She obviously thought that cycling 1,500 km would be much harder work than walking, and nothing I said could persuade her otherwise. As far as she was concerned, cycling was the Tour de France, a sport best left to young men. I tried to explain that the beauty of cycling lay in the fact that everyone, whatever their age, sex or state of fitness, could enjoy it at their own pace and their own level. We don't have to belong to the high-speed Lycra brigade. She shrugged. 'If you do manage to reach Compostela on that dreadful machine, pray for me!'

I watched the Bastille Day fireworks over my delicious dinner of roast pork and green Le Puy lentils, one of the specialities of the region. It was a particularly noisy display, as the bangs ricocheted off the surrounding mountains and sent the city's birds whirling and squawking into the night sky. Then a band struck up in the square just as I was going to bed. Two competing orchestras soon joined in, and a lively troupe of folk-dancers. From the grandstand of my attic window, I watched the celebrations well into the early hours. It was not a restful preparation for my journey, but it was great fun.

Like Bishop Gottschalk, who led the first pilgrimage from Le Puy to Santiago de Compostela in AD 951, I started out from the black stone bulk of the cathedral. Its gloomy, rather Arabic architecture loomed over me as I scrambled down the steep cobbles of the Rue des Pèlerins (Pilgrim Street) into the Rue St Jacques, scarcely able to control my wayward bicycle over the bumps. It was far too steep to cycle. In fact, for the first few days the drops and climbs were so sheer that I walked almost as much as I rode. But once I had accepted that my bicycle was little more than a glorified baggage-trolley, I was content to amble along, enjoying the sights and scents of the countryside.

The Way of St James cuts across the grain of the country. Rivers rise in the mountains of the Auvergne, swell to torrents and crash with force through deep rocky gorges. Le Puy lies in a loop of the fledgling Loire, and my first test was the watershed between that river and the Allier. I toiled uphill from Le Puy's 625 m to Montbonnet at 1,108 m, then swooped down to Monistrol on the banks of the Allier, only to have an even more killing climb up to the next plateau. This would be the pattern. After the Allier came the Lot, the Dourdou, the Auze and the Tarn, not to mention the minor rivers no one has ever heard of, all encased in vertical cliffs which had to be scaled. But there were scenic delights at every bend in the road. The gorges were thick with oak, ash, beech and lime, which gave welcome shade on the upward plods, and the high, rolling plateaux were alive with songbirds and butterflies. Despite the exhaustion involved (my own fault, as I never train), it was a magical, exhilarating ride.

On the stiff climb out of Monistrol, a Swiss boy overtook me, swanning up the cliff on his bicycle as if he were taking a leisurely spin in Regent's Park. He was naked to the waist and there was not a surplus ounce of flesh on him.

'Are you going all the way?' he shouted as he breezed past. There was no need to ask where. He said he was aiming to reach Compostela in a fortnight.

I made it to Sauges in the early evening – a ride of 44 km which had taken me a shaming seven hours. In the Hôtel de la Terrasse, they had a special tariff '*pour nos amis pèlerins*'. I expected the cut-price rooms to be the worst in the hotel, but the opposite was the case. My bathroom had a proper bath, with oodles of hot water, because pilgrims need a relaxing soak at the end of their day's toil. A nice touch was the carving of the bedhead and wardrobe with clusters of St James's cockleshells.

The villages in the Auvergne stand on hilltops, with stone towers and fortress-like churches as grim reminders of the Hundred Years War. In many ways, foot pilgrims along the Way of St James across France have an easier time than cyclists, because Le Chemin de St Jacques is maintained as a long-distance walkers' path, the GR 65, which follows the rivers down in their valleys and skirts most of the villages. I could see coloured anoraks bobbing merrily along in the shelter of the trees below, while I was climbing up my parallel tarmac, exposed to the elements, to reach some skyscraping village. Of course, my passing envy melted away completely when I hurtled in triumph down the next descent, oversweeping all those earthbound sunhats.

Although it was mid-July and sunny, I was cycling at some altitude across the Aubrac Plateau and needed my anorak against a chill southwest wind. It was a harsh, rugged landscape with low granite outcrops, unsuited to mechanised farming. Scythes, hay-forks and rakes were clutched in gnarled hands, but the faces were friendly and even the farm dogs, normally the cyclist's bane, seemed to be smiling.

I took shelter for a while in the small Chapel of St Roch on the windswept border between Haute Loire and Lozère. St Roch is a French pilgrim saint, who became so popular as a healer in the fourteenth century that many of St James's chapels along the Way to Compostela were rededicated. St Roch was on a pilgrimage to Rome when the plague swept across Europe. With his miraculous powers, he healed scores of victims, until he himself was struck down in Piacenza and nursed back to health by a dog. His statues are less attractive than those of St James, as he is usually sculpted pointing to his hideously diseased thigh, which also seems to be an object of prurient interest to his long-snouted dog.

On my third day, I climbed to 1,340 m at the Col d'Aubrac. This would be the highest point of my journey until I crossed León. I began the morning feeling stiff and low, but once I was over the col and bowling across the wildest stretch of the plateau, with its broom, heather, kestrels and songbirds, my spirits soared and I sang along with the exaltation of larks.

The hotel in Aubrac was full and the pilgrim gîte was the grim granite Tour des Anglais (named, like so many of these village towers, after the English troops who rampaged through the Auvergne during the Hundred Years War). I decided to press on to St Chély d'Aubrac, reckoning that if I had to resort to pilgrim accommodation, I would be more comfortable at the milder altitude of 808 m than shivering in a mediaeval tower on the edge of a windswept upland. In fact, I found a small hotel in Chély. At first sight, my room was a Black Hole of Calcutta, airless and depressing. But once I had opened the two windows and thrown back the shutters, it was transformed by the flood of sunlight and the magnificent views of wooded hills in both directions. It was one of those small hotels which still exist only in rural France. There was overblown floral wallpaper on the ceiling and cupboard doors as well as the walls, a mottled brown carpet, a gold candlewick bedspread, transparent with washing, and paintwork of a most unattractive faecal brown. I was in the land of pigs' trotters, tripe and quail stuffed with duck pâté, but luckily there was trout on the menu too, fresh from the nearby stream. Preceded by a *salade soleil* (lettuce, tomato and sweetcorn) and followed by home-made bilberry sorbet, the whole washed down with half a litre of very acceptable local wine, the meal was a fitting close to an excellent day's cycling.

On the great climb out of St Chély, which nestled in the densely wooded hollows of the Foret d'Aubrac, I actually managed to stay on my bicycle. I even made an uphill detour that afternoon to see St Pierre Bessuejouls, one of the earliest mediaeval churches on the way. Two days ago, I would have given the most magnificent cathedral in the world a miss if it had involved extra cycling, but the mountains of the Auvergne were pulling me painfully into shape.

At St Côme d'Olt, I met the river Lot and cycled along its spectacular rocky gorge through Espalion to Estaing, sharing the waterside path with the GR 65. After days of high, breezy moorland, the heat in the valley struck me like a slab of concrete. I staggered into the Hôtel aux Armes d'Estaing, flopped down on my bed and slept for two hours. At 4 o'clock, I ventured out to the church to see the pilgrim altar with St James to the left and St Roch (pointing to his festering thigh) to the right, but it was still too hot for comfort. Even at 9.30, when the music of the *Carmina Burana* drew me out to a neighbouring café, the stones of the riverside wall were still too hot to touch. But at least I could read the café menu. I had broken one of the arms off my reading glasses in Le Puy on Bastille Day, when the shops were shut. Since then, my spectacles had wobbled precariously on my nose through a succession of small shopless villages, until I finally found an optician in Espalion.

Up from the Lot, down to the Daze, up from the Daze and headlong down to the Dourdou, the roads on my map were demented worms, pirouetting on their tails like corkscrews, the sort of D-roads Michelin loves and marks in green for beauty. They led me gasping into Conques, a mediaeval city with some authentic buildings, but so well restored that it looked more like Disney's film set of Paris in *The Hunchback of Notre Dame*. It was bursting with French tourists and there was no room at any of the inns. So, for the first time on my pilgrimage, I fished out my official pilgrim's record and presented it to the Premonstratensian White Friars in the delicious coolness of the Abbaie Ste-Foy.

Following the tradition of the monastic orders, the White Friars provided accommodation for pilgrims. Their lay manager, M Alain, was most welcoming, but regretted that there were no single or double rooms left. He stamped my pilgrim passport with an image of the strangely pop-eyed Ste Foy, then escorted me to my lower bunk in a huge mixed dormitory. Everyone there was French except two Cambridge Modern Linguists, who were making the pilgrimage in the Long Vac to improve their spoken French and Spanish. With the energy of the young, they rushed off in the afternoon for their first ever ride on horses, while I rested my weary legs on my bunk.

I attended evening service with the Brothers in the Abbey chancel. There were just eight of them. The abbot was old and rotund, as an abbot should be. Then there were two middle-aged monks and five young ones. It was a perfect service – just twenty minutes of plainsong and responses, with one reading and no sermon, followed by a brief organ voluntary. The singing was slightly out of tune, but they were monks, not musicians, and their devotion was palpable. It was an intimate, almost family affair, as we sat in the glow of the chancel lamps, lapped in our small circle of light and warmth beneath the echoing splendour of the vaulted tribune. After dinner in the whimsically named 'Tentations de Charlemagne', I re-entered the abbey on a tide of Bach, which rolled majestically from the organ loft and resounded through the great Gothic arches. There was a Bach organ and baritone recital, which gave me an opportunity to sit in peace and let my eye wander over the detail of the stone and wood carving. I noticed the cockleshells of St James lovingly carved on every pew end.

It was a hot, stuffy, mosquito-ridden night on a bunk which creaked and swayed whenever the man on the top deck shifted his considerable bulk. Many of the walkers set off before dawn, to escape the worst of the heat, and I rose early too, eating my morning bun in the shower block by the open window, to catch what little breeze I could. Unfortunately, when I tried to make my coffee, the plug of my electric water-heater exploded in the shaver socket, fusing all the lights in the dormitory wing. I made a swift tactical exit.

Most of the pilgrims from Le Puy had passed along the way some weeks before, aiming to reach Santiago in time for the Feast of St James. But the fellowship of the road was still alive among the rest of us stragglers. In the café in Noilhac, where I found my first badly needed cup of coffee, I was greeted enthusiastically by Alain and Giselle, and a rather quieter Swedish couple, all pilgrims I had met the previous afternoon. Because the GR 65 took a short cut from Conques, they had covered the stretch on foot in exactly the same time as it had taken me to cycle up one of my steepest climbs to date. They were making the pilgrimage in stages, two weeks a year, as part of their annual holiday, and had booked their hotels along the way. I described my less provident night with the White Friars, and this led to a discussion of monastic orders and colours of habits.

'There's even a red order in Spain,' said Alain.

'Red habits?' said I. 'That's rather *galant* for monks, isn't it?'

At this, the woman behind the bar chipped in. 'Perhaps it's for the bullfights?'

'That's it,' said Alain, twirling an imaginary cape. 'Toreador monks!' He was a merchant banker from Paris with a nice line in fantasy.

At the highest point of the route to Decazeville stood another small chapel to St Roch. On that baking hot morning its dim interior was an oasis of coolness, and I realised how important these sanctuaries must have been to pilgrims in the days before air-conditioned cafés and cold drinks from the fridge. But the shrines were not simply cool places to linger, or find a bed for the night. They brought a comfort to mediaeval pilgrims which is beyond the comprehension of the modern mind. For true believers, completing the pilgrimage to Santiago de Compostela earned them remission of half their time in purgatory. In addition, they would be entitled to extra deductions for prayers in roadside shrines; and if they were unlucky enough to die, as many did, before they reached the end of their pilgrimage, they would still qualify for their remission, provided they were suitably devout and had visited all the 'places of obligation' along the way. In the days when the clergy preached fire and brimstone, and the torments of hell were depicted in all their grotesque horror in churches the length and breadth of Christendom, the fires of hell and purgatory were as real to believers as the fires in their own hearths at home. So remission was of unimaginable value. As the mediaeval church became more corrupt, pardoners made a fortune out of selling indulgences, deducting the odd day or week from purgatory, depending on the amount of money paid. It was disgust at these 'papal indulgences' which sparked off Martin Luther's Reformation.

This particular statue of St Roch the Pilgrim displayed St James's cockleshells on his cloak and hat, for good value, as well as sporting his usual disgusting thigh. I was joined in my inspection of it by Jan, a Belgian boy from the bunk next to mine in the abbey. He had already walked from Antwerp to Le Puy, starting his journey in mid-May. I sat on the grass outside the chapel and watched him stride purposefully down the hill on his long, lean legs, his blond hair flying in the upland wind, but I soon overtook him as well as my French and Swedish friends. I had met with such good companionship in Conques that, despite the smell of sweaty socks in the dormitory, my stay in the abbey was one of the highlights of my pilgrimage, a positive experience full of spiritual calm, friendship and encouragement.

The newspapers wrote of *les canicules*, the desperately sultry dog days, but I didn't mind them at all. I would much rather be hot than cold. In any case, I had reached a welcome stretch of level plain – a rarity on this journey. In Figeac, I chanced on a hotel run by two cycling brothers, so that Condor had the company of their smart racing bikes in the riverside courtyard. They were amused to hear that I had fused the abbey lights and even more amused when I didn't know the French for my electric boiler and referred to it as my *truc*, the French for 'thingy' (I later learned that the correct word is the cumbersome *thermoplongeur*). They immediately volunteered to repair it for me, and I returned later in the day to find them happily soldering. '*Votre truc!*' they cried, waving my boiler merrily in the air.

My hotel room looked out across the river towards the old town, sleepy now, but at one time a city of such importance that King Philip IV granted it the right to mint its own money in 1302. I got my pilgrim passport stamped in the ancient Hôtel de la Monnaie, now occupied by the tourist office. I had had enough of churches for the time being, so I concentrated on the squares. There was La Place de la Raison (who but the French would name a square after an abstraction?) and the fascinating Place des Écritures, the Square of the Scripts. Jean-Francois Champollion, who deciphered Egyptian hieroglyphics, was born in Figeac, in a house which now contains a fine collection of Egyptian antiquities. The nearby Place des Écritures has a stunning floor of polished basalt, engraved with the writings on the Rosetta Stone, the parallel texts in Greek, Egyptian hieroglyphics and demotic Egyptian, which provided Champollion with his key. It's a brilliantly appropriate memorial, simply and accurately executed – as far as I could judge from the Greek, at least, the only script I could read.

The road from Figeac to Cahors wound through the deep, luxuriant canyon known as the Val du Paradis, cut by the Cele river and much frequented by canoeists. It was hot enough to fry eggs down on the river bank, and I found that my week spent alternately walking uphill and freewheeling down had been poor preparation for 85 km of constant pedalling on the flat. I was glad to wheel into Cahors for the start of my short holiday.

My friend Daphne, who had been deputy headmistress and a much valued colleague when I was head of St Felix School in Southwold, now lived in Tournon d'Agenais. She and her husband, Bryan, had migrated from Suffolk with their greyhound, Luke, and their twitchy cats, Hector and Sukie, to a beautiful grey stone mansion with orchards and a *pigeonnier*. I left my bicycle in Cahors and travelled there by bus. It was an idyllic three days, with tours of the countryside in their car (it takes a week's cycling over mountains to appreciate that particular luxury!), a visit to the Saturday market and drinks with local friends. Our evening swims were followed by a couple of Ricards, an excellent dinner, and half an hour or so of the French two-step beside the pool to the accompaniment of *Le Petit Chaton* on the accordion.

And this was not my only treat. When I got back to Cahors, I found my good friend and travelling companion Heather waiting for me in the Hôtel Terminus. Strangely, this hotel was not named after the nearby railway station. It was built as a sumptuous bourgeois home by a wealthy citizen of Cahors who wanted comfort at the end of his days, the terminus of his life. Sharing the cost of a room, I could go up a few notches in the standard of my accommodation, so we enjoyed his exquisite art nouveau monument and *les menus gastronomiques* in the hotel restaurant, enhanced by the dark velvet Cahors vintage, Château Eugenie, which was the favourite of the tsars of Russia.

'I think Hugh might like this hotel, don't you?' asked Heather. 'He has such grand ideas about accommodation that I never know where to take him. I'm always trying to find suitable places.'

'I think it's a lovely hotel. And he could hardly object to the dinners.'

We did our sightseeing, then Heather hired a bicycle, buying a red baseball cap and some amazing red goggles to go with it. The next day, we set out for Moissac.

Poor Heather! We crossed the powerful fourteenth-century Pont Valentré, which guards the western crossing of the river Lot, its three impregnable towers making it a fortress in its own right. Then we began the ascent of one of the longest, hardest hills on my entire journey. Heather had no chance at all of cycling up it on her first day and, despite my week's practice, I soon had to join her on foot. When we were down by the river Lot, which loops protectively round the city of Cahors on three sides, we could see the motorway striding on its concrete piers across the limestone crags high above our heads. We little realised that we would have to walk right up to it, under the piers, then keep on climbing until the traffic on it turned to dots in an eagle's eye. We were rewarded with a beautiful ride along a gently undulating plateau, following the river Bargelonnette through orchards and fields of sunflowers into Montcuq.

Travelling with Heather always changed my routine. Apart from buying food and essentials, I am a total non-shopper, whereas Heather could shop for England, if not for Europe. We made a purchasing tour of Montcuq, with me tagging along behind, helping to carry Heather's parcels, and spent a pleasant half-hour with Elspeth and Sophie O'Neill, an English mother and daughter, both members of the Confraternity of St James, who run the Chimera Bookshop. Then we were collected in the town centre by Dame Merle Park, the prima ballerina who had been principal of the Royal Ballet School when Heather was a governor there.

Merle and her husband, Sid, spent the summers in their charming little house and garden just outside Montcuq. After lunch, Merle drove us to see the mediaeval frescoes in Rouillac Church and the distinctive iron-beaded, filigree crosses in the churchyard. Sid, meanwhile, stayed at home, listening to music and wearing his grey tabby kitten, Felix, round his neck like a silken collar. He had recently suffered a stroke and found walking difficult.

We had entered duck territory, so they took us out to dinner that evening in a country restaurant, high in the hills, where there was nothing but duck on the menu – an amazing array of duck starters and duck main courses. They stopped just short of duck puddings (ice-creams in duck-shaped moulds?), but they did have duck pictures, duck ornaments on every table and even china duck lavatory-brushes.

We were entertained royally by Merle and Sid. Merle talked of her childhood in Southern Rhodesia, as it was then, where her father was an engine-driver. She had left home young and come over to England to dance. Sid was a solicitor, but his talents didn't stop there. He had trained as a cordon bleu chef, bred Jersey cows and ridgeback pigs, and was generally dotty about animals. His eyes glistened when he talked about his pets and how they 'give all the time'.

It was a happy evening, when we were unaware of the gathering shadows. Sid Bloch died shortly afterwards, and my wonderful friend for forty years, Heather Brigstocke, was mown down by a motorist in Athens as I was writing this account. She has appeared in a number of my books and it is a great sadness to know that she will never star again.

Needless to say, Heather and I made rather a late start the next day, arriving in the bastide hill town of Lauzertes just in time for lunch at the Hôtel du Quercy. A scooped-out melon filled with red berries and liqueur granita was followed by a risotto with wild mushrooms and delicate rings of smoked belly pork, crisply fried. Sophie O'Neill, from the Montcuq bookshop, was married to Frédéric, the young chef who had taken over the hotel at the age of 22. His mother and father, who was a maths teacher and the deputy mayor of Lauzertes, waited at table in the evening, so the hotel was quite a family affair. Sophie came over for a chat as we were tucking into our dinner, our second feast of the day, and brought us a gift of wild-flower postcards painted by her mother, Elspeth.

'This could be another Hugh hotel,' I said.

'Possibly,' said Heather doubtfully. 'The bedrooms are a bit small, though they are well appointed. But he wouldn't like that dingy lino on the stairs.'

'Well, Frédéric says he's doing up the stairs and corridors this winter. Perhaps you should wait till next year. I'm sure Hugh would enjoy the food here.'

'Hugh is good at enjoying his food – as are we.'

'*A tavola non s'invecchia*, as the Italians say. You don't grow old at the table.'

Quercy once belonged to England. It was part of the magnificent dowry – almost one-third of France – which Eleanor of Aquitaine brought to our future King Henry I. We lost it all eventually, but it sometimes seems as if we are reclaiming our heritage, house by house, village by village, as more and more English idyll-seekers buy properties in southwest France. We heard English voices everywhere, whenever we stopped to buy bread or a coffee; and English number-plates flashed maddeningly by as we laboured over the hills between the Lot and the Tarn to reach Moissac. Our room had a splendid view over the river and the nine substantial arches of the Pont Napoleon, but it was the abbey church of St Pierre that we had come to see – where my pilgrim passport qualified us both for half-price admission.

Since the Middle Ages, Moissac Abbey has been one of the most important stops on the road to Compostela, and it is simply stunning. It would take a year to examine the mediaeval carving in detail, and a lifetime to appreciate it fully. We began in the cloisters, completed in 1100, with their 76 alternating single and double marble columns. The marble is worn in places, but fortunately the capitals were carved in a hard grey stone, which has preserved the sharpness of the lively scriptural scenes. Peeping out from the jungle of foliage and animal grotesques, there was Daniel in the lions' den, Noah in his ark, the decapitation of St John the Baptist, fishermen casting their nets on Lake Galilee – all exquisitely incised and rather Byzantine in character.

But for me the abbey's jewel is the south porch, with its magnificent tympanum of Christ in His glory, flanked by angels and the symbols of the Evangelists. Below Him are ranged the 24 Elders of the Book of Revelation (or as many of them as could be crammed into the available space), each one a distinct individual but all gazing up at the Saviour with the same startling eyes. Many of the other biblical characters are portrayed with charming naïveté. I particularly liked the carving of Lazarus in Abraham's bosom, where the aged, long-bearded patriarch nurses little Lazarus, a grown man the size of a baby, on his lap. Below the fan-shaped tympanum, the central supporting pillar is carved with St Paul and the Prophet Jeremiah, he of 'The Lamentations', whose mournful face and lean, sinuous form seem laden with all the sorrows of the world. I saw some wonderful churches along the way of St James, but nothing to compare with that jewel of an abbey at Moissac.

We were drawn back for a second long tour on Sunday morning. Heather had a particular interest in sculpture, and was far more knowledgeable about it than I am, so she treated me to an illuminating walking tutorial. Then she went mad in the market, scooping up two shirts, a basket, jars of soup, olives, aioli, a string of garlic and a miscellany of small glittery objects which caught her magpie's eye. Though highly discriminating in many respects, she could also be an Autolycus, 'a snapper-up of unconsidered trifles'. She had left a large suitcase in Cahors, which was just as well!

Lunch was fruit and a bottle of Badoit water. It helped to dispel the faint liverish headaches lurking after Saturday evening's *menu gastronomique* and get us back into shape for Sunday's. We went into our holiday dinners full of good health and diet resolutions, but our gourmandise always seemed to get the better of us. We egged each other on.

Merle had arranged to pick up Heather and her bicycle, to drive them back to Cahors, so after ten days' good company and an escape from my spartan routine, I mounted my faithful Condor and cycled off along the north bank of the Tarn. I can still see Heather standing in the sunshine by the river, waving until I disappeared into the trees. When the Tarn flowed into the Garonne, I followed the south bank to Auvillar and admired its mathematical oddity – a round mediaeval market-hall in the middle of a triangular square. So far, the morning's ride had been agreeably flat, but then came the Gers.

It is said that of the three great Christian pilgrimages in the Middle Ages, Jerusalem and Rome were significant because of their shrines and the sacred relics they contained, but the pilgrimage to Santiago de Compostela had a different emphasis. Of course, the shrine of St James in the cathedral was important, but the main point of the Way of St James was the journey itself. A true pilgrimage is a long, arduous struggle across difficult and some-times dangerous terrain; so much so, that the pilgrimage to Compostela was sometimes offered to mediaeval wrong-doers as an alternative to a spell in prison. In fact, I understand that the Belgians offered that choice to convicted criminals until the end of the nineteenth century.

Pilgrimage, in all religions, is such a powerful experience that it has come to stand as a metaphor for human life itself – life's journey, with all its hardships and temptations. The laboured, mechanical setting of one foot in front of the other, day after day, with blisters, sunburn and doubtful accommodation, becomes such an all-absorbing effort that the mind is emptied of its usual trivial concerns. The sheltering structures of habit are swept away and we have nowhere to hide from the eternal questions. Santiago de Compostela is remote enough and the road sufficiently hard to provide the required elements of endurance and danger. It is such a challenging, and therefore such a supremely satisfying road, that the pilgrimage along it has maintained a continuum from the Dark Ages through the wars in Europe, through the Reconquest of Spain, through the Reformation (which denounced pilgrimage and the worship of relics), through flood, famine and natural disaster to the present day. At times in the past, the movement of pilgrims has dwindled to a trickle, but there has been a boom in recent years.

Even in a secular age, the trials of this particular Way seem to satisfy some deep longing, some need to test ourselves, to prove that we can manage outside our safe little cocoons and meet harsh challenges, relying on our own resources. The movement of pilgrims along the Way of St James has swelled again to a tide, a mighty river, in which we are all no more than droplets, tiny spherules of an unbroken historical and religious tradition.

I might not be struggling along the way myself on blistered feet, but cycling it was no doddle either. It was not a journey for the idle or unfit. I had conquered the mountains of the Massif Central, mostly by walking up them. Now I had to tackle the relentless Gers. It was beautiful country, a delight to the eye with its golden corn, brilliant yellow sunflowers and vine-covered slopes. But it undulated at just the wrong gradients. The cliffs of the Lot and Tarn were short and vertical, and I had strolled up them with a clear conscience, enjoying the coolness of the wooded gorges. But the hills of the Gers were longer and more exposed. The ascents were too steep for comfort, but not steep enough to justify walking; and the sunflowers and vines, though pretty to look at, offered no shade at all. The sun beat down on my head as I toiled up one slope after another, with never quite enough speed on the descent to carry me up the next incline. And between the undulations were a few really serious climbs – to historic hill towns like Flamarens, Lectoure, Condom (famous for its Armagnac) and Larresingle. In many ways, the Gers was a more gruelling ride than the mountains of the Auvergne – and my self-indulgent holiday had squandered the fitness I had gained in that first week. It was a stretch of country where I ended my days too shattered to eat. A few nectarines, a salad, a *demi ficelle* with ham, or a small pizza and a glass of wine, was all the dinner I could manage before I crashed into bed.

But gradually life improved. The gradients of the hills eased off as I approached Les Landes; and there were morning mists in the valleys, even one or two showers to cool the air. Studying my map over coffee in Aire-sur-l'Adour, I saw that the route ahead snaked its way across 150 km of relatively unpopulated country, where it might be difficult to find accommodation. So I decided to abandon the path I had been following so far from Le Puy and cut across country through Geaune to join the Vézelay route at Hagetmau.

My restful time on the fringes of Les Landes, cruising along the flat through scented pines and sandy heathland, proved to be short-lived. Once over the Adour, whichever route I followed, the ground began to rise again, with steep hills spiking the general incline, which I knew was now leading up to the Pyrenees. But there was one major consolation. I should soon be in Basque country, enjoying a change of diet. I was heartily sick of seeing duck, and nothing but duck, on every menu. And on my last night in duck territory, the restaurant in Sault de Nouailles offered me the ultimate in duckish horror – braised duck hearts as the evening special. I ordered the steak instead, and it was very tough.

I left Sault de Nouailles in thick early-morning fog, along a roller-coaster road which dipped down to one small stream, then climbed over the watershed and down to the next. In Orthez, once the capital of Bearn, I saw the first signs posted in Basque as well as French. The town has the most spectacular mediaeval bridge over the boulder-strewn Gave de Pau. It spans a deep, tumbled gorge, and I paused near the bridge's central gate-tower to watch the tumult of the waters below. My hair and cagoule were still dripping moisture, but as I sprinted out of Orthez to L'Hôpital d'Orion, the sun touched the hilltops and the last shreds of mist dissolved to reveal a magnificent landscape of hills and valleys, some thickly forested and others dotted with beige and white cattle grazing contentedly on rich pastures. Dominating all was my first distant view of the Pyrenees. The small Gothic church in L'Hôpital d'Orion was an important pilgrim sanctuary, but it was closed that morning and the whole village seemed to be asleep, so I climbed the steep hill up from the stream, crossed a ridge of farmyards and Michelin viewpoints, then swept down to Sauveterre de Bearn, one of my favourite French towns. The region goes in for dramatic mediaeval bridges. The one in Sauveterre, like the more famous bridge at Avignon, is wildly picturesque but of no practical use, as only one arch and the gate-house tower remain.

It was still only mid-morning and I had covered a considerable distance. I was obviously getting into shape again after the gastronomic indulgences of Cahors and Moissac. I sat outside a café within sight of the Romanesque church and rewarded myself with a large coffee and a croissant. It was almost a perfect moment, marred only by the racket of the town loudspeakers (an innovation since my last visit), which were bellowing rap for the enjoyment of the tourists. There were loudspeakers in St Palais too, where my hotel overlooked the main square, but these were playing gentle folk music, interrupted from time to time by tourist-office announcements.

The Musee de Bas Navarre et des Chemins de St Jacques in St Palais stamped my pilgrim passport when I called in to watch their slide show on the routes to Santiago. The stamp displayed the nearby Stele de Gibraltar, which was my first stop the next morning.

Gibraltar seemed a bizarre name for a spot in southwest France. It had nothing to do with the Rock of Gibraltar, which takes its name from Jebel-al-Tarik, the Arabic 'Hill of Tarik', and is a natural corruption. The British have never been very skilled at getting their tongues round foreign place names, and have usually changed them into something simpler (I think our most comic corruption is the British sailors' 'Leghorn', for the port of Livorno). But it seems that the Basques are even more inventive than we are. The locals told me that their Gibraltar was a corruption of Mont St Sauveur. Now I know that Basque is a weird and wonderful language, but even so, it seems a twist of the tongue too far to get from the soft and silent consonants of the French Mont St Sauveur to the smart snap of Gibraltar.

But however the Basques came by the name, Gibraltar is a significant point on the Way of St James, as it marks the spot where three of the four main routes converge – the routes from Paris, Vézelay and Le Puy. The modern sculpture, which stands at this dramatic meeting of the ways like a large stone keyhole, is a traditional Basque discoid, engraved with a stylised sun for the living and a moon for the dead, as well as a cockleshell for St James. From its grassy knoll, paths lead off into the distance in four directions, including the long straight onward pull to the summit of Mont St Sauveur. There are some authorities who say that nearby Ostabat, not Gibraltar, is the actual meeting place of the three routes. I was in no position to judge between the arguments, so I cycled through Ostabat too, just to be on the safe side. If it was not the actual junction, today's tiny village was certainly a very important town in the Middle Ages, as its hospitals and inns could accommodate around five thousand pilgrims a night.

I was the only pilgrim at either place that morning, but it was easier in the solitude to imagine the bands of mediaeval penitents, staggering along with their staffs, than it was to picture them in the cities. The Massif Central had been touched in a special way by the pilgrimage. The hard path from Le Puy was the path the pilgrims had trodden through the ages, and I heard the echo of their footsteps across the lonely heights of the Aubrac and deep in the Auvergne gorges. But I had lost those resonances shortly after Conques. They were drowned out, partly by my own social life, and partly by the disturbing waves of holidaymakers, French and foreign, who crammed every sight worth seeing in these attractive regions of southern France. I hoped that tranquility would return once I reached the Pyrenees, restoring the lost space for reflection. And I hoped to find more pilgrims on the way, who would rekindle my sense of purpose and sweep me along with them towards our common goal.

Meanwhile, I joined the mediaeval pilgrims in spirit, as they made their way along the path to the Chapel of St Nicholas at Harambels. They would be treading joyfully, happy to have met up with fresh groups of people to talk to, and feeling considerably safer as members of a larger band. France west of the Rhone had been united under one ruler, and more or less stable, since the time of Louis I (814–840), Charlemagne's successor. This new-found security was the reason why Bishop Gottschalk felt confident about leading his flock on the first pilgrimage from Le Puy to Santiago in 951. But brigands, highway robbers and small-time thieves were still a danger to life and pocket, so no pilgrim ever travelled alone – and the bigger your group, the happier you were. The chapel at Harambels was the first sanctuary they would all visit together after the merging of the three ways at Gibraltar. Showing its age now and a bit ramshackle, it stands in the quiet village, looking more like the neighbouring barns than a place of worship. It is one of the oldest pilgrim churches in Western Europe, mentioned in Ameri Picaud's guidebook, *Liber Sancti Jacobi* in the *Codex Calix-tinus* of 1149. Inside is a statue of St James, dressed as a Compostela pilgrim.

After Harambels, I had to rejoin the main road as far as St-Jean-le-Vieux. An artless wayside cross, with the unpronounce-able name of La Croix de Galzetaburu, marked a junction where pilgrims from numerous country paths joined the main flow (I was told that Galzetaburu was Basque for 'head of the road', but it looked to me like another variation of Gibraltar). Shortly afterwards, I branched off along the walkers' route through La Magdeleine. I made no notes at the time, but I have a lingering memory of shady trees and a stream, and the relief I felt at escaping the busy, sun-hammered highway.

At last, I climbed up to St-Jean-Pied-de-Port, entered the citadel through the pilgrims' Porte St Jacques and wheeled my bicycle over the cobbles of the ancient Chemin St Jacques. So far, my journey had been half pilgrimage, half holiday – an extremely leisurely 725 km in four weeks. Now the serious phase was beginning. I had arrived at the foot of the *port,* or pass, where the pilgrims rested before their dangerous crossing of the Pyrenees.

THE PASS OF RONCESVALLES

Cumpainz Rollant, sunez vostre olifan,
Si l'orrat Carles, ki est as porz passant,
Ne placet Deu, co li respunt Rollant,
Que co seit dit de nul hume vivant,
Ne pur paien, que ja seie cornant!

(Roland, my comrade, sound your horn. Charles will hear it, going through the pass. Roland replied, God forbid! Let no man living say of me that I sounded the alarm because I was afraid of pagans)

La Chanson de Roland (c 1100)

St-Jean-Pied-de-Port was full of singing, dancing, bagpipe-playing Basques, the men in white with red sashes and the women in multicoloured swirly skirts, predominantly red. Guidebooks, of whatever country, have pictures of merry locals dancing in traditional costumes; but in all my travels, I had never seen such people in the flesh until I arrived in the Basque Country. Basques were dancing in the square in St Palais; and in St Jean they were dancing down the middle of the streets, causing traffic chaos. Centuries ago, Voltaire said: '*Les Basques sont un petit peuple qui saute et danse au sommet des Pyrénées.*' Nothing had changed. The little people were still leaping and dancing, looking rather silly, like Morris dancers. And the French holidaymakers looked even sillier, decked out in cartwheel Basque berets and sashes from the market stalls. The French like to enter into the spirit of things. I remember a planeful of men in kilts, sporrans and tam o'shanters, whom I took for a Barmy Army of Scottish football supporters returning from a match. They turned out to be a group of Frenchmen, kitted out for a coach tour of Scotland!

My hotel had a party of twenty Belgians, cycling to Santiago with a mechanic in a support vehicle. The Basque in reception, whose French was as awkward as mine, told me they were doing the pilgrimage from Brussels in two weeks. Cycling was popular with the Belgians, while the Germans tended to go on foot, he said. At last, I was meeting some other pilgrims again, particularly in the church, where a forest of candles glimmered in the gloom, representing prayers for safe passage. And I saw others, when I climbed the winding cobbled streets of the old city to visit the

Pilgrim Reception Centre at the Societé des Amis de Saint-Jacques, the French equivalent of our Confraternity of St James. There I signed the register and bought their own *Carnet de Pèlerin* or *Credencial del Peregrino*, partly to be on the safe side (just in case my English document was not recognised in rural Spain) and partly to help their funds. 'The Path of St James is the path of liberty,' they told me as they stamped both pilgrim passports. I hoped they were right.

It was time for my weekly 'day off', and I liked St Jean so much that I decided to spend the weekend there. I had my dérailleur realigned and my brakes tightened in preparation for the mountains, failed to get money from the out-of-service ATMs and enjoyed the Basque cuisine. Many of Spain's most famous chefs hail from the region, where fresh ingredients are combined with imagination. Chicken or pork with onions, tomatoes, sweet red peppers, olives and herbs were such a relief after the endless duck of southwest France. And then there were eggs and ham in a spicy cheese sauce; and sea bream and squid, salt-water fish, so tasty after weeks of inland trout. I was usually unadventurous and stuck to Irouleguy wine, as I could just about manage to get my tongue round the name. The rest of the wine list was difficult even to read, let alone pronounce. How would I ask for a bottle of *txakoli*? Basque, or Euskera, is that rarity in Western Europe, a language outside the Indo-European family. I had no mnemonic or pronunciative pegs to hang my words on.

The origin of Euskera is as mysterious as the origin of its people, who are proud to say that they have never been conquered, not even by the Romans or the Moors. They straddle the Pyrenees from the French region of Pyrénées-Atlantiques to the Spanish provinces of Navarra, Guipuzcoa, Vazcaya and Alava (more Euskera names!). Ameri Picaud described them in his twelfth-century guidebook as a barbarous people, whose speech was like the barking of dogs – but then he was rather a grumpy monk, with a low opinion of everyone, French, Basque or Spanish, who was not from his native Loire. Parthenay-le-Vieux was the centre of his universe and the yardstick against which all people and places were measured and found wanting. In fact, I thought the Basques were kind and very jolly, even if I couldn't cope with their arcane language.

This will be my last mention of Ameri Picaud and his *Liber Sancti Jacobi* or *Codex Callixtinus*, as other writers who have made the pilgrimage along the Way of St James have kept him in their backpacks and followed him on their travels. He is often referred to as the first travel writer ever, but classicists know better. Herodotus, the Father of History, wrote his guidebook to Egypt fifteen hundred years before Picaud; and Pausanias was the original Mr Lonely Planet, with his detailed, practical guides for Romans who wished to visit the antiquities of Greece. Compared with these, Ameri Picaud was a late-comer, though his prejudices make him an amusing companion.

The day dawned bright for my ascent of the green mountains. I was off to the fabled Roncesvalles, to the pass where Roland fell, sounding his horn in vain. His heroic death, along with the massacre of all his paladins, became the stuff of legend, the source of one of the earliest *chansons de geste*, the *Song of Roland*. The event is well chronicled. Around 777, when the Muslims were firmly established in Spain, Charlemagne led an army there, to serve as mercenaries in a war between rival Moorish princes. It was not a particularly successful campaign, so Charlemagne decided to cut his losses and make for home in France. As his army was crossing the Pyrenees in August 778, the Basques swept down from the surrounding mountains to the Pass of Roncesvalles, where they ambushed the rearguard, led by Roland, Lord of the Breton Marches. It was a revenge attack for the sacking of the Basque city of Pamplona by Charlemagne's marauding army. The tale was far from glorious, but it was taken up by wandering minstrels and embroidered. What began as a straightforward military defeat – well deserved, some might say – blossomed into a legend of Christian knightly chivalry. In the minstrels' song, the Basques became dastardly Moors and Roland grew enormously in size and acquired a magic sword, Durandel. At first, he was too proud to sound the alarm, to play the coward in the face of attack by a gang of mere pagans. He and his rearguard fought with amazing valour against overwhelming odds; and when he did finally blow his horn, it was too late. The doleful sound echoed through the pass and Charlemagne galloped back to his aid. But Roland and the flower of Western chivalry lay slaughtered to a man.

In fair weather, walkers over the Pyrenees, and the tougher brand of mountain-biker, can deviate from the tarmac and take the spectacular Route Napoleon, now a rough path through dense forest to the Port de Cize at 1,480 m I had no interest in this route, as I was dreaming of Roland. The road through Valcarlos (the Valley of Charlemagne) was far more to my romantic taste. In any case, main roads are often the oldest, as they follow the line of least resistance, and I felt in my bones that the D933 was the route which the mediaeval pilgrims would have taken. What pilgrim in his right mind would climb to 1,480 m when he could cross the watershed at 1,057 m?

I left St Jean over the river Nive, then pedalled along beside one of its burbling tributaries to the deserted Spanish border post at Valcarlos. It was such an easy ride that I got there long before the banks opened. So, still without cash, I began the climb to the Ibañeta col, expecting a pimple of a pass. But I had been lulled into a false sense of security by the gradual ascent to Valcarlos. A few bends later, the road became a vertical wall with forest on either side. I was soon plodding up the pass, which narrowed at every turn, in no danger of ambush, but pestered by flies and almost buckling in the heat. It took me four hours to reach the col at Ibañeta, where I must have looked as shattered as I felt, because a young Spanish cyclist, who had just sprinted effortlessly up from Pamplona on a day's spin, looked at me in a very worried way and advised me to stop in Roncesvalles for something to eat.

Ibañeta was the most crowded col I had ever seen. Pilgrims who had climbed to the Port de Cize were rushing down to merge with those of us who had taken the easier road, and we all collapsed gratefully into the cool of the modern chapel. The dancing Basques were at it again, leaping and singing round the memorial on the spot where Roland fell. It was a chunk of rough-hewn stone, with an iron Durandel poised behind an iron saltire and two horrendous spiked missiles. The view to the north, back down the densely forested pass, was stupendous, well worth the effort of the climb; and the invigorating breeze across the open grassland explained the crowds of picnicking Spanish families, escaping for the day from the torment of their burning plains. Quite apart from the pilgrims, the spot was such a magnet for summer walkers and holidaymakers in general that I feared for my bed in Roncesvalles.

The village lay just below the col on the Spanish side, and my first view of it was the monastery's higgledy-piggledy zinc roofing, which sloped and toppled at worrying angles round the massive square tower. I had expected something more impressive of this twelfth-century Augustinian foundation; but once I reached ground level, I revised my bird's-eye view. The monastery was almost a town in scale, a magnificent collection of Gothic buildings, part fortress and part church. Failing to get into a hotel, I joined a young German who was reclining on a stone bench in the monastery porch, resting his weary legs. I stretched out on the opposite bench and we dozed together, waiting for the refuge to open at 4 o'clock.

The monastery at Roncesvalles was founded as a hospital to care for pilgrims on the Way of St James, but the monks' welcome was wider than that, if a popular mediaeval song is anything to go by:

> Porta patet omnibus, infirmis et sanis,
> Non solum catholicis verum et paganis.
> Judeis, hereticis, ociosis, vanis,
> Et ut dicam breviter, bonis et profanis.

(The door lies open to everyone, both the sick and the healthy; and not only to Catholics, but even to pagans – to Jews, heretics, the lazy and the feckless. In a word, to everyone, whether good or evil.) The song goes on to praise the treatment that pilgrims receive there. They sleep in soft beds, get nutritious meals, have hot baths, have their beards shaved, their hair cut and their wounds tended. The sick are nursed back to health, no matter how long it takes; and their friends may stay with them. If they die, they are buried in the monastery chapel.

This splendid tradition is maintained, but in a suitably modified way, because the Pass of Roncesvalles no longer presents the same dangers and hardships. There are restaurants in the village and the sick can be sped off in ambulances. But it is still a *refugio*, a refuge from which no pilgrim is turned away.

By the time the doors opened, there was a great crowd of us waiting to gain admittance, so the wardens were strict about credentials. No pilgrim passport, no bed. We were led down stone corridors to one of the oldest parts of the complex, where flights of rickety oak stairs led up to our dormitories, right under the zinc roof. A kind Brazilian boy carried my panniers. There were far too many of us for the available bunks, so women and families were given priority. The rest were told to lay their sleeping mats wherever they could find a space.

I attended evening service in the sombre Gothic church, consecrated in 1219 and modelled on Notre Dame de Paris. The service ended with a special pilgrim blessing. It was a moving experience and I felt privileged to be there – a tiny, insignificant speck in a twelve-hundred-year tradition. I tried to put myself into the shoes of those mediaeval strugglers up the pass, for whom the monastery was not just a shining beacon of security in a dangerous world, but a place of profound devotion. For in an age when relics were worshipped with fervour, the monastery held the most potent of them all, fragments of the True Cross. The reliquary is now called 'Charlemagne's Chess Set', because the fragments lie in an enamelled box inlaid to resemble a chessboard, with crystal lights revealing the pieces of the True Cross beneath. To die while worshipping such a relic would be a guarantee of paradise. The modern mind is overawed by such towering faith.

Fresh batches of pilgrims kept arriving throughout the evening. The refectory these days is for monks only, so I had to pad round the village until I found a restaurant which would accept credit cards. By the time I got back to the monastery, I could scarcely pick my way through the mass of sleeping bodies on the floor. There was no bed-linen, and the three-tier bunks were well below the standard of comfort so warmly praised in the mediaeval song, but there was hot water and laundry facilities. And it was all offered free of charge (donations gratefully received): another generous aspect of the tradition.

The man in the bunk above me tossed and snored all night. I could see why his wife shared her bunk with the children. If the man belonged to me, he would never have got as far as Roncesvalles – he would have been strangled years ago! There was no possibility of sleep, so I was happy to get up with the walkers at 5.30. I packed my panniers by torchlight and we all crept out of the silent monastery. The village cafés were still closed. I cycled off towards Pamplona, stopping to unpack my cagoule for warmth in the dark, cold dawn. There was a bitter wind and I was pining for my morning coffee, but everything was shut fast until I reached the Erro junction and saw a welcoming light. But disaster struck! I still had no cash, and the café refused my cards.

I was saved by a fellow pilgrim, a French boy who was also on a bicycle. He held out a few coins, and when I hesitated, he said, 'Go on. Take them. Buy yourself some breakfast. You won't be able to pay me back, but pass the money on to someone else who needs it.'

I was now on the Camino Frances (the French Way), the ancient route from France across northern Spain to Santiago de Compostela. The red GR 65 signs, which I had followed from Le Puy to the border, were now replaced by the dazzling blue and yellow signposts of the Camino de Santiago, or Donejakue Bidea in Basque, emblazoned with the stylised scallop-shell of St James and the European ring of stars. They announced that my route was a European Cultural Itinerary. Cyclists followed the roads, while walkers and the occasional horseman followed the yellow arrows along paths too rough for bikes, but we were all heading in the same direction, hundreds of us, both the living and the souls of the dead who had died along the way. I was just one fish in a great shoal, where fellow pilgrims, like the boy in the café, could be counted on for help, and the people I passed on the road would often say 'Pray for me in Santiago!' It was everything I had hoped for. I was now embraced in a community of purpose.

I finally managed to change some money in a bank in Zubiri. 'Robin Hood!' said the teller, when he spotted my Nottingham origin in my passport. There were two cols between Roncesvalles and Pamplona, but they were doddles after yesterday's climb, and I was soon cruising through grim industrial suburbs. The Confraternity's booklet directed me, street by street, along the camino to the heart of Pamplona, the capital of Navarre and birthplace of St Ignatius of Loyola, the founder of the Jesuit Order. My pilgrim route led inevitably to the cathedral, but it was closed until 6 o'clock. I was to find these Spanish siestas a great problem. In France, it was easy to visit the churches along the way; but in Spain, when I was simply passing through a town, I often missed a fine church and failed to get my pilgrim passports stamped. In Pamplona, a major halt along the camino, I decided to try the city hall. It was such a magnificent sixteenth-century edifice that I hesitated on the threshold, afraid that the liveried flunkies would chase me off in my dusty, disreputable state. But I took heart at the message engraved over the portals: 'These doors are open to everyone.' And so they were. The desk staff were pleased to stamp my passports. 'Pray for us in Santiago!'

Pamplona was a gracious city, but suffocating in the August heat, so I followed the Confraternity's directions to the outskirts and treated myself to a very smart, air-conditioned hotel. After the effort of the pass and the night in a monastery bunk, I felt I deserved it.

THE PLAINS OF SPAIN

There's no discouragement
Shall make him once relent
His first avow'd intent
To be a pilgrim.

John Bunyan

From my bedroom window, I could see forty wind turbines striding majestically along a bleak western ridge. They were whirling away, far off in the distance, and I never dreamed that I should have to climb right up to them. In England, we tend to be rather disgruntled about wind turbines, seeing more minuses than pluses in this clean, renewable source of energy. But in Spain they are proud of their wind farms, calling them by the delightful classical name of 'aeolian parks' (Aeolus being the god of the winds). This particular procession was 'El Parque Eolico del Perdón', with a welcoming visitors' centre and café.

It was a long pull up to the ridge, the Alto del Perdón, along an undulating road, but the gradients were gentler than the monstrosities in France. I could stay in the saddle all the way up, without too much effort – and then there was the magic of the long runs down, when the wheels spun faster and faster, yet I felt so safe on the broad hard shoulder that I rarely had to apply the brakes. I sped like the wind. Aeolus had nothing on me!

Down a dusty path across harvested grain fields, I made a detour to visit the lovely little Romanesque chapel at Eunate. Modelled on the Church of the Holy Sepulchre in Jerusalem, it stood peacefully in the middle of nowhere, its sturdy hexagonal walls surrounded by a cool arcade and capped with a lantern of the dead. It was a pilgrim hospital and burial chapel. There was a romantic melancholy about the place, and I was lucky to be able to appreciate it in silence that morning. My previous visit, when I was cycling the Vézelay route with my friends Diana and Francis, had been blighted by a succession of noisy Spanish coach parties.

One more hill to climb, then I swooped down to Puente la Reina on the river Arga. There a bronze pilgrim, traditionally clad and cockleshelled, with his staff in his hand, marks the spot where the route over the Somport Pass from Arles joins up with the other three. *'Y desde aqui todos los caminos a Santiago se hacen uno solo'* (From now on, all the paths to Santiago merge into one), said the inscription. I wheeled my bicycle across the elegant pilgrim bridge built by an eleventh-century queen of Navarre and sped across the rolling acres of her realm to the Monastery of Irache.

All the way across Spain there are fountains, constructed by the charitable, to provide fresh water for the parched throats of pilgrims. But a vintner in Irache had an even more generous idea. He built a wine fountain. In a small courtyard just below the monastery, two cockleshell taps dispense streams of glowing ruby, under the smiling gaze of a stone pilgrim in a niche. It was quite a palatable Navarrese wine, but I still had a long ride ahead of me and the midday sun was fierce. Dehydration loomed, so I took only a taste. A notice beside the fountain said that pilgrims were very welcome to refresh themselves, but without abusing the gift. If they wanted to take wine away with them, they should buy it at the company's bodega nearby. It seems that even pilgrims can be freeloaders.

I reached Los Arcos in the early afternoon, had a beer and a sandwich in the bar, then retired gratefully to my bed for a three-hour siesta. I never sleep in the afternoons at home, but I can always drop off in the Spanish heat. Everything is shut fast, except the bars – and even there the bartenders drowse over their deserted counters. I read for a while, then drift off with ease, totally relaxed because I know that no one will be ringing on my doorbell or disturbing me with a telephone call. The Spaniards are all asleep; I never carry a mobile; and no one at home has the faintest idea of my address. I am wonderfully, blissfully free.

The Hotel Monaco, where Diana once broke a tooth on an olive pit, was one of the many hotels along the Camino which provided special half-price meals for pilgrims. The portions were so generous that my pile of green lentils, meat-balls, chips, bread, half a cantaloupe melon and a carafe of rosé sent me staggering round the streets that evening to work it off. Los Arcos was a very traditional small Spanish town. The men were drinking in the bars, or sitting in taciturn groups on benches under the trees; the boys were whizzing around on mountain bikes or playing football in the plaza. There was not a female to be seen. I eventually found the women and girls in the outer residential streets. They were standing in their doorways, dressed to kill and chatting with their neighbours. Some had brought out a chair to work at their crochet while keeping an eye on their toddlers. Apart from the pilgrims, there were no mixed groups. The church was decorated for a wedding, so presumably young people had some way of meeting the opposite sex, but when and where was a mystery. The only couple I saw that evening was a couple of storks, clattering their beaks at each other in their nest on the church lantern. It was my last night in Navarre. Early next morning, in Logroño, I entered the rich wine-growing region of La Rioja and turned south to Clavijo for my first rendezvous with St James.

In the early eighth century, the Berber Muslims of North Africa swept across the Straits of Gibraltar and conquered Spain, proclaiming the sovereignty of the Caliph of Damascus in Toledo in 713. They met with little resistance, because they were, on the whole, more cultured and tolerant than their Gothic predecessors, and less keen on pillage. The Spaniards were allowed to practise their own religion and keep most of their own possessions, without having to pay the hefty tribute previously demanded of them. For centuries, the majority were content, trade and scholarship flourished and the country's wealth was poured into the foundation of universities and the building of architectural wonders in Cordoba, Granada and Seville. Under the Moors, Spain reached glittering heights of civilisation, while the rest of Europe languished in the gloom and superstition of the Dark Ages. So superior were the Muslims of Spain that their progress seemed unstoppable. Under Abd ar-Rahman, they poured into France over the Pass of Roncesvalles, captured Bordeaux and swept north. The squabbling Franks were forced to unite in self-defence and their combined armies, under Charles Martel, routed the Moors at the Battle of Poitiers (732). Christianity in Western Europe had come through by the skin of its teeth.

Their victory at Poitiers reinvigorated the Christians. With the help of Charlemagne, they recaptured Pamplona and Lisbon. Galicia and León followed Asturias, forming a belt of Christian resistance in the mountains of northern Spain. Then the miracle occurred. A hermit by the name of Pelagro noticed a great star one night, surrounded by a cluster of smaller stars, which seemed to be leading him to a particular spot in Galicia. When it was excavated, on Sunday, 25 July 813, a stone sarcophagus was found, containing a body and a severed head. It was obviously St James, whose martyred remains had been hidden 800 years ago and subsequently lost. King Alfonso of Asturias, one of the militant Christian rulers, rushed to the spot and built the first shrine there, the Church of St James, or Santiago, at Compostela. There is a fanciful derivation of the name. Compostela is said to mean 'the field of stars', after the sign which pointed to the holy relics. I wish I could accept this delightful suggestion, but as a Classicist, I find it hard to swallow. I cannot see *campus stellarum* contorting its vowels and slipping its consonants to form 'compostela'. I fear that the name might well derive more prosaically from the Latin *composita*, things which have been interred, particularly as excavations under the cathedral in the 1940s uncovered a Roman necropolis.

However that may be, news of the rediscovery of St James spread like wildfire throughout Christendom. Charlemagne was one of the first pilgrims to his shrine, to be followed by bands of knights, inspired by the miracle to carry arms for the Christian kings of northern Spain. Then, to crown all, St James himself awoke from his long sleep.

For many years, an annual tribute of one hundred virgins had been paid by the kings of Asturias to the caliph in Cordoba. In 844, Ramiro I rebelled. He gathered his forces on the plain below the citadel of Clavijo and fought a desperate battle with the Moors. The Christian army was outnumbered and just about to capitulate when St James himself appeared on a white charger, leading the heavenly hosts into battle. He carried a white banner emblazoned with his red swordlike cross and cried '*Santiago – y cierra España!*' (St James – and close up Spain!) Wielding his mighty sword, the saint personally slaughtered 70,000 Moors that day, earning for himself the title of Santiago Matamoros (St James the Moor-slayer). His prowess established him as the patron saint of Spain, and the long, slow Reconquest continued. At the time of the crusades, Spanish knights were forbidden to travel to the Holy Land, as their paramount duty was the defeat of the Moors at home; and knights from other parts of Christendom were entitled to the same indulgences for fighting in Spain as crusaders in the Middle East.

Spain was finally closed to the Moors in 1492, when the Catholic Monarchs Ferdinand and Isabella rode in triumph into Granada, the last city to be freed. Later that year, their protégé Columbus sailed out of the port of Palos to discover the New World, and Spain's great age of empire began. The Reconquest had taken more than 600 years – and it started with St James on the battlefield of Clavijo.

Statues of Santiago Matamoros can be found in churches throughout Spain. The triumphant saint brandishes his sword while his horse tramples on the beheaded corpses of his Moorish foes. *Rubet ensis sangine arabum* (The sword is red with the blood of Arabs). For some years, this ferocious image of St James has been an embarrassment to liberal churchmen; and more recently, in the heightened tension between Christians and Muslims throughout the world, Santiago Matamoros has come to be perceived as a downright provocation. In the wake of the 2004 train bombing, when Islamic terrorists killed 190 people in Madrid, the cathedral authorities in Santiago de Compostela decided to transfer their statue of Santiago Matamoros from its chapel to a museum and replace it with another image of the gentler Santiago Peregrino. According to the leading Spanish newspaper *El Mundo*, they feared that 'the expressive image' could attract the anger of the Arab world: 'The pilgrim apostle is a universal image, whereas the other sculpture was related to a historic epoch and very particular circumstances.' As the basilica receives visits from people of various traditions, they wished to avoid a situation in which 'persons of other cultures felt offended'. To the anger of traditionalists, political correctness – and perhaps half an eye for tourism – has won the day.

I visited Clavijo on a cool, overcast morning, when cycling was a pleasure. I was almost the only visitor prowling round the battlefield in the shadow of the castle, and there was not a great deal to be seen, but I got my usual buzz of excitement. Momentous events leave a tingle in the air, a stirring of ghosts. Whether or not there was a battle there (and some authorities dispute it), and whether or not St James appeared on his charger, Clavijo changed the course of Spanish history, and established the shrine of Santiago de Compostela as a pilgrim destination to rival Rome and Jerusalem.

In Najera, I pedalled back and forth, round and round through twisting alleys, searching in vain for the pantheon of the kings of Navarre, Castile and León. There were plenty of signs to the Convent of Santa Maria la Real, but they always petered out at the last moment, as signs have a nasty habit of doing. I knew it was hiding somewhere at the base of the city's red granite cliff, but my best efforts failed to find it. I gave up. In any case, I was getting to the stage where I had seen so many churches and monasteries that I didn't care if I never saw another one again as long as I lived – and I still had the important pilgrim Cathedral of Santo Domingo de Calzada to 'do' that day.

I love the impressive names the Spaniards give to very modest places. 'Saint Domingo of the Highway' was named after an eleventh-century Benedictine monk who was a great friend to the Compostela pilgrims. He built a refuge, a hospital and a bridge for them, and he paved parts of the way to ease their journey. But tourists are drawn to the town these days chiefly to see the cock and two hens, which are housed in a magnificently ornate cage inside the cathedral as reminders of another miracle of Santiago (or possibly Santo Domingo).

A mediaeval couple and their teenage son were passing through Santo Domingo on their pilgrimage to Compostela. The handsome boy took the fancy of a young woman in the inn. When he spurned her advances, she was so enraged that she planted some silver in his scrip, then accused him of robbery. He was convicted and hanged. His grieving parents continued on their way and made their offerings at the shrine of St James. On the way back (for mediaeval pilgrims had to walk both ways), they passed the gibbet, where their son was hanging. 'Thanks to St James,' said the innocent boy, 'I am still alive.' His parents rushed to the magistrate who had condemned him to death, to tell him of the miracle and ask him to release their son. The magistrate was just about to tuck into his dinner of a capon and two fat hens. 'If your story is true,' he declared, brandishing his carving knife, 'these fowl will leap up and crow!' Which is exactly what they did. The innocent boy was cut down from the gallows and the reunited family of pilgrims went home rejoicing.

The living reminders of the miracle are caged high up in the nave, where their crowing and squawking occasionally interrupts the most sacred moments of the Mass. I was pleased to learn that their caging in the dark cathedral was not a life sentence. The cock and hens are members of a dedicated battery, who work shifts.

The pilgrim hostel built by Santo Domingo is now a parador, one of the chain of historic buildings owned by the state and run as extremely expensive hotels. It is way beyond the means of today's pilgrims, so I joined my fellows in the Hospedería Santa Teresita, a brisk place with the scent of polish on gleaming tiles, run by nuns, partly as a modest hotel for pilgrims and partly as an old people's home. It's a combination which works really well, as the old people enjoy seeing new, younger faces and having the stimulus of conversation with outsiders. The Hospedería was a living community, not some sort of a ghetto where the aged were hidden from sight in a television room with the same somnolent group for company, day after day.

As I climbed over the wooded Montes de Oca (the Goose Mountains) and cruised down the long descent to Burgos on the Rio Arianzón, I felt the adrenalin surge of my first major city. I am never so happy as when I leave tedious arable land and find myself strolling down tree-lined boulevards of shops, with architectural gems on every corner. Burgos has a particularly fine promenade along the river, where the outdoor cafés are the focus of the city's social life. Inevitably, the exterior of the cathedral was under scaffolding; and I regretted the Spanish practice of boxing in the choir and high altar, which in Burgos meant that I lost the full sweep of the austere Gothic nave, viewed from the west end. But I saw the tomb of Rodrigo Diaz, the great 'El Cid', in the transept crossing. A native of Burgos and second only to Santiago Matamoros in the slaying of Moors, his black equestrian statue also dominates one of the city's bridges. It is a grand portrayal of the warrior, with his mighty sword, 'La Tizona', raised and his cloak flying in the wind, but I was disappointed at his long patriarchal beard. I had always imagined him as a dashing knight in his prime. His prancing steed, Babieca, came up to expectations, though, being suitably huge and mettlesome.

The porter at the Hospedería Santa Teresita had recommended a hotel near the cathedral, which catered for pilgrims and Spanish Darby-and-Joan clubs on their holidays. The restaurants in town didn't open their doors until about 10 o'clock, so I shopped for a picnic supper of ham, cheese, tomatoes, fruit and wine, which I enjoyed in my hotel room while the intense heat of the last few days erupted in a violent storm. There was a dazzling display of electrics, but little rain to cool the air.

The lateness of the dinners in Spain was one of my greatest problems. After a demanding day's cycling, I was too hungry to wait until 9.30 or 10 for my main meal, and too tired to digest the food if I did, because Spaniards seem to have no dishes which don't involve frying in oceans of fat. If you robbed them of their frying-pans, they would suffer total culinary breakdown. As hanging around, staving off famine with a hunk of bread and a portion of La Vache qui Rit processed cheese, while waiting for a heavy 10 p.m. fry-up, is not my idea of a pleasant evening, I often went in for picnics, or an early visit to a bar for a meal of tapas and a *bocadillo* – usually a giant submarine stuffed with tuna or cheese, which was almost as indigestible as the fried dinners. Spain is not gastronomic heaven, which is a pity, as dinner is normally the highlight of my travelling day.

But Burgos was a gracious city, as befits the ancient capital of Castile (and the capital of Franco's Spain for two years after the Civil War), so I forgave its culinary shortcomings. I took a day off from cycling and strolled along the elegant Paseo del Espolon, catching up on my correspondence at café tables and watching kingfishers watching frogs in the Rio Arianzón's reed beds. Sated with churches, I visited only one monastery, the former summer palace of the kings of Castile, now the Monasterio de las Huelgas, founded by the Cistercians to house a hundred nuns of noble birth. The Chapel of Santiago was said to have a very special statue of the saint with an articulated right arm, which could be moved to dub knights of the Order of Santiago and even to crown kings of Castile on occasion. But the chapel was closed for restoration. Travellers' luck again!

When I cycled away from Burgos it was spitting rain, but I was sheltered by an avenue of plane trees. Then it cleared to a fabulous day. Blue sky, sun and a slight breeze from the west, enough to cool the face without impeding motion – that was the morning. By noon the air was trembling in a heat haze and objects were shifting in and out of focus. I had left the red soil of La Rioja behind me and entered the province of Castilla-León, a landscape of white chalk outcrops among endless fields of blond stubble. The paleness was blinding, an ocean of white gold, with nothing to serve as a landmark except a rare church tower in the far distance or a wavering line of emerald along the bed of an invisible stream. As the hours ticked by and the horizon melted in a blurred intensity, I felt I was losing my moorings, becoming somehow disconnected from reality. I was alone in that pale, infinite space, empty of everything but my thoughts. I had reached the floating, almost disembodied state where saints see visions.

So this was pilgrimage. And if I had discovered transendence at the speed of a bicycle, what must be the experience of walkers who would take a whole week to cross this shimmering, remorseless landscape before they caught their first glimpse of the towers of León? Spain is a vast, empty country, the last remaining wilderness in Europe.

My own ride from Burgos to León took two and a bit days, with overnight stops at Carrión de los Condes and Mansilla de las Mulas. Strangely, I met no other pilgrims across this stretch, so with no one to talk to I had ample leisure to think about my own pilgrimage and my reasons for making it. At the *refugio* in the Monastery of Roncesvalles, I had been asked to complete a questionnaire. What was the motive for my journey to Compostela? Was it religious, spiritual, cultural, leisure or sport? I could tick as many boxes as I liked, so I ticked the first three. With all those hills and mountains to climb, cycling to Compostela was definitely not a leisure activity; and I've always hated sports. Of the three I ticked, culture was easy, because the Way of St James is lined with the most stunning ecclesiastical architecture, and I like nothing better than a nice prowl around a Gothic cathedral or a drool over Romanesque carving. But what about religious and spiritual?

At this point, I suppose I should come clean and confess that I am not a practising Christian. In my years of travelling, I have been welcomed by people of many religions and have come to see the positive side of their faith, whether it be Islam, Buddhism, Hinduism or Zoroastrianism, as well as Christianity. I can no longer accept that there is just one vision of God and creation, one divine revelation suitable for all men. 'There are many paths up the mountain, but we are all striving towards the same summit.' In Pakistan, on the northwest frontier, a massive outcrop on the main road through the Hindu Kush from Afghanistan is engraved with the Edicts of Ashoka, the warrior king who is thought to have reigned from 256–238 BC. After years of fighting to extend his empire across northern India, he converted to Buddhism and renounced his bloodthirsty ways. He confessed his wrong-doing. He said that he had sought to bring peace through war, but had instead inflicted only misery, death and destruction on hundreds of thousands of innocent people. One of his edicts reads: 'Never think or say that your own religion is the best. Never denounce the religion of others.' More than two millennia have passed since those edicts were formulated, yet we are still fighting wars to impose our own beliefs, both religious and political, on other nations. We have still not learned the lessons of Ashoka.

I am not sure that I understand the difference between 'religious' and 'spiritual'. I was not on the way to Compostela in order to pray at the shrine of St James, to ask a boon, give thanks to the saint, or repent of my sins, so my pilgrimage was not religious in the accepted sense of any religion I know. But I was trying to read the route with mediaeval eyes, to discover its profound significance for committed Christians. Was this a religious, a spiritual or an intellectual exercise? I found no answers, but I did create a quiet space around myself and a freedom from mundane preoccupations, when I at least had time to formulate the questions. I was embraced in the devotion of the Middle Ages, in the beauty of its architecture and liturgy, and the warmth of my fellow pilgrims. It was a journey of reflection, a joyful, completely satisfying, otherworldly experience, quite different from any cycle ride I had previously undertaken.

In the Hindu Vedas, the earliest Sanskrit hymns, the feet of the pilgrim are described as 'flower-like'. The pilgrim's sins are said to disappear, 'slain by the toil of his journeying'. Or, in a more modern poem by Swami Vivekenanda:

The water is pure that flows,
The monk is pure who goes.

As I cycled along, I did not have the faith to believe that my sins were being slain, but I at least gained the clarity of vision to recognise them.

I am fearful of the Camino's boom in popularity. When I see it advertised in holiday brochures as one of the 'must-do' long walks or mountain-bike challenges of Europe, I am saddened by the inevitable loss of its unique quality. Can these cross-country fiends not test out their muscles and will power on other difficult tracks? Can the carloads of tourists not see that there is an element of desecration in their well-fed, air-conditioned progress from one parador to the next? It will be a sad day if the Camino becomes totally commercialised and secular.

Of course, even in mediaeval times, there were Santiago pilgrims whose purpose was not entirely religious. The Romans invented holidays, but the art of holidaymaking was lost with the fall of Rome. There were no more summers in seaside villas, no more cultural tours of the Greek ruins, or trips undertaken just for the fun of them. With the collapse of the Pax Romana, the roads became far too dangerous for non-essential journeys. If you wanted to see something of the world in the Dark Ages, your only protection against brigands, cut-throats and miscreants generally was to sign up with a group for a pilgrimage. The Wife of Bath, who went 'Thrice to Jerusalem, at Rome, at Boloyne and in Galice at Seynt Jame', comes across in Chaucer's *Canterbury Tales* as quite a gadabout. I can see her today – a regular customer of Saga Holidays, travelling the Way of St James in a coach and taking Mediterranean cruises to Rome and the Holy Land. She would still have safety in numbers, but she would no longer have to justify her jaunts on holy grounds.

Carrión de los Condes, where I spent my first night out of Burgos, is a small town with almost as many churches and monasteries as people. But its chief claim to fame lies in its centuries-old connection with El Cid. One of the counts of Carrión de los Condes, who were powerful rulers in those days, arranged for the marriage of his sons to El Cid's daughters. These callow youths made the grave mistake of ill-treating their brides, for which El Cid wreaked terrible vengeance, not only on them but upon their entire family. His rival in slaughter, Santiago Matamoros, has a blood-curdling statue in the former Church of Santiago, now a museum. The curator was clearly embarrassed, more or less apologising for it as she led me swiftly by, eyes averted. 'We prefer to think of Santiago as the pilgrim saint,' she said, 'bringing peace and brotherhood.'

With no diversions across the endless, undulating plain, I was covering something like 100 km a day, which meant that I spent my next night in Mansilla de las Mulas, just short of the city of León. It was a poky little place, with nothing to see but its crenellated battlements. But it sticks in my mind because I laid out everything I needed for the night on my spare bed, then sat down on the foot of it. The bed tipped up, hurling its contents on to the floor. One of the items was a silly Pyrex mug, which had enchanted both Heather and me in a French supermarket. It had a flock of little woolly white lambs jumping about on a bright green meadow, under the sort of trees and blue sky that children draw. As a non-shopper, I can be absolutely ravished by things I see on the shelves, but quite happy to leave them there, whereas Heather always had to buy them. I tried to dissuade her, without success, and every evening she drank her pre-dinner whisky, looking defiantly at me over the top of this ridiculous mug. But my scorn soon changed to gratitude, because I accidentally left my own travel mug behind in Lauzerte, so Heather passed the gambolling lambs on to me when we parted in Moissac. When the mug crashed on to the tiles, its heat-proof glass shattered into a million crystals which swept across the floor, covering it completely, like frozen rain. By that time, the idiotic mug had become my very favourite possession and I was devastated to lose it.

Mugs seemed difficult to find in León, and I spent half the afternoon tracking down a replacement, having spent most of the morning searching for a hotel with a vacant room. I ended up with art nouveau lilies on white china and a bed in a back street, where Condor was suspended lovingly from a hook in the cellar, alongside the proprietor's racing bike. Then I set off to León's magnificent Gothic cathedral, where the evening sun was streaming through the massive rose window of the west façade.

The stained glass of León Cathedral is the finest in Spain. It dates back to the thirteenth century, to that glorious period of Gothic architecture when the builders gained such mastery over their materials that they seemed to be working in light and air rather than earthbound matter. Their vaulting structures sprang towards heaven in staggering walls of glass, supported only by the most delicate suggestion of stone tracery. It was the triumph of art and mechanics, harnessed to the glory of God. León's stained glass has been compared to that of Chartres, and the French inspiration is plain to see; but the colours are quintessentially Spanish. Instead of the jewelled reds, blues and purples of France, León's walls of glass explode in bursts of vivid golds and yellows, intensified by the deep amber glow of the setting sun. And to crown all, the dark wood of the boxed-in choir, which broke the majestic sweep of the nave in other Spanish cathedrals, had been replaced in León with a glass screen, so that the light flooded unbroken from the west end down the entire length of the mighty nave to the high altar. The cathedral that evening was one dazzling, blinding display of refracted radiance.

Almost as impressive in its more modest Romanesque fashion was the pantheon of the kings of León and Castile, where the stone carving was on the very cusp of the transition from pure Visigothic foliage to the figured, narrative sculpture emanating from France, which travelled into Spain along the pilgrim way. The building's twelfth-century frescoes were as fresh as when they were painted, and I was pleased to see that the central dome was filled with the positive, joyful image of the Pantocrator, Christ as ruler of the world, sitting on His heavenly throne in glory. I wondered at what period in their history the Spanish became obsessed with cruci-fixion, martyrdom and suffering, those gory aspects of Christianity which produce such dark images in their churches. The early Church accepted martyrdom, but it was the trial through which Christ and His saints passed to achieve glory, and it was that final glory which was celebrated. The later Church, especially in Spain, seems to have drowned in gore, depicting the suffering with almost prurient interest, for its own sake. Some Spanish churches can be positively frightening. Was the ferocious brand of Christianity they exported to the New World a tool for terrifying their benighted subjects into submission?

The vibrant street life of León soon dispelled the brooding. It was a city of elegant shops and cafés, the pleasantest I had met so far in northern Spain. But I was too weary to wander with the Spaniards late into the night, so I cheered myself with a fine dinner, as early as I could find it, and the promise of a short ride next day, just 40 km to Astorga. My 100 km a day across Castile had taken their toll.

Of all the monasteries and refuges along the Way of St James, one of the very grandest was the Monasterio de San Marcos, which I passed just outside León. Built in 1168 for the Order of the

Knights of Santiago, its outside walls are plastered with patterns of raised cockleshells and the main entrance is dominated by one of those statues, so embarrassing to the Spaniards today, of Santiago the Moor-slayer. The arms of the Spanish throne are also in evidence. For the Knights of the Order of Santiago became so powerful that they began to constitute a political threat to the throne, so Queen Isabella came up with the cunning idea that her husband, King Ferdinand, should put himself up for election as Grand Master. Voting duly took place and, not surprisingly, the king was elected. So the power and wealth of the Knights of Santiago came under the control of the Catholic Monarchs. Mediaeval pilgrims would rest in this magnificent building, to get up their strength for the bleak mountains ahead. But inevitably, it has now become another Parador, a hotel for well-heeled travellers, which today's pilgrims find difficult even to visit.

Astorga reminded me of Conques, and I hated it on sight. It looked like a restored, mediaeval theme park inside its Roman walls. It bulged with Spanish tourists, and the only arresting feature was the eccentric episcopal palace, designed by the Catalan architect Antonio Gaudí. So despite my weariness, I pressed on to Murias de Rechivaldo and its refuge.

I was about to cross the mountains of León, La Maragateria and El Bierzo, a high, windswept region of great beauty, where some of the villages are abandoned, and improvident pilgrims who set out without emergency rations can find themselves in difficulties. I checked into the refuge and dumped my gear on the bottom bunk of a pair, where my neighbours were a nonagenarian, doing the pilgrimage with the aid of his walking stick, and four young Polish men. The language we had in common turned out to be French, though we confused one another utterly with the variety of our accents. When I took my pilgrim passport to the undergraduate wardens for stamping, one of the girls drew a little stick pilgrim and a cockleshell beside the name Murias de Rechivaldo, instead of wielding the usual die-stamp.

About 15 km beyond Murias the pilgrim way enters the village of Rabanal del Camino, where Britain's Confraternity of St James of Compostela, together with the local El Bierzo Association, have created a pilgrim refuge, El Refugio Guacelmo, out of the ruins of the parish house opposite the Church of Santa Maria. It is a typical stone-built Maragato house, with a large upstairs dormitory and a shady garden. I rang the doorbell at about 10 a.m. The two English wardens had waved off their overnight pilgrims, cleaned the refuge and were just about to sit down to breakfast on the patio. They invited me to join them for delicious coffee, newly baked bread and jam. Both were teachers, who were fitting in a spell of voluntary refuge-running during their school holidays, and we laughed about some of their trials, such as coping tactfully with loudly snoring pilgrims in the dormitory. I described my cycle ride to date.

'All the way along,' I said, 'I've been relying absolutely on the guides that Alison Raju has produced for the Confraternity – the one from Le Puy to the Pyrenees and the one I'm using now on the Camino Frances, from the Pyrenees to Santiago. They've been my bible. They are absolutely excellent. Thoroughly reliable. By far the most useful books on the route.'

The two wardens started to giggle and one of them pointed to the other. 'She's Alison Raju!'

I was delighted at the coincidence, as I'm sure Alison was too. I had praised those guidebooks to the skies, obviously having no idea that their author was sitting right next to me at the breakfast table. What greater compliment can you pay?

The road was ascending now towards the highest pass on the Camino, and just beyond Rabanal I spotted a familiar figure striding up the mountain. It was Jan, the Belgian boy I had met on a hilltop just outside Conques. He had left Antwerp in May, reached Conques in July and now, only a month later, was already in the Maragateria, only about 170 miles short of Compostela. I caught up with him and dismounted.

'Jan! I'm amazed to find you so far along the road. How on earth have you managed it?'

Jan greeted me warmly enough, but didn't stop walking, so I hurried along on foot beside him. He was desperately thin. His blond hair was bleached white by the sun, contrasting sharply with his weather-beaten face and limbs, which were burned almost black. His faded T-shirt was hanging in shreds and he was striding along in scuffed boots, oblivious to the beauty of the heathland with its profusion of wild flowers and heather. Looking neither to right nor left, his long legs worked mechanically, like pistons. He had become a well-oiled robot.

'I enjoyed France,' he said, 'because of course I can speak French and I made lots of friends in the refuges. We often walked together in groups during the daytime, which was fun. But since I crossed the Pyrenees, I've been really lonely. My Spanish is basic and I find it difficult to make contact with people. In any case, there are such crowds here now, in August, that it's difficult to hear yourself think in some of the refuges, let alone have a sensible conversation. There are gangs of rowdy Spanish students, most of them with no interest at all in the pilgrimage. The refuges are free, or modest in price, so I'm afraid it's just a cheap holiday for them. They're exploiting the charities which provide for genuine pilgrims. I get very angry sometimes. In fact, I'm so fed up, so keen to finish now that I'm walking further and further every day, so I never meet up with the same pilgrims two evenings running. I just can't wait to get to Santiago!'

I sympathised, because my Spanish too was much more basic than my French. I could order my meals and ask the way without difficulty, but what I missed were the jokes. There's so little humour at elementary level. I had been travelling across Spain, immersed in my guidebooks and my solitary thoughts until that very morning, when I had actually had two proper conversations – with the Rabanal wardens and Jan – and even shared a few laughs.

'I shall never travel in a Spanish-speaking country again, until I've improved my grasp of the language,' I said. 'Riding a bicycle alone during the day is one thing. But spending every evening on my own, with no possibility of a friendly exchange, is quite another. Fortunately, my journey across northern Spain will take less time than yours, even though you're going at a phenomenal rate for a walker.'

'The way I feel at the moment,' grunted Jan, 'I never want to speak Spanish or see anything of Spain ever again! I just want to get home.'

We plodded on up the mountain, with me puffing and panting to keep pace with his long mechanical stride. On the crest, he did stop for a moment. We had reached La Cruz de Ferro, the tall Iron Cross, which stands at 1,504 m, just before the summit of the highest pass through the Montes de León, and the highest point of my whole journey. Its soaring perpendicular was rooted in a huge mound of pebbles, because it was the tradition for every passing pilgrim to add a stone. Jan and I scrabbled around in the scrub, found our pebbles, then clambered up to place them on top of the pile. It was probably a *montjoie* in origin, a cairn which the Normans raised after a victory, so that their leader could climb up and be 'King of the Castle' – whence the children's game. They were later used as markers along the road to Compostela. Writing in the early seventeenth century, Samuel Purchas notes that the way was 'marked with *montjoie* from Englande to Saynt Jamez in Galise'. La Cruz de Ferro above Foncebadon is the last survivor.

My climb up to the cross had been almost as slow as Jan's, but Condor now came into his own. The descent was perilously steep. I sped through semi-deserted villages, where the streets were skiddy with cowpats, then steeled my nerves on the stretches between, with their blind bends and potholes. I reached Ponferrada in a flash, whereas Jan was not expecting to arrive until the next afternoon, despite his muscled, robotic legs.

My own rather feebler legs had one more challenge before them in the province of Castilla-León – the climb up to the pass at Pedrafita de Cebreiro on the border with Galicia. It was one of my hardest days ever. The road to Cacabelos was uphill and half-unpaved. Higher up, at Villafranca del Bierzo, I stopped at the Romanesque Church of Santiago. In mediaeval times, pilgrims who were ill or injured could enter this church through the Puerta del Perdon and receive the same pardons and indulgences as they would have received had they been able to continue all the way to Santiago de Compostela. I wondered who decided on the authenticity of their illnesses. Faking it must have been a great temptation.

Beyond Villafranca, I had a choice of route. The guidebooks strongly recommended the old road to the summit; the newer NVI had siphoned off most of the traffic and left the ancient route safe and peaceful for cyclists. Of course, I chose the old road and was very happy with my choice, because it tootled along a shady river valley, while the new NVI climbed the fearsome mountains above. I looked up at it from my agreeably flat road and gloated. But the terrain soon got its revenge. I might have known that my old road would have to join the new one at the pass, and join it up a spectacularly steep five-mile grind. I had to reach the same altitude in half the distance, and I nearly collapsed in the heat. I faded out beside a hotel just two or three miles below the pass, checked in and fell into a stupor on my bed. When the evening cooled, I had a warm bath to relax my aching limbs, but I was still wobbly from the exertion. By the time dinner was served at 10 p.m., all I could manage was a bowl of soup. Perhaps Galicia would be physically kinder.

GALICIA AT LAST

What country has sent you safely back to us, covered with shells, laden with tin and leaden images, and adorned with straw necklaces, while your arms display a row of serpents' eggs?
I have been to St James of Compostella.
What answer did St James give to your professions?
None, but he was seen to smile and nod his head when I offered my presents, and held out to me this imbricated shell.
Why that shell rather than any other kind?
Because the adjacent sea abounds in them.

Erasmus, The Colloquies

Exposed to every icy wind that blows, the village of O Cebreiro crowns the Pass of Pedrafita. Here stood the makeshift camp where hundreds of British soldiers died of starvation and exposure in the Peninsular War. It was the depths of the winter of 1808/9, and they were retreating to A Coruña to embark for home. Their leader, Sir John Moore, was mortally wounded in a French attack on the port and famously buried at midnight.

> Not a drum was heard, not a funeral note,
> As his corse to the rampart we hurried . . .
> We carved not a line, and we raised not a stone,
> But we left him alone in his glory.

'The Burial of Sir John Moore at Corunna' was the only poem ever published by the Reverend Charles Wolfe (in the *Newry Telegraph* in 1817), but its heroic lines have earned it a place in almost every anthology of English poetry since.

O Cebreiro is now a village of only nine inhabited houses, but it is a national monument because of its ancient *palozzas* – squat stone dwellings with thatched roofs, Celtic in origin. Such is the current popularity of the pilgrimage to Santiago that over a thousand people pass through this tiny place every day in the summer, cramming themselves into its state refuge and its one small hotel. The day I passed through was no exception, as I had to use my bike as a battering-ram to force my way through a battalion of tented French teenagers and their convoy of support vehicles. The cafés and souvenir shops were crowded, so I retreated to the tranquillity of the small tenth-century Church of Santa Maria la Real, where Dr Elias Valiña Campedro is buried.

This parish priest was the scholar of the Camino, and it was on his initiative that the system of yellow arrows was instituted in 1984. Enthusiastic volunteers painted them by hand on trees, rocks and the sides of buildings all the way from the Pyrenees to Santiago; and volunteers keep the paint fresh to this day. As well as learned treatises on the history of the pilgrimage, Dr Elias produced a booklet of sketch maps of the route, which I found an invaluable complement to Alison Raju's written guides. His bronze bust stands outside his church, and his family maintains the connection with O Cebreiro by running the modest hotel there.

From my eagle's eyrie on the edge of the village, I looked down on a ravishing landscape. The burning plains of Castile and León were behind me. In front stretched the emerald hills of Galicia, the rainiest corner of Spain. It looked just like Ireland, its Celtic sister across the sea.

I swooped down from the Puerto Pedrafita do Cebreiro in the cool of a golden morning, then climbed the next pass, the Puerto de San Roque, where an expressive bronze pilgrim leaned at an angle of 45 degrees into a winter gale, his head bent and his cloak flapping out behind him. From there I hurtled down again, then up to the highest pass of the three, the Puerto do Poio at 1,337 m (4,386 ft). It was only ten miles, but it was a tough mountain ride, which took me most of the morning. From Puerto do Poio, the land fell away, down to Santiago and the north Atlantic, and I was hoping for easier cycling. But I simply exchanged mountains for steep hills, where the notorious Galician west wind blew into my face from the ocean. At least there were plenty of trees to provide shelter and shade.

I stopped for the night in Sarria and watched the world go by over a glass of chilled white wine at a riverside café. Sarria was so keen on the Camino that there were cockleshells worked into the wrought-iron railings along the river, and lovely litter-bins shaped like iron shells in every street. It was another red-letter day. Having been starved for company all the way across northern Spain, I found congenial people – and English ones too – for the second day running. Up on the pass by the pilgrim statue, I got into conversation with a young couple who were on a motoring holiday in Spain, with some walking. And in my hotel dining-room that evening, I was delighted to hear more English voices. Stuart and Di were walking the Camino Frances over two summer holidays, and we swapped experiences over our puddings and a few extra glasses of wine. We talked late into the night, as we felt considerably less tired in the cooler air of Galicia. And with Santiago now within striking distance, we were already in holiday mood.

In its bowl of green hills, Sarria lay under a veil of thick mist which only cleared at the top of a long, long climb. The next town, Portomarin, took me by surprise, as it was a 1960s brutalist complex of glass and concrete, a strange sight in this ancient corner of Spain. Then I realised that the old Portomarin had been flooded when the river Minho was dammed, all except its Templar castle and the Romanesque Church of San Nicolas, which were carried uphill, stone by stone, to be re-erected in the new town centre. I stopped to admire the portico of the church, a fine piece of sculpture by Master Mateo, the builder of Santiago's magnificent Portico de la Gloria. Then I climbed again, up and up a seemingly endless hill. How I longed for a nice flat walk along Baker Street!

A day's ride from Santiago de Compostela, just when I should have been at the peak of fitness and brimming with joyful expectation, I woke up with a bad cold. My nose ran, my throat was sore, my legs ached on the hills and, though the countryside was cool and green, the pine woods did nothing for me. I looked down at the tarmac, counted the revolutions and willed myself to struggle from one kilometre marker to the next. I gave up when I saw an inviting modern hotel just beyond Arzua, and took myself to bed for the afternoon with lemon tea, whisky and aspirin. I was only 15 miles short of journey's end, but I couldn't have cycled that last little distance to save my life.

In the evening, I went down to the bar for a light supper. Surrounded by local men, I tried to eavesdrop on their conversation, but could pick up scarcely a word. They were speaking *gallego*, a sort of cross between standard Castilian and Portuguese. In the depths of the Galician countryside, few people speak anything else; the language is taught in schools; and road signs are normally written in *gallego*, with Castilian Spanish underneath. The Portuguese definite article turns La Coruña into A Coruña, and the Spanish letter 'l' becomes the Portuguese 'r' – *praza*, instead of *plaza*, and *praia* for Spanish *playa* (beach). When we got into conversation over our tapas, the men switched to Castilian.

'So you're from England, are you? Then you'll know all about A Praia de Winston. It's named after your great leader.'

'No. Where is it?'

'It's any beach where the smugglers bring in foreign cigarettes. There are masses of Praias de Winston, all down the coast. So don't think those picturesque little boats you see out there are all out fishing. Of course, what bothers us is not the small-time tobacco smugglers. Tobacco and alcohol running have been with us forever. What we're really worried about now is the cocaine. It's a wild coast, a hard place to catch smugglers, and the Medellín boys have moved in. We've always been poor here, so contraband is a great temptation. Either that – or emigrate.'

The last lap. Like any great city in the world, Santiago has undistinguished outskirts, which spread for miles and are made worse in this case by the airport, which now occupies most of the suburb of Lavacolla (Wash your Neck) – the place where pilgrims traditionally washed and spruced themselves up before entering the city. From there I cycled on to Monte del Gozo, originally the *montjoie* from which the joyful pilgrims got their first glimpse of the great towers of Santiago Cathedral. 'The King of the Castle' here was not the victorious champion in a battle, but the first pilgrim to spot the towers and cry '*Mon Joie!*' Today, the area is rather a utilitarian mess, with refuges built by the Xunta de Galicia to shelter 2,000 pilgrims, car parks and cafés, not yet softened by the newly planted trees or improved by the most unsightly modern sculpture. And recent building has hidden the cathedral towers from view. Still to be crossed was a new motorway with futuristic car-parking. Then I finally cruised down to the Puerta del Camino, the Gate of the Way, the traditional entrance for pilgrims into the walled city of Santiago de Compostela.

A brief shower, followed by a burst of sunshine, had set the golden granite alight, and it sparkled with refracted raindrops. I pushed my bicycle through the streets and squares of the city's mediaeval heart, where arcades, palaces, churches and statues were all cut out of the same glowing stone to present one harmonious, magical whole. And in the centre lay the vast Praza do Obradoiro, acres of glistening granite flagstones in the shadow of that overwhelming baroque fantasy of a cathedral. Pilgrim or not, that first sight must be one of the crowning moments of all travel. Of course, with my usual luck, I found the great Obradoiro façade clad from top to bottom in scaffolding! But the twin towers I had failed to see from the *montjoie* peeped coyly out from bell level, so I got a passer-by to record my arrival with a photograph of myself and Condor in their lee. Then I checked into the Hostal Suso, a well-known meeting place for pilgrims near the cathedral. My spirits were still on the low side, but I celebrated my arrival as best I could with a ham *bocadillo* and a glass of beer, then took my coughs and sneezes to bed for the afternoon.

My pilgrim passport had an impressive array of stamps – 24 in all, from the Black Madonna of Le Puy to a very fine purple cockleshell from Palas de Rei. All it lacked was the ultimate stamp, the accolade from the Cathedral of Santiago. This was not given automatically, and I knew that I had to make a good impression. I threw away my travel-weary cycling clothes and presented myself in a freshly laundered outfit.

The canon in the cathedral's pilgrim office examined my stamps and entered in his ledger that I had cycled along the Way.

'What was your motivation for making the pilgrimage?' he asked.

I was expecting the question and had given careful thought to my answer.

'I made this difficult journey alone, because I needed time for reflection. I have reached the stage in my life where I need to come to terms with my past and work out my priorities for the future. The pilgrimage has been a great spiritual experience. It has freed me from my everyday preoccupations and given me the space to consider God and the eternal questions – the things that really matter . . .' or words to that effect. I felt it necessary to be utterly honest, so I refrained from mentioning Christianity. If I had lied about my beliefs, my whole journey would have seemed a cheat, and I would know in my heart that I had not deserved my accreditation. Fortunately, the canon seemed satisfied with my reply. We chatted for a while, then he put the cathedral's stamp of St James on my pilgrim passport and, more importantly, handed me the greatly sought-after Compostela.

My Compostela now hangs, suitably framed, in my hall. It is a certificate printed in sepia on cream paper, and the wording is surrounded by a frieze of cockleshells, topped with a somewhat sentimental, Victorian-looking image of St James the Pilgrim. The canon filled in my name in the middle of the Latin text, and I was impressed, as a classicist, to note that he entered my name with grammatical accuracy in the accusative case. I appear as 'Doñam Annam Mustoe', and it is certified, signed and sealed that I have come as a pilgrim, in a spirit of devotion and piety, to the most sacred shrine of St James.

St James's remains have had a chequered history since they first drifted on to the shores of Galicia in their miraculous stone ship. Hidden in Iria Flava from the pagan Queen Lupa, they were lost for centuries until the hermit Pelagro was led by a group of stars to their burial place on 25 July 813. King Alfonso of Asturias rushed to the scene and built a modest shrine to house them. Then in 844, the newly rediscovered saint led his Spanish Christians to a glorious victory over the Moors at the Battle of Clavijo. But fortunes ebbed and flowed during the centuries of La Reconquista. The vanquished Muslims, under their leader, El Mansur, soon won back the north of Spain, capturing Iria Flava in 977 and razing it to the ground. Fortunately, the sacred remains were unharmed and, once the city was recaptured by the Spaniards, its name was changed to Santiago on the orders of Pope Urban II, and work began on a cathedral magnificent enough to house the country's patron saint. But that was not the peaceful end to his problems. Enter Sir Francis Drake and his marauding English, who arrived off La Coruña in 1589. So fierce was their reputation that St James was hastily exhumed and rushed off to safety in the neighbouring spa town of Orense. Once again, his remains were lost by his absent-minded rescuers. But in 1879, three corpses were somehow discovered in the course of building work in the crypt of Santiago Cathedral – where St James should have been lying all along – and authenticated by Pope Leo XIII as the true remains of the apostle and his two disciples, Saint Theodore and Saint Athanasius. Pope John Paul II's pilgrimage in 1982 was presumably the final seal of approval.

As my last act in Santiago, I made my way to the cathedral to pay homage to the remains of the apostle who had been the inspiration for my journey. I started from the far end of the Praza do Obradoiro, to give myself the longest possible view of the daring, fantastical *churriguresque* (Spanish baroque) west façade. Spanish architecture, from Gothic to Gaudí, has always had an astonishing freedom of style, traditionally marrying the rich decoration of Muslim art with the structure of Christian building. So the Spaniards were bound to respond with more enthusiasm than most when the baroque revolt from the tyranny of the architect's ruler swept across Europe. They took the spirit of the new overblown, curvaceous style to their own wild heights of spontaneity and passion.

The guidebooks were ecstatic about the profusion of embellishment and statues on the façade, but Santiago Peregrino with his angels, saints, kneeling kings, disciples and father, Zebedee, were all sadly hidden behind the forest of scaffolding. All I could see were the twin towers, crowned with their elaborate cupolas, and the cathedral bells themselves. These ancient bells, like the saint they celebrate, have had their own share of adventures. When El Mansur conquered Iria Flava and stripped Santiago's shrine of its treasures, he forced a band of Christian prisoners to march, shouldering the bells, across the entire Spanish peninsula to Cordoba, where they were inverted and used as oil lamps in the Great Mosque. In the final years of La Reconquista, King Ferdinand entered Cordoba in triumph and found the bells. In a sweet act of revenge, he loaded up a band of Moorish prisoners and marched them all the way back to Santiago with the bells on their shoulders.

I climbed the double stairway into the cathedral. It was a great surprise – a cathedral within a cathedral. The baroque façade was simply its shell. Inside lay a simpler Romanesque basilica in the form of a Latin cross. And the original west doorway, the eleventh-century Portico de la Gloria of Master Mateo, stood inside the present baroque entrance, which was a great pity, as it was dark in there and impossible to stand far enough back from the masterpiece to study it.

I began the traditional rites observed by all pilgrims. First, I approached the statue of St James under the central figure of Christ in the carved portico. He sits on a column of grey marble, of which the capital represents the Trinity and the shaft the Tree of Jesse. Just at hand level there are five holes, which have been hollowed out over the centuries by millions of pilgrim fingers. I queued to stick my own into the tree. Opposite the portico, against the central jamb of the main door, is the Santo d'os Croques (the Saint of the Skull-taps), said to be a portrait of Master Mateo. Like the other pilgrims, I tapped my head on his crown. This ritual is not known to benefit adults, but the mental agility of children and their memory for facts in exams are said to improve significantly after this meeting of skulls.

With my usual bad luck, I found the high altar covered in sheets of tarpaulin! But along with the rest of the pilgrims, I climbed the stair behind it, which was lit by a lamp forged from weapons of the Reconquest, and approached the seated figure of the Most Sacred Image of Santiago from the rear. His simple thirteenth-century statue was adorned in 1765 with a halo and a silver cape, encrusted with diamonds and precious stones. We all gave him a hug, kissed his cape and stroked the shells on his back; then I went down to the crypt beneath the high altar, where the apostle himself rests in a silver casket, along with the two disciples who brought his body to Spain. Here, the devout said their prayers and I stood for a moment in silent contemplation, picturing the people along the way who had asked me to pray for them in Santiago. Then I lit a candle for them all, and for my own dead.

I emerged to a crowded cathedral and the Lord's Prayer in an American accent. A cruise ship had just docked at A Coruña and spilled its usual load of well-heeled, elderly transatlantic voyagers.

'Honey, just look at all that marble!'

'Charlene, did you see those cute little choirboys?'

'Why don't you join us for the service?' asked what seemed to be a priest in a multicoloured jumper. 'We've got something very special arranged.'

I sat down with the group and listened to one of their number reading a passage about James and his brother John from the Gospel According to St Matthew. The two brothers went privately to Jesus and asked if they could sit in the places of honour in His kingdom, on His right and left hands. Jesus replied that it was not He, but His Father, who was in charge of the heavenly seating arrangements. So the two brothers gained nothing from their forward behaviour, apart from the annoyance of their fellow disciples. I didn't think the story showed Santiago in his best light.

At that moment a hush fell on the congregation, for two hefty men, robed in crimson, appeared in the south transept, carrying the immense *Botafumeiro* on a wooden yoke. This 'King of Censers' is swung only in Holy Years (when the Feast of St James, 25 July, falls on a Sunday), and on a few other very significant occasions in the church calendar. But money talks, and I suppose the cruise line had made arrangements for a private display. I couldn't believe my luck.

Gently smoking, the world's largest censer was placed in the middle of the transept crossing, all six feet of it and one hundredweight of silver. It was then hooked on to a ceiling pulley by a rope, thicker than my arm, which dangled down from the soaring transept. A posse of crimson-robed acolytes stepped forward, hauled the *Botafumeiro* just above head height, and began to swing it back and forth. The cathedral's mighty organ joined in, rising to a crescendo as the censer swung higher and higher. In flight, it described a terrifying arc, from the rafters of one transept to those of the other, barely skimming above the heads of the congregation in its downward swoop and stopping just short of the ceiling as it flew up again. The cathedral was lost in a pungent, intoxicating fog of incense. The censer's swing reached its apogee and the organ thundered so loudly that it shook the whole building. But just in the nick of time, just when it seemed that all this violence must end in disaster, the *Botafumeiro* began to slow down, the organ softened in tone and the wild adventure was over. It was almost pagan in its excess – the Church as theatre, with baroque knobs on.

I reeled out with the dazed Americans and made my way across the Praza do Obradoiro to the Hostal de los Reyes Catolicos for a celebratory aperitif. The Catholic Monarchs, Ferdinand and Isabella, founded what is now a most costly hotel as a hospital for pilgrims, sparing no expense to make it a building worthy of such an important holy site. Nothing but the best would do. Its restrained granite exterior was relieved by the most delicate sculpture in the Spanish plateresque style, while its interior was arranged around four elegantly fountained courtyards, one for each of the four Evangelists. It was such a sumptuous hospital, and so popular, that pilgrims had to be restricted to a three-day stay, unless they were sick and in need of medical care.

Unfortunately, its role these days could not be further from the intentions of the Catholic monarchs. The Hostal is yet another of Spain's historic buildings which has been converted into a parador, an expensive international hotel. But the three-day tradition still lingers on in a vague kind of way. The first ten pilgrims to show up with their Compostelas at meal times are admitted to the hotel kitchens, where they are fed, together with the staff, free of charge. They used to be entitled to three meals a day for three days, but rumour has it that the allocation has now been reduced to one single meal.

According to some students I met, who had taken advantage of their entitlement, the pilgrims enter by the tradesmen's entrance and are led down a maze of tiled corridors to a wretched little room, where they serve themselves with a tray of adequate, but pretty basic fare. I decided not to bother. If I ate in the Hostal de los Reyes Catolicos, it would be as a pampered, paying customer in the beautiful garden restaurant. I studied the mouth-watering menu, but my cold had taken away my appetite along with my sense of taste, and the listed delights would have been wasted on me. So I walked into the next street and found a small eatery, where I dined quite reasonably for one tenth of the price. One day, I shall go back to Santiago, with a different wardrobe and no cold, and treat myself magnificently.

But my Compostela did have one significant use. When I went to a travel agency to book my flight home, I found that I was entitled, as a genuine, Compostela-carrying pilgrim, to a fifteen per cent reduction on the Iberia air fare. Unlike the mediaeval pilgrims, who had to walk home, I stowed my bike on the bus to Lavacolla Airport and went back to London the easy way.

It had been a difficult ride over arduous terrain, physically punishing and very lonely at times, but pilgrimages were never meant to be easy. The mountains of the Auvergne, the hills of the Gers, the Pyrenees, the burning Spanish plains and the towering passes of León were all challenges which I had met and overcome. Even my restless nights in dormitory bunks seemed somehow appropriate, for they had added the element of sackcloth and ashes to what might otherwise have been too comfortable a time. I had struggled, but I was richly rewarded for my pains. My arrival in Santiago de Compostela, when I found it glittering in the sunshine after rain, was one of life's glorious moments. I had felt a tremendous sense of satisfaction, even joy. It had been a journey *sui generis*, unique, unlike any other, and I would not have missed it for the world.

BIBLIOGRAPHY

THE AMBER ROUTE

Cary, M, *The Geographic Background of Greek and Roman History*, Oxford, 1949.

Charlesworth, M P, *Trade-routes and Commerce of the Roman Empire*, Cambridge, 1924.

Magris, Claudio, *The Danube*, Collins Harvill, 1989.

Marcus Aurelius, *The Meditations*.

Navarro, J M de, 'Prehistoric Routes between Northern Europe and Italy defined by the Amber Trade', *Geographical Journal*, Vol LXVI, 1925.

Oxford Companion to Decorative Arts.

Penguin Atlases of Ancient Greece and Rome.

Penguin Dictionary of Decorative Arts.

Ross, Andrew, *Amber. The Natural Time Capsule*, Natural History Museum, 1998.

Schama, Simon, *Landscape and Memory*, Fontana Press, 1995.

Spekke, Arnold, *The Ancient Amber Routes and the Geographical Discovery of the Eastern Baltic*, M Goppers, Stockholm, 1957.

Tacitus, *Germania*.

Wheeler, Sir Mortimer, *Rome Beyond the Imperial Frontiers*, Penguin Books, 1954.

Many additional classical sources, including Artemidorus, Cassiodorus, Homer, Martial, Pliny the Elder and Strabo.

The Internet, which was especially useful for 'The Mystery of the Amber Room'.

THE SANTA FE TRAIL

This is not a scholarly account, as I did not draw on original sources. The historical background was picked up largely from museum pamphlets along the trail, in particular Jack D Rittenhouse's *Trail of Commerce and Conquest. A Brief History of the Santa Fe Trail*, University of New Mexico Press, 1971.

Also:

Casey, Robert L, *Journey to the High South West*, Globe Pequot Press, Connecticut, 1983.

Frazier, Ian, *Great Plains*, Faber and Faber, 1990.

Kamen, Henry, *Spain's Road to Empire*, Penguin Books, 2002.

THE WAY OF ST JAMES

This route is very well documented. The travel section of any good bookshop will provide a wide range of useful books. More scholarly publications can be obtained through The Confraternity of Saint James of Compostela, 45 Dolben Street, London SE1 0UQ. Tel: 020 7403 4500 www.csj.org.uk

APPENDIX – BICYCLE SPECIFICATIONS

My old faithful Condor, built by Monty Young and his team for my first ride round the world, had a make-over a couple of years ago. It started its life with randonneur handlebars, which were later changed to straight ones. Both had their disadvantages. This time, we decided to give butterfly bars a try and I have found them perfect. With new handlebars, a new chain set, new pedals and a brilliant orange respray, my well-travelled Condor rose like a phoenix from the ashes. Its startling new colour has simplified my life. I just have to say, 'It's the orange one', and it's found immediately in airports and garages. And I feel more secure, because robbers would surely hesitate before riding off on such an eye-catching machine.

Frame	Reynolds 631 Mixte, butted tubes
Transmission	Shimano Deore. Front 28-38-48. Rear 13-15-17-20-23-26-30
Wheels	Deore LX hubs
	Mavic TS19 rims
	DT stainless steel spokes
Tyres	Continental Top Touring 2000
Handlebars	Humpert Pro Bars
Pedals	Shimano M324 SPD
Saddle	Brooks B17 STD
Mudguards	SKS
Pannier rack	Blackburn Ex1
Rear panniers	Karrimore Iberia

INDEX